"I owe a shallow knowledge of the Dulles name to having [...] one would often hear mention of the Dulles family in news reports. When I came to study theology with John Foster Dulles's youngest son, Avery Dulles, SJ, my interest was piqued. The then Father, and later Cardinal, Dulles was discreet in speaking of his father when I would ask, alluding only to his advocacy of a 'religiously grounded public consensus.' Thus, I was enriched in reading *God's Cold Warrior* not only to see the depth of John Foster Dulles's thinking and religious commitment but also to deepen my appreciation of the Dulles intellectual dynasty."

— **Robert A. Sirico**
president, Acton Institute

"At a time when many associate Christian nationalism with evangelical Protestantism and regard the religious right as a threat to liberal democracy in the United States, John Wilsey's astute and thorough biography of John Foster Dulles is a good reminder of what faith-based politics looks like. A lifelong liberal Presbyterian who played a major role in the United States' Cold War strategies as secretary of state in the Eisenhower administration, Dulles had the rare combination of tolerant religion and militant nationalism. This book helpfully shows the access to power and significant influence that mainline Protestantism had on the United States' policy as the nation rose to a global hegemony."

— **D. G. Hart**
author of *Damning Words: The Life and Religious Times of H. L. Mencken*

"Wilsey illuminates the important role of Christianity in the life and work of John Foster Dulles, the towering and controversial US secretary of state in the Eisenhower administration. The book highlights how Dulles's progressive faith guided his ecumenical church service in the 1940s and his work as America's leading diplomat in the 1950s. While some scholars view Dulles as an inflexible moralist who intensified the Cold War with the Soviet Union, Wilsey's biography offers a helpful corrective, providing a sympathetic account of this influential public servant."

— **Mark R. Amstutz**
Wheaton College

"John Foster Dulles looms large in the pantheon of Cold War foreign policy leaders, yet the apparent space between his inner life and outer presentation have long rendered him an enigmatic figure. Wilsey's warm and deeply researched volume offers an intimate portrait of Dulles, capturing the man in all of his contradictions and complexity. Blending spiritual and intellectual biography, Wilsey reveals much about Dulles's internal world, teasing out the roots of his pragmatism in matters of faith as well as diplomacy, and highlighting the relationship Dulles saw between moral laws and the natural world. With this work, Wilsey has added tremendously to our understanding of the ideas and values that shaped Dulles's worldview and thus US politics and foreign policy."

— **Lauren Turek**
Trinity University

LIBRARY OF RELIGIOUS BIOGRAPHY

Mark A. Noll, Kathryn Gin Lum, and Heath W. Carter, series editors

Long overlooked by historians, religion has emerged in recent years as a key factor in understanding the past. From politics to popular culture, from social struggles to the rhythms of family life, religion shapes every story. Religious biographies open a window to the sometimes surprising influence of religion on the lives of influential people and the worlds they inhabited.

The Library of Religious Biography is a series that brings to life important figures in United States history and beyond. Grounded in careful research, these volumes link the lives of their subjects to the broader cultural contexts and religious issues that surrounded them. The authors are respected historians and recognized authorities in the historical period in which their subject lived and worked.

Marked by careful scholarship yet free of academic jargon, the books in this series are well-written narratives meant to be read and enjoyed as well as studied.

Titles include:

*Duty and Destiny: The Life and Faith of **Winston Churchill***
by Gary Scott Smith

*A Short Life of **Jonathan Edwards***
by George M. Marsden

*One Soul at a Time: The Story of **Billy Graham***
by Grant Wacker

*A Christian and a Democrat: A Religious Life of **Franklin D. Roosevelt***
by John F. Woolverton with James D. Bratt

George Whitefield: *Evangelist for God and Empire*
by Peter Y. Choi

For a complete list of published volumes, see the back of this volume.

God's Cold Warrior

The Life and Faith of John Foster Dulles

JOHN D. WILSEY

WILLIAM B. EERDMANS PUBLISHING COMPANY
GRAND RAPIDS, MICHIGAN

Wm. B. Eerdmans Publishing Co.
4035 Park East Court SE, Grand Rapids, Michigan 49546
www.eerdmans.com

27 26 25 24 23 22 21   1 2 3 4 5 6 7

ISBN 978-0-8028-7572-3

Library of Congress Cataloging-in-Publication Data

Names: Wilsey, John D., author.
Title: God's cold warrior : the life and faith of John Foster Dulles / John D.
    Wilsey.
Other titles: Life and faith of John Foster Dulles
Description: Grand Rapids, Michigan : William B. Eerdmans Publishing
    Company, 2021. | Series: Library of religious biography | Includes bibli-
    ographical references and index. | Summary: "A religious biography of
    John Foster Dulles, focusing on how his faith commitments shaped his
    evolving views on America's role in the world"—Provided by publisher.
Identifiers: LCCN 2020033818 | ISBN 9780802875723 (paperback)
Subjects: LCSH: Dulles, John Foster, 1888–1959. | Dulles, John Foster,
    1888–1959—Religion. | Presbyterians—Washington (D.C.)—Biography. |
    Statesmen—United States—Biography. | United States—Foreign rela-
    tions—1945–1953. | United States—Foreign relations—1953–1961. | Foster
    family. | Washington (D.C.)—Biography.
Classification: LCC E748.D868 W55 2021 | DDC 973.921092 [B]—dc23
LC record available at https://lccn.loc.gov/2020033818

To Mandy, Caroline, and Sally
Amor Vincit Omnia

John Foster Dulles, 1958

Contents

Preface   ix

Acknowledgments   xi

Abbreviations   xv

Introduction: "He Being Dead, Yet Speaketh"   1

1. "Don't Let the Little Ones Forget Me"   19

2. "His Character Is Straightforward and Sweet" (1888–1912)   44

3. "Does the Ark Need the Sustaining Hand of Uzza?" (1912–1926)   67

4. "Work, for the Night Is Coming" (1927–1939)   97

5. "Everything Is Fine until You Relax" (1940–1946)   122

6. "Give a Man a Revolver" (1946–1952)   145

7. "A Faith Linked with the Pursuit of Justice" (1953–1959)   169

Epilogue: Civil Religion, Progressive Christianity, and John Foster Dulles   188

Notes   205

Index   235

Preface

This treatment of John Foster Dulles will explore his worldview as informed by his religion. Dulles was one of the most significant American diplomats in the early years of the Cold War, but this book is not a diplomatic history. He was also a principal leader in the Federal Council of Churches during the 1940s, but this book is not an institutional history. This book seeks to identify and trace intellectual, moral, and religious patterns as they appeared in various familial, ecclesiastical, and diplomatic contexts throughout the life of a lawyer, churchman, and diplomat. I have also tried to focus this study on features of Dulles's life that have been less comprehensively considered by previous biographers. Consequently, I have intentionally avoided exploring some areas in Foster's career that have been thoroughly covered by historians and biographers since the 1960s.

Acknowledgments

Acknowledgments sections are likely the most overlooked in a book like this. That is a shame, because no author can endeavor to make sense of another's life without help. I am no exception, and I have been blessed beyond measure to have enjoyed the assistance and companionship of many people along the path to describing John Foster Dulles as a man with a dynamic faith.

I owe a debt of gratitude to Heath Carter, who first believed in the legitimacy of this project and who has been a constant source of encouragement. My editor, David Bratt, is also a source of encouragement and inspiration, and I have so appreciated his friendship.

I conducted most of my research as 2017–2018 William E. Simon Visiting Fellow in Religion and Public Life in the James Madison Program in American Ideals and Institutions in the Politics Department at Princeton University. I am grateful to Robert P. George, Bradford P. Wilson, and Matthew J. Franck for accepting me into the program and befriending my family and me with all sincerity. The Madison Program staff, Debby Parker, Evy Behling, Ch'nel Duke, and Duanyi Wang, provided invaluable support, without which no part of this book could have been written. And I cannot forget my wonderful colleagues in the program, who offered their criticisms and encouragements over the course of the year in formal and informal settings: Adeline Allen, Anton Barba-Kay, Keegan F. Callanan, Allen C. Guelzo, Boleslaw Z. Kabala, Thomas W. Merrill, Mark L. Movsesian, Deborah A. O'Malley, Michael Stokes Paulsen, Nathan Pinkoski, Andrew R. Porwancher, Charles T. Rubin, Matthew W. Slaboch, Carl R. Trueman, David L. Tubbs, and Kevin G. Vance. Thanks to John F. Doherty and Luis E. Tellez of the Witherspoon Institute for their help with this project. And the Undergraduate Fellows of the James Madison Program provided me with challenging questions and feedback during my time at Princeton.

I am profoundly grateful to Special Collections Assistants April Armstrong, Brianna Heverly, Lynn Durgin, Christa Cleeton, and Rosalba Varallo Recchia at Princeton's Seeley G. Mudd Manuscript Library. Their assistance and professionalism were outstanding. In addition to research at the Mudd Library, I consulted the beautiful and extensive archive of the Presbyterian Historical Society in Philadelphia. My thanks go to Beth Hessel, who served as Executive Director of the PHS while I was conducting my research; also Allison Davis, Charlene Peacock, Lisa Davidson, Jennifer Barr, Bill Brock, Cecilia Figliuolo, Sharon Reid, Ray Scaletti, David Staniunas, Yvonne Wathen, Elizabeth Wittrig, and Gabriela Zoller. This book just would not exist without them.

At the Watertown Presbyterian Church in Watertown, New York, I enjoyed the support and hospitality of Rev. Fred G. Garry on my visit there in the fall of 2017. I also benefited immensely from the guidance of church archivists Doug and Mary Sanford, who opened the church's historical resources to me and drove me to Henderson, New York, to see what was once the Dulles/Lansing family compound on the Lake Ontario shore. Since then, Dr. Doug Sanford, a longtime Watertown ear, nose, and throat physician, has passed away. We honor his memory. I also express gratitude to John Johnson, the chief executive officer of the *Watertown Daily Times*, for providing me with helpful insights and resources on the Dulles, Foster, and Lansing families.

My wife, daughters, and I took a visit to Main Duck Island in Lake Ontario, the island the Dulleses purchased in 1941. We went during the spring of 2018 to explore the island (now inhabited mostly by snakes), walk where Foster walked, and see where he and Janet had their cabin. Thanks to Terry Sprague, who introduced us to Dave Harrison, who took us out to the island from Port Milford, Ontario, in his fishing vessel. Herb Cooper, a fisherman and teacher from Prince Edward County who knew the Dulleses personally, came along and gave us tremendous insights and stories. My friend of over thirty years, Philip Bennett, drove us, took pictures, and charmed our way through the US/Canadian border. We have deep gratitude to each of these friends for facilitating that trip, which was so memorable and necessary to the development of this project.

Acknowledgments

Profound thanks to the Cushwa Center for the Study of American Catholicism at the University of Notre Dame. Thanks to Ben Wetzel, Pete Cajka, Kathleen Sprouse Cummings, and MaDonna Nowak for their assistance in providing me with the opportunity to share my research in the fall of 2018. Thanks also to the Acton Institute for the Study of Religion and Liberty, which gave me opportunities to lecture as an affiliate scholar. In addition to the Madison Program, Acton provided necessary research funding. And without the sabbatical leave provided by my institution, The Southern Baptist Theological Seminary, I could not have completed this project.

Many fine friends and colleagues have provided me with feedback on this project after reading drafts of the manuscript. Sincere thanks to Emilie Dulles, Baron Christopher Hanson, Lauren Turek, Marian Strobel, Phillip Luke Sinitiere, Stephen Presley, and my father, David L. Wilsey. And I was richly benefited through discussions about Dulles with Cara Burnidge, William Inboden, Mark Edwards, Joseph Torigian, Trey Dimsdale, Zach Carter, Ronald Pruessen, Mark Toulouse, Michael A. G. Haykin, Dan Hummel, and Nicholas Sileo. Will Crawford, a member of the Undergraduate Fellows of the James Madison Program and of University Cottage Club at Princeton where Foster Dulles also held membership, gave me a fine tour of the house and grounds. He showed me the memorial gazebo dedicated to Foster as well as the tiger skull cigar caddy presented to Foster by Field Marshal P. Pibulsongkran of the Thai government in 1956. Thanks also to Pascual Arias Jiménez of Hispanic Initiatives at Southern Seminary for his translation help.

Of course, I would not have been in a position to do any of this without the love, patience, and support of my wife, Mandy, and our two daughters, Caroline and Sally. John Foster Dulles has been something of a third wheel in our family for a long time. His has been a silent presence among all of us, and he has provided us with many adventures. My family accompanied me just about everywhere I went on research trips along what we affectionately called "the Dulles trail" up and down the East Coast from Lake Ontario to Washington, DC. We lived just off the Princeton University and Princeton Theological Seminary campuses—stomping grounds for Dulleses from the 1870s to today. We even named our tabby cat, a very sophisticated fellow, after Secretary Dulles. Foster the cat, reminiscent of the secretary, is accustomed to command. My family's love for me is my most precious possession, and this is their project as much as it is mine. They share in whatever good it represents. I alone bear the responsibility for its shortcomings.

Glory be to the Father, and to the Son, and to the Holy Ghost, as it was in the beginning, is now, and ever shall be, world without end. Amen.

JOHN D. WILSEY
Louisville, Kentucky

Abbreviations

AFME	American Friends of the Middle East
ANZUS	Australia, New Zealand, and the United States
CFM	Council of Foreign Ministers
CIA	Central Intelligence Agency
CIL	*Corpus Inscriptionum Latinarum*
ELDP	Eleanor L. Dulles Papers, Public Policy Papers, Department of Rare Books and Special Collections, Princeton University Library
FCC	Federal Council of Churches
FEC	Far Eastern Commission
FPC	First Presbyterian Church
JFDOHC	John Foster Dulles Oral History Collection, Department of Rare Books and Special Collections, Princeton University Library
JFDP	John Foster Dulles Papers, Public Policy Papers, Department of Rare Books and Special Collections, Princeton University Library
NAACP	National Association for the Advancement of Colored People
NSC	National Security Council
PACC	Philip A. Crowl Collection on John Foster Dulles, Department of Rare Books and Special Collections, Princeton University Library
PHS	Presbyterian Historical Society
SCAP	Supreme Commander for the Allied Powers
UNCF	United Negro College Fund

"He Being Dead, Yet Speaketh"

Seeing the dead affords practice in seeing the living.

—Beth Barton Schweiger[1]

I couldn't tell you much about the weather on March 19, 2018, except that it was cold outside. I had spent most of the day in the Seeley G. Mudd Manuscript Library at Princeton University going through folder after folder containing documents and pictures pertinent to John Foster Dulles's life in the late 1920s and early 1930s. About twenty minutes before closing time, I decided to open one more folder and then pack up and head home. The folder contained some photographs from 1933, and it was thin—just a few pictures to look at, I thought, and then I could stretch my legs and give my bleary eyes a rest.

One photograph in that folder gave me a start. It showed a large reception room filled with people. The people were dressed in formal attire. They were smiling, enjoying conversation, and making their rounds to friends and associates around the room. Here, a young woman wearing a hat was smiling warmly—perhaps she was meeting someone for the first time and introducing herself. There, a man looked to be making his way through the press of people, perhaps trying to catch someone on the way out with a greeting, or to get some quick clarification on a question. Everyone in the photo looked to be enjoying themselves. It was a party. A notation on the back of the photo simply said, "JFD, 1933."

Right in the center of the photograph, among all the partygoers in the room, was the unmistakable face of the German chancellor, Adolf Hitler. He was dressed in a white tie and tails, with a pin depicting the Nazi Party insignia proudly displayed on his lapel. And there he was, talking to John Foster Dulles. The broad smile on Hitler's face as he talked with Foster (the name he went by from early childhood) demonstrated that he was relishing the moment.

This was one of those times when blood rushes so quickly through your body that you can hear your own heart beating. Up to that point, I had no idea that Foster had ever met Hitler. I had not seen any other biographers mention it. His brother Allen had met Hitler—one biographer described how Allen had met Hitler on an official visit to discuss Germany's massive outstanding World War I debt reparations at Nazi Party headquarters in the early 1930s. Allen cracked a joke with the chancellor about the British and the French. At first, Hitler didn't get it, but when someone explained the joke, he broke out into body-contorting guffaws. Allen said that Hitler "had a laugh louder than Foster's. I always thought my brother brayed like a donkey when he was amused, but I now know he sounds like a turtle dove compared with Hitler."[2]

The mystery of Foster's meeting with Hitler in 1933 was deepened by the fact that the photograph had no notation except "JFD, 1933." But a few days later, I came across an unreleased statement from Foster, dated many years later: January 21, 1952. It said, "I was in Germany in 1933 as representative of American bondholders to induce the German government to resume payment on U.S. dollar bonds. I never had any discussion with anyone anywhere with reference to 'supporting Hitler,' whose coming into power in Germany I deeply deplored."[3]

This statement was helpful in providing some needed context to the photograph, but in many ways it raised more questions than it answered. Was there more to Foster's 1933 trip to Berlin and meeting with Hitler than his 1952 explanation indicated? Was he a Nazi sympathizer? Was he an anti-Semite? Was this the only meeting Foster had with Hitler, or were there others? And why did not Foster release his 1952 statement to the public? What was the real nature of his ties to Nazi Germany? What does this meeting, shrouded in obscurity, say about Foster's religious, political, social, and personal convictions? And then, there was the cynical question I tried in vain to suppress, but it persisted in crowding up all the space in my mind—*was Foster hiding something?*

As I continued to collect resources, as I learned more about Foster's 1933 visit to Berlin, I discovered that he was accused by some fairly prominent figures many years later of divided loyalties because of his dealings with Germany in the 1930s. It occurred to me that the work of writing a biography—and in this particular case, a religious biography—is fraught with the peril of having Jovian power over the subject. The power is perilous because with such power comes serious responsibility. How easy it is for us in the present to neglect our responsibility to those who are dead. The dead can no longer explain themselves, defend their actions, express regret over their decisions, ask forgiveness, or receive praise. It is up to the biographer to make sense of the life of a dead person for a present audience living in a different time than that which is past. To do this responsibly, the biographer has to take the whole person and his times into account as much as is possible, considering the past in all its complexity.

The subject of this book is John Foster Dulles, President Dwight D. Eisenhower's secretary of state, who towered over American foreign policy like a colossus from 1953 to 1959. He was born in 1888 and died in 1959. The subject is, obviously, historical. I am a Christian historian, so I try to approach the craft of writing history with the search for truth animated by what the apostle Paul called the "fruit of the Spirit" in Galatians 5:22. Also, I am cognizant of the fact that we in the present have a perspective on the scope of Foster's life that neither he nor any of his friends, enemies, or observers of his day could possibly have had. From the frigid winter day of his birth at his grandparents' house at 1405 I Street, NW, in Washington, DC, in February of 1888 to the bright spring day when his friends and family laid him in his grave on a hilltop in Arlington Cemetery in May of 1959, we see the sweep and span of John Foster Dulles's life. In many ways, we know his end from his beginning.

When I consider that photo from 1933 showing Hitler having a laugh alongside Foster, and all the questions it raises, I remember that I possess the awesome power of perspective. I know the details of what to them was the uncertain future. I know what Hitler will go on to perpetrate against humanity. I also know how Foster will react to Hitler's actions in his future, and how World War II eventually would shape Foster's most profound convictions—things he could never have known then. Finally, I have access to knowledge about the consequences of decisions Foster made as a central figure in the twentieth century, consequences about which Foster could only speculate at points during his lifetime. Many of those consequences—good, bad, and indifferent—continue to have their effects in contemporary times. And we are all compelled to live with those consequences today, as grievous or enriching as they may be. Foster and his contemporaries could never have dreamed of having the power of such perspective.

Certainly, we don't know everything. We are still just people, and our knowledge is limited, even though we now have access to vast stores of evidence from Foster's life. But as we look back on Foster's life as he lived it, from 1888 to 1959, we do see things in ways he never did. The power of perspective gives us a decided advantage over Foster, and this advantage translates into another kind of power—the power to stand in judgment over him. Historian Beth Barton Schweiger reminds us to use this power charitably. We do not shrink back from critical evaluation of a life like Foster's, but we remember to evaluate it circumspectly. Just because our subject is dead does not mean he loses his humanity. And just because he is dead does not mean that his living students are omniscient, or immune to their own failings and limitations.

The dead continue in their humanity, just as the effects of their lives continue to sway we who live among the living. In this way, the dead still speak. As a Christian by God's grace, I employ the fruit of the Spirit in my interactions with those I encounter in life—love, joy, peace, patience, kindness, goodness, faithfulness, gentleness, and self-control. And by God's grace, I also employ such fruit in my interactions with the dead. Schweiger eloquently and rightly calls us to adopt a "pastoral imagination" in our interaction with the dead, to be "open to being formed by those encounters with the past" and "to deny knowledge of the past as power and to practice knowledge in love."[4] As a Christian religious historian of the nineteenth-century American South, Schweiger knows how to put her words into practice.

John Foster Dulles, though dead, still speaks. His life meant something, for good *and* for ill. The effects of his actions reverberate today in ways that redound toward righteousness, evil, and everything in between. He was a person of many complexities, just like us. He lived in the past, and much has changed since his day. Given his complexities as a human being, it is fitting for those of us who seek to understand the meaning of his life to exercise empathy and charity, even as we do so critically.

So who was he? It's a question that would not have been asked in the middle of the twentieth century. John Foster Dulles was a household name in those days. Some folks today of a certain age can call him to mind pretty readily. Still, it seems that today, many more remember the name Dulles only in association with one of two things: either one of his other famous relatives or the big DC airport named after him. Many, for example, think of Allen W. Dulles, his younger brother. Allen was director of the Central Intelligence Agency from 1953 to 1961—in those days, he was often called "America's Spymaster." Allen was a charismatic, outgoing, charming, sophisticated, pipe-smoking bon vivant who dwelt under the shadow of his older brother for most of his life.

Other people who hear the name Dulles go immediately to Avery Dulles, the youngest of Foster's three children. Avery was a Catholic theologian, a member of the Jesuit Order, whose academic and public career spanned five decades. Beginning in 1960, Avery served at various times as a member of three university faculties, namely, Woodstock College, the Catholic University of America, and Fordham University. He was a visiting professor at nearly a score of other universities and the author of hundreds of articles and almost two dozen books on theology and church history. Avery was made a cardinal by Pope John Paul II in 2001.

Other famous Dulleses were John Watson Foster Dulles, Foster's eldest son, who taught history at the University of Texas for nearly fifty years, and Eleanor Lansing Dulles, Foster's sister, who was a scholar of European economics and ran the State Department's Berlin desk from 1952 to 1959. Beloved in Europe, she was known during that time as "the Mother of Berlin."[5] The necessity of clarifying one's meaning when referring to "Dulles" is understandable, but Foster's life has largely been either forgotten or oversimplified.

When Foster died on May 24, 1959, the whole world mourned him. His state funeral was the largest since President Franklin Roosevelt's in April 1945. (The somber funeral for the slain president John F. Kennedy four years later surpassed Foster's in both size and pathos.) Eisenhower wrote that he was "a champion of freedom," "a foe only to tyranny," and "one of the truly great men of our time."[6] "No one," Eisenhower wrote in a 1956 diary entry, "has the technical competence of Foster Dulles in the diplomatic field."[7] Most Americans of the Eisenhower era agreed. Just after taking office as secretary of state, a 1953 poll showed that only 4 percent of Americans disapproved of Foster's handling of his job. In 1962, a few years after Foster's death, President Kennedy dedicated a newly completed commercial jet airport on ten thousand acres of land outside Washington as Dulles International Airport.[8] Kennedy praised Foster and the Dulles and Foster families in his speech for their tradition of service to the United States at the highest levels.

But over time, Foster's star fell. At the airport dedication ceremony, Kennedy presided over the unveiling of an imposing bronze bust of Foster. After about three decades, the bust was removed and stored away to prepare for renovations. It was never returned. The bust's removal was to the chagrin of, well, virtually nobody. One of Foster's recent biographers, Stephen Kinzer, found the missing bust stashed away in a conference room, looking "big eyed and oddly diffident, anything but heroic."[9] By the early 1970s, biographies began to cast him as an overbearing Presbyterian, an arrogant and obstinate simpleton, a man with a binary view of the world, uncritically regarding Americans as the good guys and the Communists as the bad guys. In 1981, the editors of *American Heritage* left Foster off their list of the ten best secretaries of state in American history. And by 1987, Foster was ranked as one of the five worst people to hold the office.[10]

Foster's star has fallen to the extent that today, he has come to serve as a scapegoat for American foreign policy failures of the 1950s, '60s, and '70s. To be fair, Daniel W. Drezner of the *Washington Post* wrote in 2016 that Foster was superior to any secretary of state since the Clinton administration.[11] But Kinzer had no use for subtlety in his contempt. In a 2014 interview on his dual biography of brothers Foster and Allen, Kinzer hissed that Foster was "very off-putting. He was arrogant, self righteous, and prudish . . . even his friends didn't like him." Kinzer even dropped the whole burden of responsibility for the Vietnam debacle squarely in Foster's lap. "John Foster Dulles," Kinzer averred, "was more responsible for the U.S. involvement in Vietnam than any single individual." To drive the point home, he improvidently asserted, "we could have avoided the entire American involvement in Vietnam" absent Foster's decisions at the Geneva Convention of 1954.[12]

Foster was a man of many ironies. He was a private man, preferring the company of his wife Janet and lapdog Pepi over anyone else. He kept his inner life largely hidden from outsiders. The historians who know him best describe him as an elusive figure. Smug and simplistic pronouncements distort our understanding of both the man and his times.

Foster was one of the longest-serving secretaries of state in the department's history, serving from January 1953 until April 1959. His experience in international politics began remarkably early. He was nineteen years old and finishing his junior year at Princeton when his grandfather, John W. Foster, invited him to attend the Second Hague Convention in 1907. "Grandfather Foster" was serving as representative of the Chinese government, and young Foster went along as his private secretary. He graduated from Princeton University in 1908, served a yearlong academic fellowship at the Sorbonne in France under the philosopher Henri Bergson, and graduated from George Washington University Law School in 1911. After law school, he went to work for the prestigious Wall Street law firm Sullivan and Cromwell. And he served on many subsequent diplomatic missions representing the United States—to Panama in 1917; to the Versailles Conference in 1919–1920; to London, Moscow, and Paris in the years immediately after World War II; and to the first four sessions of the United Nations General Assembly.

His most notable foreign policy achievement prior to 1953 was successfully crafting the peace treaty with Japan from 1950 to 1952. It was a triumph. Foster received praise from all over the world, even from historic critics of American foreign policy in Latin America. President Harry Truman once called Foster a "stuffed shirt" and personally detested him, but even he had to admit that the treaty was a striking success.[13] "You have conducted these long and difficult negotiations with devotion and outstanding skill," Truman wrote Foster five days after the Senate ratified the treaty on March 20, 1952. "That they have been brought to so successful a conclusion and one which has commanded overwhelming support both in our own country and abroad is the greatest of all tributes to your work."[14] Secretary of State Dean Acheson, who also personally disliked Foster, sounded a similar theme. "It has been a joy to work with you over these past years," Acheson said. "Your grasp of the problems, your resourcefulness in solving them, and your dedication to the task has made our association a very happy one."[15] Foster's leadership on the treaty was so effective that President Truman offered him the ambassadorship to Japan. But preferring not to be "at the end of a transmission line if the powerhouse itself was not functioning" but rather "at the powerhouse," Foster declined. He had his eyes on the 1952 presidential election and the ultimate prize of the office of secretary of state, a prize he had desired for most of his life. Foster became Eisenhower's official choice to head the State Department just over a year later.[16]

Religion played a crucial role in Foster's career. His legal and diplomatic experience was directly related to an aspiration he had as a young man to be what he described as "a Christian lawyer" in the mold of his grandfather Foster, who took him to The Hague in 1907 and served Benjamin Harrison as secretary of state from 1892 to 1893. One evening in the summer of 1908, shortly after graduating as valedictorian from Princeton, Foster was talking with his parents about his career plans. He had seriously considered becoming a minister like his father. In the end, he decided against it. "I hope you will not be disappointed in me if I do not become a minister," he said to his parents. "But I've thought about it a great deal and I think I could make a greater contribution as a Christian lawyer and a Christian layman than I would as a Christian minister."[17]

Foster blended his vocation as "Christian lawyer" with that of diplomat in order to serve his country and his church, as he understood it. In 1937, he attended the Oxford Ecumenical Church Conference, one of the most significant events in the developing ecumenical movement of the twentieth century. Prior to attending this meeting, Foster despaired of the church ever having any real effect on world problems. But the meeting inspired Foster. He became convinced that Christianity was the fount from which the solutions to humanity's most pressing problems bubbled forth. As a fifty-four-year-old looking back on his thirties, the fruitful years of his career as an international lawyer, he wrote a short piece entitled "I Was a Nominal Christian." Referring to his career in the 1920s and early '30s, he said, "I became only very nominally a Christian during the succeeding years." But after the Oxford Conference, Foster realized that "the spirit of Christianity, of which I learned as a boy, was really that of which the world now stood in very great need, not merely to save souls, but to solve the practical problems of international affairs."[18]

Shortly after France fell to the Nazis in 1940, Foster was chosen to lead the influential Commission for a Just and Durable Peace of the Federal Council of Churches. This body would help frame the moral vision of the United States after World War II. Foster's experience leading the commission had a direct bearing on his vision for the Japanese peace treaty. He believed that God had given America the responsibility to lead the world into an international order that lived under the supremacy of moral law. "As I pondered the problem [of crafting the peace treaty], my thoughts went back ten years to the time when the Federal Council of Churches had organized its commission on a just and durable peace and I had become chairman of that commission. . . . Would it be prudent and possible, now that I had a national responsibility actually to practice what we had preached?"[19] Shigeru Yoshida, prime minister of Japan at the time, stressed Foster's trustworthiness throughout the process of hammering out the treaty and credited Foster with the success of Japanese-American relations since the war.[20]

Foster's tenure as secretary of state began January 26, 1953, just a few days after Eisenhower's inauguration. He was a uniquely peripatetic secretary. He liked to boast of logging more air miles than any of his predecessors. He presided over the French defeat in Indochina, the Quemoy/Matsu crisis, the Suez crisis, the Soviet invasion of Hungary, and the launch of Sputnik. He was famous for coining the term "massive retaliation" and inspiring the term "brinkmanship." In doing so, he gained the reputation among some, such as the popular *Washington Post* cartoonist Herblock, for being reckless in dealing with America's rivals and being willing to risk nuclear war and the annihilation of human civilization for disproportionate ends. Herblock also sought to create the impression through his cartoons that Foster made things up as he went along, using provocative language but having no intention of backing it up with action. The cartoonist had a point. Foster was a sharp critic of the Truman administration's policy of containment and instead favored a policy of "liberation" during the late 1940s. He thought it immoral to simply abandon to their fate those countries absorbed into the Soviet orbit and thought it was America's duty to roll Communism back. But during his tenure as secretary of state, Foster made sure that American foreign policy remained consistent with containment.

This book is about Foster's religious commitments, and how he articulated his fundamental beliefs about God, human dignity, and moral law during his life as a lawyer, a churchman, and a diplomat. For most of his life, Foster regarded his religion as his animating force. No evaluation of Foster's life and career, whether we end up admiring him or disdaining him, is complete without a careful consideration of his religious attitudes, beliefs, and practices. He was brought up in a devout Presbyterian family in Watertown, New York. Foster's father was the pastor of Watertown's First Presbyterian Church, and from his earliest days, both his mother and father taught him an abiding confidence in the ethical teachings of Christianity. Foster's religious commitments ebbed and flowed throughout his life—he was not unfailingly devoted to his faith from childhood to the end of his life—but his Presbyterian upbringing established enduring attitudinal patterns. His faith commitment lay somewhat dormant in his early adulthood but awakened into a sharply articulated and developed form from his middle to late career.

Foster's religion can be succinctly described as liberal, although he held some conservative attitudes and practices. Most importantly, Foster put the practical always above the abstract; for him, the dynamic prevailed over the static. To him, change, not stasis, was the normative feature of time. Moral forces—the power of right over wrong—were invincible. The churches were indispensable to peace. Peace, like war, must be actively waged to be secured and advanced. He believed that America was chosen by God, not passively, but to actively champion human freedom and protect peoples who were vulnerable to tyranny—mainly Communist tyranny. Providence—God's activity in the world through human and natural agency—was prominent in Foster's thinking. He understood America's mission in terms of Christ's teaching from the parable of the faithful servant, especially in Luke 12:35–48: to whom much is given, much is required. And he believed that God had given him the special purpose of calling Americans to their divine mission. He thought theology had its place in the pulpit, but the essence of Christianity was operational, not dogmatic; ethical, not theological. In short, Foster's Christianity was fortified with a Tocquevillian American pragmatism:[21] it was a hands-on religion, a religion stressing the importance of duty, one that solves everyday problems and that gives human dignity and freedom the place of highest prominence. As his son Avery put it, Foster believed that "religion at its best could create a sense of obligation to promote universal harmony and to transcend the interests of the group to which one belonged."[22]

Foster's observers, both during his life and after his death, often cast his religious identity in absolute terms. They perceived him at times as a fundamentalist, a Puritan, a liberal, an atheist, or one who simply used religion for political means. But there is rich complexity to Foster's religious thought and activity because it evolved over time. In the first part of his career from 1911 to 1936, Foster separated his religious from his professional life. It is tempting to think of this period of Foster's life as irreligious. While it is accurate to say that from his undergraduate days at Princeton until the 1937 Oxford Ecumenical Conference his religious involvements became less and less public, it is a mistake to think of Foster as irreligious. His friend of many years, New York governor and presidential candidate Thomas Dewey, had the impression that Foster was an atheist prior to 1937.[23] This is not correct. Foster was an elder at the Park Avenue Presbyterian Church (which merged with Brick Presbyterian in 1928) during the 1920s, and his children Avery and Lillias both fondly remembered going to church regularly on Sundays and coming home to Sunday dinner. In those days Foster looked dapper to his children, wearing a top hat and tails and carrying a cane to church. Afterward, the family would enjoy a hearty meal followed by home-made ice cream—a Dulles favorite. But given Foster's own reflections, and those particularly of his daughter Lillias, Foster's attitude toward the church was that it was important, but it lacked the vision to make a difference in international affairs. And diplomacy was the arena that captured Foster's imagination more than anything else. But during his later public career from 1937 to 1959, Foster built a public reputation as a churchman and as a diplomat guided by his faith mainly because he changed his mind about the usefulness of religion as an antidote to international problems.

Foster probably never had a deep devotional life, but he loved the New Testament and he had several favorite hymns. He memorized large portions of the Scripture as a child and continued the habit of reading the New Testament regularly into his adulthood. He carried a copy of the New Testament with him most of the time.[24] At home growing up, his father would rise early and awaken the family by walking through the house singing "When Morning Gilds the Skies." On Sundays, Allen Macy would require his children to take notes on his sermons, and then over Sunday dinner call on them individually to raise points they had observed from their notes. Allen Macy would assess the quality of his sermons based on that of the notes his children took—if they did not take good notes, he thought, then his sermon must not have been clear.[25] Foster carried the memories of his childhood—austere and disciplined but happy, animated by the preaching of his father and everyone taking part in the regular singing of hymns as his mother played the piano—to his last days. When he was on his deathbed at Walter Reed Hospital, suffering from the final stages of colon cancer, he wanted to sing with those gathered around him the hymns that had been his favorites since his boyhood days—"The Spacious Firmament on High," "God of Our Life, through All the Circling Years," "Work, for the Night Is Coming," and "All Praise to Thee, My God, This Night."[26]

There is another element that formed Foster's religious and intellectual worldview—nature. From a very early age, he developed a love of the outdoors. His grandfather Foster and his uncle Robert Lansing (who served Woodrow Wilson as secretary of state) owned houses adjacent to one another at Henderson on the Ontario shore, just twenty miles or so from Watertown. These houses formed something like a family compound, and from his earliest years, Foster joined everyone in the family as they spent their summers on the lake fishing, sailing, reading, camping, swimming, and playing tennis. Every May or June, both sides of the family would load up a wagon with a stove, furniture, and trunks of clothes and proceed in several groups along the dusty tracks leading to Henderson. Foster's sister Eleanor recalled races to the shore—"there was a certain amount of competition as to who would get to the cottage first and who would have the most adventures on the way."[27]

Early in his life, Foster cultivated the skill of sailing. As a boy, he had a small craft he named *No. 5*. As an adult, he enjoyed taking long cruises on his forty-foot yawl, the *Menemsha*. He took his children sailing and taught both of his sons to sail. They cruised as far west as Lake Superior and as far east as Long Island Sound. Avery in particular learned quickly. He recalled how his father taught him to navigate by dead reckoning, and that he had once navigated successfully across the Bay of Fundy with his father in a thick fog. A number of biographers characterized Foster as a cold and distant father. Townsend Hoopes wrote in his critical biography that Foster's three children "were classic cases of parental neglect."[28] But what cold and distant father teaches his son to navigate a sailing vessel across the Bay of Fundy by dead reckoning? "It was one of my great triumphs," Avery said, describing navigating against a powerful current and in fog so thick that visibility was down to just a few feet—with his father, Foster, at his side.[29]

In addition to sailing, Foster owned an island on the Canadian side of Lake Ontario called Main Duck Island. Foster regarded Main Duck as a sanctuary, and to the end of his life the island was his most cherished place. After Lillias married Robert Hinshaw, he invited the newlyweds to honeymoon on the island, which they did. He and his wife, Janet, would spend weeks at a time on Main Duck living in a cabin that he hired a local First Nations tribe to construct for him. The cabin had no running water, no electricity, and no direct contact with the outside world. Foster loved the outdoors, and he always saw nature as a classroom for learning how to navigate difficult problems in diplomacy. He cultivated relations with the local Canadian fishermen, often buying some of their fish and giving them access to the waters surrounding the island and its harbor. Herb Cooper, a longtime fisherman and teacher from Prince Edward County, Ontario, recalled how Foster maintained good relations with Lake Ontario fishermen and earned their respect and admiration. As local fishermen with whom Foster had regular contact, Herb and his older brother George were occasionally the Dulleses' guests on the island. Herb remembered that George and Foster both enjoyed a round or two of Old Overholt (Foster's whiskey of choice). But since Herb was a lad of only eighteen at the time, Mrs. Dulles would let him have no spiritous libations. "You're too young," she said, and gave him a cup of tea instead.[30]

These details describing Foster's family relationships, religious upbringing, and love of the outdoors are essential to understanding him as a man, not just as the powerful diplomat, churchman, or lawyer. He was famous for his love of a good joke, and his laugh was as legendary as it was contagious—associates and friends describe him as laughing all the time, throwing his head back and roaring peals that reverberated throughout a room. Those who worked for him had a particular affection for him because he treated them with respect and even affection. Phyllis Bernau Macomber, one of his secretaries at the State Department, described everyone in his office as a "family." They worked to exhaustion, traveled with him all over the world, and saw him at his best and his worst. Macomber was so devoted to him that she stayed by his bedside in the last weeks of his life. One evening as he lay in his hospital bed just before his death, he invited her to move on, to leave his staff if she saw him as something of a falling star. "I said no, I was going to stay. That was it. I wouldn't think of doing otherwise," Macomber said.[31] Foster's humanity was most clearly evident to those closest to him, and especially to those who worked under him.

At the same time, Foster could be calculating and cunning. As indicated above, Foster had close business ties to German industry and finance in the 1930s, which brought him into contact with Adolf Hitler. Since Foster was not a public figure until the late thirties, his activities escaped wide notice. But in 1944, it was evident to the media that if Thomas Dewey were elected president, he would surely nominate his good friend Foster as secretary of state. This brought Foster's past into the public eye.

A muckraking journalist named Drew Pearson wrote a number of pieces calling Foster's activities into question, most notably his relationships with cartels and banks that did business with Nazi Germany. Pearson also asked questions about Foster's relationship to the America First Committee, the isolationist group that preferred America sit out World War II while the British faced Hitler alone. "Right up to the outbreak of the war in 1939, John Dulles [sic] took the attitude that Germany was a misunderstood nation which had shown great investment promise and now should be treated with sympathy and understanding until she got back on her feet," Pearson charged.[32]

Foster did, in fact, defend Hitler as late as 1937 against those who considered him a warmonger and a lunatic. In a letter to Henry Leech, the editor of the *Forum*, Foster wrote, "One may disagree, as I do, with many of Hitler's policies and methods. But such disagreement should not lead one into the error, as I conceive it, of disparaging his abilities. One who from humble beginnings, and despite the handicap of alien nationality, has attained the unquestioned leadership of a great nation cannot have been 'utterly lacking in talent, energy, and ideas.'"[33] It is also true that Foster was reluctant to close Sullivan and Cromwell's Berlin office after Hitler came to power in 1933. Foster was the only voice among the firm's partners that advocated for keeping the Berlin office open. Even his brother, Allen, wanted the office closed and Sullivan and Cromwell out of Hitler's Germany. Foster was worried about the financial loss that would result from such an action—"What will our American clients think, those whose interests we represent in Germany, if we desert them? It will do great harm to our prestige in the United States."[34] Only after his colleagues at the firm threatened to quit and form a competing firm did Foster relent. In a 1935 meeting called to consider moving out of Germany, Foster, facing rebellion from his partners, finally said, "Who is in favor of closing down our operation in Germany?" Every single hand was raised. "Then it is decided. The vote is unanimous."[35]

Still, when he was subjected to criticism in the 1940s during the beginning stages of his public career, Foster rarely missed a chance to boast that he took the lead in his firm as they moved out of Germany once Hitler had established himself in power, even though that was not true. He wrote in 1946, "My firm's attitude toward Hitler can be judged from the fact that promptly after Hitler's rise to power, my firm decided as a matter of principle not to act for any Germans. . . . That was in 1935, several years before our government broke with Hitler."[36] Twisting the narrative to favor his own role did not seem to be problematic for him. It is true that Foster could claim with credibility to have no direct association with Hitler's government. But he did maintain ties to powerful cartels that did business with Hitler's Germany—International Nickel, chemical producers like I. G. Farben (German), Imperial Chemical Industries, Ltd. (British), Solvay and Cie. (Belgian), and Dupont (American). Foster was also a director of the Consolidated Silesian Steel Company, which owned stock in the Upper Silesian Coal and Steel Company. Friedrich Flick, who was later tried for war crimes at Nuremburg, owned two-thirds of Upper Silesian's stock. Foster found it extremely difficult to divest himself from those powerful lucrative interests, despite the fact that they were indispensable to the development of the German military machine during the 1930s.

Foster always vehemently denied that he was in any way a supporter of the Nazi regime. He carefully distanced himself from any ties to Germany during the 1930s when he was scrutinized, not only by the media but also by figures ranging from United States senators like Claude Pepper of Florida to everyday church people and pastors around the nation who wrote letters to the FCC expressing their concerns about Foster as a prominent churchman and the head of the FCC's Commission for a Just and Durable Peace. But as Dulles biographer Ronald Pruessen reminds us—these matters are fraught with their own complications and complexities. If people like Drew Pearson were correct and Foster knowingly supported the Nazi regime, even indirectly, any actions he took to do so would reveal much about Foster's intentions and character. If not, and Pearson only represented those who were seeking to undermine Foster in the 1944 election season, then he can be relieved of suspicion. But evaluating Foster's attitudes and actions with regard to Germany in the 1930s can be tricky. While Foster's denials of direct association with German businesses that strengthened Hitler were technically true, he still maintained indirect ties with those interests up until the outbreak of war in 1939. Pruessen wrote, "As one historian has suggested, a far more accurate gauge of the sentiment of American businessmen toward Germany during the 1930s is a measurement of their actions rather than their words: this is certainly true of John Foster Dulles."[37]

If we can say anything certain about Foster as we evaluate his life, it is that he represented many paradoxes and ironies. Personally, he was known for being principled, but he was eminently pragmatic. He was devoted to his children, but he was often distant and hard on them when they disappointed him. He could be a father figure to his siblings, and at times a sibling figure to his children. He was witty and gregarious but also withdrawn. He boasted that he knew the Bible better than anyone in the State Department, but he rarely read the Old Testament. He was proud and vain, but he also welcomed opposing ideas and was open to criticism. He was adventurous but not athletic. He loved to court danger, but his idea of a good time was a game of backgammon with his wife and a good mystery novel. He inspired lifelong loyalty, devotion, and affection in friendships dating back to college days, but some of his friends at Princeton had little to no recollection of what he was like in college when they were asked about him years after graduation. He was deeply knowledgeable in political philosophy, economics, the law, and diplomacy but incurious when it came to history and theology. He could be urbane and sophisticated but easily impressed with simple perks like getting a free haircut during his brief stint as a US senator. He enjoyed wealth and power, but he never lost touch with his provincial upstate New York roots. He loved competition but rarely competed in sailing or tennis, his favorite sports. He was devoted to his wife, but he encouraged his sister not to marry her partner because he was Jewish. He readily broke from the ministerial tradition of his family, but he personally struggled when his children charted their own paths away from other Dulles traditions. He was rigid and stubborn but often changed his mind on issues of religion and diplomacy. He was sensitive and gentle with his staff but drove them hard and inspired awe and fear among them. He was an introvert but loved the campaign trail and press conferences. He was a tireless worker, but he was home every night for dinner and games with his wife and children. He could be serious and grim, but he had a quick sense of humor that was sometimes streaked with mischief and playfulness.

In his public life, Foster could be sanctimonious, but he was not pious. He frequently preached on natural law, but he was not a theologian. He was a committed internationalist, but he believed in American hegemony and indispensability. He was suspicious of alliance systems but constructed them around the world to isolate the Communist threat. He admired the dynamism of Communism, recognized it as a religion unto itself, but condemned it as godless and committed himself to its eradication. He was disparaging of those whom he believed reacted emotionally to the Nazis in the 1930s, but he also exhibited emotionally charged reactions in his opposition to the Communists after 1945. He favored international control of atomic weapons prior to becoming secretary of state, but as secretary of state he advocated for a strategy he called "massive retaliation" and dared America's rivals to go to the brink of nuclear war. He gave the United States a lasting and just peace with Japan but had little imagination to fashion a similar peace with the Soviets or the Chinese. He was a political operative but not a politician. And at various points during his career, he was accused of being both a warmonger (by Senator Claude Pepper) and a pacifist (by fundamentalist Presbyterian Carl McIntire). He lacked public charisma and was bland behind a podium. But he had a magnetic presence; he filled a room, he was tall and muscular, and people found him irresistible. Women were frequently drawn to him, but he was famously ardent in his love for and attention to his wife.

As our narrative unfolds, we will see that five patterns of religious belief emerged and took shape as Foster's thought and career developed. Those belief patterns, simply stated, were: (1) the dynamic prevails over the static; (2) Christianity's essence is operational rather than theological; (3) moral law is supreme, and the power of moral forces is irresistible; (4) dynamic change means that peace must be actively waged like war; and (5) nature reflects a morally ordered world. Foster held to these five principles throughout his life. But he was not a theologian, nor was he a philosopher. Foster was pragmatic and a realist, so he reacted to circumstances as he encountered them. As a result, Foster's understanding and application of these principles evolved as change occurred. Thus, Foster was a man whose vital beliefs were marked by three features, sometimes simultaneously—paradox, change, and constancy. When evaluating Foster both as a public figure and a private human being, these features are helpful to remember.

Louis Jefferson, Foster's bodyguard while he was secretary of state, reflected on how Americans assessed him nearly thirty years after his death. "History has put a cold face on John Foster Dulles. The image we are given is, more often than not, inhuman. Yet Foster Dulles was, if nothing else, a very human man."[38] There is no better way to describe Dwight D. Eisenhower's secretary of state. Part of the reason that the popular image of the dour Puritan endures is, simply, that Foster projected that image to the world. He was serious and thoughtful and drew a hard line separating the personal from the professional, the trivial from the substantial, the recreational from the industrious, and the jovial from the solemn. But his religious upbringing, ideas, motives, imagination, rhetoric, and practices— for what they were worth—offer us a window into his soul. John Foster Dulles's humanity, animated by his religion, is the subject of this book. In understanding Foster in this way, we can come closer to grasping our own humanity. And in communing with the dead, perhaps we can come to a sound understanding of our own nature before our Creator.

1

"Don't Let the Little Ones Forget Me"

But perhaps it is all to accomplish some great purpose of the Almighty. If this great rebellion had been crushed out last spring . . . slavery would have remained in *statu quo*. But the prolongation of the war . . . will compel a different policy; and to use the language of Frémont in his late Boston speech, "Our flag will cover none but free men."

—Matthew Watson Foster[1]

On a golden Sunday morning in early summer—June 29, 2003, in upstate New York—a Roman Catholic cardinal in full regalia led the opening processional at the First Presbyterian Church of Watertown and ascended the dais. The sunlight streamed through the windows, splashing the pews of the redbrick church with light as the congregation stood and sang the stanzas of "When Morning Gilds the Skies," a hymn possessed of profound historical significance for this congregation. It was among the favorite hymns of one of its longest-serving and dearly loved pastors who served from 1887 to 1904: the Reverend Dr. Allen Macy Dulles, who preached his farewell sermon from that spot ninety-nine years prior.

> When morning gilds the skies,
> My heart awakening cries,
> May Jesus Christ be praised!
> Alike at work and prayer
> To Jesus I repair,
> May Jesus Christ be praised!

It was a singular and strange sight indeed for the parishioners to see a Catholic cardinal prepare to give the morning sermon, but the occasion was most appropriate. The service that Sunday was in celebration of the two-hundred-year anniversary of Watertown's First Presbyterian Church. The venerable figure in the pulpit was none other than Avery Cardinal Dulles, SJ, who had been raised to the College of Cardinals by Pope John Paul II only two years earlier.

Avery Dulles, the youngest child of John Foster and Janet Pomeroy Avery Dulles, was born in Auburn, New York, in August 1918 while Foster was serving the War Trade Board as an Army captain in Washington during the final months of World War I. Avery converted to Catholicism in 1940 while finishing his first year at Harvard Law School, breaking generations of Presbyterian family tradition. He was ordained to the priesthood in 1956 and was awarded a doctorate of sacred theology from the Gregorian University in Rome in 1960, specializing in ecclesiology (the doctrine of the church). He became one of the most important post–Vatican II Catholic theologians, and the only American Catholic to be raised to the rank of cardinal who was not a bishop. He was tall, had an impressive bearing, possessed sharp features, and was once described as "Abraham Lincoln without the beard."[2] His teachings, which stressed the need to preserve ancient church tradition and order, filled the halls of Woodstock College in Maryland, the Catholic University of America, and Fordham University in an academic career spanning five decades. Despite his *auctoritas*, Avery was known for having something of a provincial, self-deprecating wit. A few months before the celebration, Avery was on the phone with Rev. Dr. Fred Garry, the pastor of First Presbyterian. Avery wanted to know what would be appropriate for him to wear when he spoke. Garry found himself a bit tongue-tied and told Avery he should wear whatever he wanted. Avery replied, "Well, I just don't want to look too Catholicky."[3]

Avery rose to preach. Speaking in a measured cadence, he observed that his grandfather had given the sermon on the 100th anniversary of the church, his father had given the sermon on the 150th anniversary of the church, and it was now his honor to give the sermon on the 200th anniversary of the church. "Scripture refers to people through their relatives," Avery said, and even Jesus's identity as Messiah was defined in part by his human ancestry.[4]

Foster raised Avery and all his children as he had been raised—in the shadow of his ancestors. Family was of central importance in the Dulles household in Avery's generation, just as it was in Foster's generation and in the generations before him. In 1863, Foster's maternal great-grandfather, Matthew Foster, gathered his son John W. Foster and his other children around him as he lay on his deathbed. "Don't let the little ones forget me," he beseeched them.[5] John, Foster's grandfather, wrote and privately published a biography of his father for his children and grandchildren in order to honor his father's wishes.

Foster hoped that his own sons would follow in the legal and international tradition of his grandfather. Avery, in his unique way, simultaneously honored the family tradition and broke from it. He followed in his grandfather's footsteps—not his diplomat grandfather, but his theologian grandfather on the Dulles side. But his pursuit of theology was not within the Presbyterian tradition but in the Roman Catholic one. For his 1977 presidential address to the American Theological Society (which Allen Macy Dulles, Foster's father, helped found), he presented a scholarly interaction with *The True Church*, an ecclesiological work published in 1907 and authored by his grandfather. In his characteristic wit, Avery titled his address "The True Church: An Exercise in Theological Nepotism."[6]

Avery's sense of his place in the ancestral line demonstrates the importance of family to the Dulleses and the Fosters. In our own day, when one of three Americans does not know who his or her own grandparents were, this is a foreign concept to many.[7] Still, to understand Foster, it is helpful to gain some insight into those relatives who had the greatest influence on him in his formative years. Foster, according to his sisters Margaret and Eleanor, was most influenced by his grandfather, his mother, and his father.[8] Who were they, and what did Foster learn from them?

John Watson Foster, Foster's maternal grandfather, was a Union officer commanding Indiana units during the Civil War, seeing action at Fort Donelson and at Shiloh, two of the most important engagements in the western theater. After the war, he headed up the Republican Party in Indiana and held diplomatic appointments as minister to Mexico, Russia, and Spain. He served Benjamin Harrison as secretary of state in 1892–1893, and he counseled the Chinese government through the negotiations leading up to the 1895 Treaty of Shimonoseki, which concluded the First Sino-

Japanese War. He was a key player in the 1898 annexation of Hawaii and represented China at the Second Hague Conference in 1907. Grandfather Foster was a central figure in American diplomacy as it rose to world power status. And he was particularly devoted to his grandson Foster, even turning down a lucrative offer from the Chinese government to remain as a permanent diplomatic consultant after Shimonoseki so that he could honor a promise he made to seven-year-old Foster to come home and "go a-fishing" with him.[9] Grandfather Foster, who was also a Washington attorney, was young Foster's prime inspiration to be what he called a "Christian lawyer."

Edith Foster Dulles, Foster's mother, helped provide a religious and educational environment that shaped his personality, worldview, and affections. She, along with Grandfather Foster, instilled in her son a wonder of nature all around him, especially at Henderson on the Ontario shore. She also took Foster on his first trip to Europe, dramatically opening up his horizons from his small-town upstate New York and Washington, DC, world. Washington, which Foster often visited, was provincial at the turn of the century, very much like any small Southern town.

In her privately published memoir, Edith encouraged her children and grandchildren to cultivate "fearlessness" and a "love of nature." Since she spent her childhood and teen years in Mexico, France, Russia, and Spain, Edith had a unique perspective on what it meant to be fearless. She was accustomed to long separations from her parents and adjusting to foreign environments, languages, food, and customs. She achieved poise among those occupying the highest stations in politics and society, learning to be flexible as she moved from place to place, facing tragedy and loss all the while. She modeled a combination of fearlessness and love of nature when she purchased the catboat *No. 5* for Foster in 1904. She did so against the express objections of both her husband and her father and despite her own profound anxieties. She believed that if the children were going to spend their summers on the shore, they needed to learn to sail. It was only after that summer had ended that Grandfather Foster reimbursed her for the cost of *No. 5*, since, as she put it, "he said that we all had survived the perils of the summer." From that summer when he was sixteen, Foster was an avid sailor to the end of his life.[10]

Allen Macy Dulles, through his preaching, example, and personal guidance at home, gave Foster a vision of the gospel that blended devoted personal piety with active work on behalf of the church and the community. While Grandfather Foster demonstrated the Presbyterian trait of duty to one's neighbor through his legal and diplomatic life, Allen Macy modeled this trait on the basis of theological and practical principles. Allen Macy was an intellectual. He also was careful to develop each of his children with a religious education that called for scrupulous attention and accountability to Sunday sermons, the memorization of Scripture and of hymns, and engagement in local missionary endeavors. Until Allen Macy's death in 1930, Foster frequently sought his father out for advice and counsel on practical, theological, and even legal issues.

Foster's grandfather, mother, and father brought their influence to bear primarily by means of regular family rituals enacted week after week and year after year. The Fosters and the Dulleses lived together at Henderson for four months every summer, and the Dulles children would often spend winters down in Washington living with the Fosters. Communal aspects of life consisted of church and community work; family meal preparation and consumption; reading, reciting poetry, memorizing and singing hymns, and the telling and hearing of stories. Also important were the various interactions outdoors at Henderson, foreign travel, and an international network of missionaries and political figures. The handing down of family traditions centered around Presbyterianism, Princeton University, and Washington, DC. Foster's elders gave him a coherent worldview that consisted of Presbyterian presuppositions that he wholeheartedly embraced. Those presuppositions included, but were not limited to, the principles of mission, piety, patriotism, divine providence, and righteousness. Foster absorbed these presuppositions from his early youth, and while his commitment to them ebbed and flowed over the course of his seventy-one years, they remained with him and he never considered them open to question. In fact, they were essential to the way in which he approached the most pressing problems of his life and career. As Dulles biographer Mark Toulouse wrote, "This posture, though it certainly developed as he matured, was rarely subject to intellectual reflection. He simply accepted it."[11]

The Dulles Family Tree

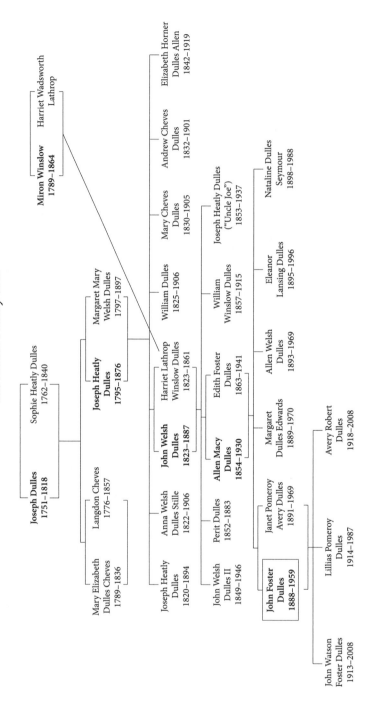

The Foster Family Tree

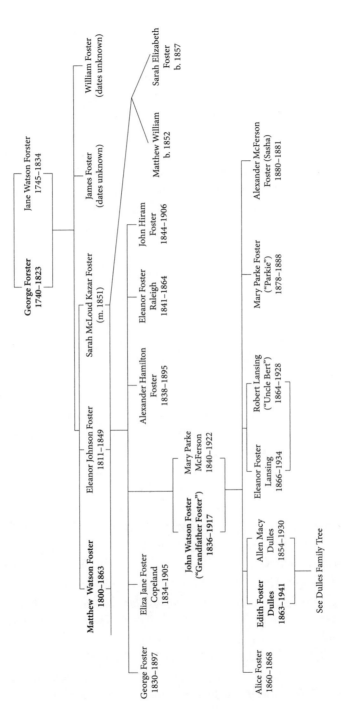

The Origins of the Dulles and Foster Families in America

The Dulles family's presence in America originated with a flight from religious persecution. Joseph Dulles (1751–1818), a Presbyterian, fled from Ireland to Holland, concealing himself in a butter churn.[12] He went from there to Charleston, South Carolina, in 1779, arriving months before the British laid siege to the city in 1780. He aligned himself with the patriot cause, took part in the city's defense, and was captured by the British in May 1780.[13]

After the war and his release, Joseph went into the hardware business and married Sophie Heatly in 1785. In 1787, he and Sophie built a shop and residence by Charleston harbor, on what is now Rainbow Row. They had two surviving children, Mary Elizabeth and Joseph Heatly Dulles. In 1810, Mary Elizabeth wed Langdon Cheves (1776–1857), an attorney who went on to become a member of Congress from South Carolina, speaker of the House of Representatives, president of the Second Bank of the United States, and an early advocate of South Carolina's secession from the Union. Joseph Heatly matriculated at Yale College and settled down in Philadelphia after graduating in 1814. Joseph and Sophie followed him, settling in Philadelphia.[14]

Joseph Heatly Dulles married Margaret Welsh of Delaware, and they had eight children who survived into adulthood. One of his children, John Welsh (1823–1887), went into the ministry, graduating from Union Theological Seminary in 1848. He was ordained by the Fourth Presbytery of Philadelphia and stepped aboard a ship in Boston headed to Madras to carry the gospel to India just over a week later. He served with the American Board of Foreign Missions in Madras and returned to America in 1853 after having suffered irreparable damage to his larynx while on the field. Once back in the United States, John Welsh became secretary for missions of the American Sunday School Union in Philadelphia, headed the Presbyterian Publication Committee, and authored two books on his missionary work, entitled *Life in India* and *The Ride through Palestine*. He was awarded the doctor of divinity degree from the College of New Jersey in 1871. John Welsh Dulles was Foster's paternal grandfather.[15]

John Welsh was married to Harriet Lathrop Winslow. Her father, Miron Winslow—Foster's great-grandfather—was also a missionary to Madras. Winslow translated the Bible into the Tamil language, a twenty-year project that he completed in 1855. He served as corresponding secretary of the Pennsylvania Bible Society, a post that was passed down to two succeeding generations of Dulleses. Foster recognized how important mission work was in his family history, particularly the work of Bible societies. In a Bible society broadcast delivered in 1950, speaking about the distribution of Bibles to American soldiers in the Korean War shortly after the devastating Chinese intervention, Foster noted the significance of his family's mission work to his own identity. "Now the Bible Society is carrying on what has been to me a family tradition. That is why I am particularly interested in being able to take part in this program," he said.[16]

The Dulles Princeton tradition began in 1871, when John Welsh was awarded the DD degree from the College of New Jersey, and continues to the current generation of Dulleses.[17] Three of John Welsh's children went to the College of New Jersey (which changed its name to Princeton University in 1896)—Joseph Heatly (class of 1873), William Winslow (class of 1878), and Allen Macy Dulles (class of 1875), Foster's father. Joseph Heatly—"Uncle Joe" to Foster—also graduated from Princeton Theological Seminary with the AM degree in 1877 and served as that institution's librarian until 1931.[18] After graduation, Foster would stay with Uncle Joe at his home just north of campus on Boudinot Street whenever he visited Princeton until Uncle Joe's death in 1937. Allen Macy also did graduate work at Princeton Seminary, completing his AM in 1878. While an undergraduate at the College of New Jersey, Allen Macy played varsity football and won first prize in senior debate as a member of the American Whig Society, the ancient debate club then in perpetual rhetorical conflict with its great rival, the Cliosophic Society. During those days, he endured the rather unfortunate nicknames of "Dools" and "Dully." Those handles didn't have too devastating an effect on Allen Macy's psyche, however—he went on to study at the University of Leipzig, the Sorbonne, the University of Göttingen, and then received a DD at Hamilton College. He pastored three churches and taught theology at Auburn Theological Seminary in Auburn, New York, until he died of a heart attack in 1930.[19]

Foster's paternal line thus embodied a missionary, pastoral, and theological tradition. His great-grandfather Winslow and grandfather Dulles were missionaries to India. They, along with Foster's uncle John Welsh II, were also active in the Philadelphia and American Bible societies. Uncle

Joe, Joseph Heatly, was an ordained Presbyterian minister and librarian of Princeton Seminary. And Foster's father, Allen Macy, was an erudite pastor and theologian.

The members of Foster's maternal side, the Foster family, were committed Presbyterian laypersons. But while the Dulles family tradition was theological, the Foster tradition was political and diplomatic. Their presence in America began with the emigration of George and Jane Forster from England in 1815. They took advantage of the peace resulting from the 1815 defeat of Napoleon and end of the War of 1812 with the Treaty of Ghent to cross the Atlantic and settle in the Mohawk Valley of New York. They came to America with three of their children but left other children in England.[20]

Once in America, the newcomers dropped the *r* from their surname, and they became the Fosters. Life was hard in New York, so in 1817 Matthew, son of George and Jane, set off west on foot in search of a place in which the family could settle and thrive. "For days and weeks he trudged along over the mountains, through the vast wildernesses of Ohio and Indiana," as Matthew's son John W. Foster (Grandfather Foster) described it, finally arriving in the booming port city of St. Louis.[21] The route Matthew took, at age seventeen, was along the Buffalo Trace, a wilderness track that ran from Albany, New York, to St. Louis. One of the waypoints on his trek was the tiny community of Delectable Hill in southern Indiana, about fifty miles north of Evansville. He made a mental note of the place, thinking it attractive and its people winsome. When he finally arrived in St. Louis, he was repelled by slaveholding, the signs of which were everywhere in the city. Deciding he could not plant roots in a town where slavery existed, he went back to Delectable Hill, Indiana, in 1819. He selected an eighty-acre parcel of land and marked it off by felling trees on each of the parcel's corners. He entered the plot on August 19 in the land office at Vincennes and immediately set to building a cabin. He made the two-room cabin of felled logs complete with "chinkin'"—clay and wood chips inserted in the gaps between the logs—and a fireplace with a chimney made with clay and wood. When Matthew finished the cabin, he made the long journey back to New York to collect his parents and brought them to Delectable Hill by way of the Ohio River to live with him there. George and Jane paid Matthew rent of four dollars per month as they lived out their days in Delectable

Hill. Their graves are still within sight of the old home place, surrounded with a wrought-iron fence that John placed there in 1899. He also erected a marble shaft at the grave, but it went missing, presumably stolen, sometime before 1955.[22]

Matthew married Eleanor Johnson, whose father was a captain in the Continental army during the American Revolution. They had six children together, including John (later Grandfather Foster), who was born in 1836. Matthew then moved his family to the larger town of Evansville, Indiana, on the Ohio River in 1846. There, what became a fruitful and varied career took off. As a wealthy merchant, a probate judge, and a prominent Whig legislator, Matthew became a pillar in the Evansville community. Matthew's wife Eleanor died shortly after they moved to Evansville, and in 1851, he married Sarah Kazar. Twelve years after marrying Sarah, Matthew died in 1863, surrounded by his children and grandchildren. John described his father as "a tireless worker" who did not "despise the day of small things." He went on to praise him as, "in the highest significance of the term . . . a patriot. Although born abroad, he came to this country in his childhood and was an intense American."[23]

Grandfather Foster, Mother, and Father

John W. Foster (1836–1917)—Grandfather Foster—initiated the diplomatic tradition in the family that Foster inherited. His personality was irresistible, and his grandchildren adored him. He was tall and imposing but had a warm and generous personality, and was always ready with a story or anecdote to bring cheer and reassurance to an intimidated stranger. He wore bushy sideburns and a full mustache, striking an iconic image.[24] And his career accomplishments were each singular and remarkable—any one of them would satisfy a reasonable person seeking an honorable reputation, but Grandfather Foster had many to his credit. As a result, he filled the imaginations of his grandchildren, and none so much as his eldest grandchild, Foster, who was his namesake.

John W. Foster and Mary Parke McFerson were married in 1859, and she accompanied him on most of his overseas adventures and served as his most trusted confidante.[25] Foster's sister Eleanor remembered her as a kindly woman, "round and plump" with hair "always in place." At Henderson, "Grandma" would refer to her husband as "Mr. Foster" around outsiders, and she was utterly devoted to him. Eleanor remembers her as happy, frequently wading while the grandchildren gleefully splashed in the water of Lake Ontario. The children were amused at what they considered her archaic clothing tastes, referring to the unyielding corset under her clothes as "Gospel armor."[26]

John graduated from the State University of Indiana as valedictorian of the class of 1855. He attended Harvard Law School for a year, passed the bar at age twenty-one, and became a law partner with Conrad Baker, who went on to become governor of Indiana. He described himself as a committed abolitionist, even though Evansville in the 1850s was a proslavery town. He was active in the first Republican presidential campaign, that of John C. Frémont in 1856, and in Abraham Lincoln's four years later in 1860.[27]

Then Fort Sumter fell. "My whole soul was enlisted in the anti-slavery cause, and when the Civil War . . . burst upon the country, my first impulse was to join the army of the Union," John remembered.[28] Ultimately John was given a major's commission by the governor, Oliver P. Morton, and commanded the Twenty-Fifth Indiana Volunteers. The Twenty-Fifth participated in Brigadier General Charles Smith's assault on Confederate Fort Donelson in February 1862, which contributed to the fort's famous "unconditional surrender" to Ulysses S. Grant. John also led his regiment at the Battle of Shiloh near Pittsburgh Landing, Tennessee, that April, the bloodiest battle in American history to that time. He was promoted to lieutenant colonel as a result of his gallantry on the battlefield. The Washington *Evening Star*, in its 1892 Grand Army Edition, produced a grandiloquent feature article on John's service at Shiloh soon after he began his tenure as secretary of state in 1892. "Again and again all through that disastrous Sabbath were his lines broken by the weight of superior numbers and each time, with the colors in his hand, did the plucky major rally the twenty-fifth until the rebels retreated," the *Star* trumpeted.[29] When reflecting and writing about his own time in the army, John was much more guarded. He wrote, "My military life greatly enlarged my knowledge of men and gave me fuller confidence in myself."[30]

After the war, John renewed his involvement in the Indiana Republican Party. By the late 1860s and early 1870s, he headed the Republican State Committee and played a significant role in delivering Indiana to Grant and also helping Oliver P. Morton, who had in the meantime been elected to the Senate, to keep his seat. Through his involvement in executive leadership within the party, he built relationships with some of the most prominent Americans of the late nineteenth century: U. S. Grant, Schuyler Colfax, Benjamin Harrison, and Frederick Douglass, to name a few. When Grant won the election of 1872, he offered John a diplomatic post through his emissary Senator Morton, out of gratitude for his Civil War service and his dedication to the party (1:10).

John was initially reluctant to accept a diplomatic post overseas, having no experience in international law. But, as he later wrote, "after canvassing the matter fully with my wife, we decided that, with our young family, a brief residence in Europe would be both pleasant and useful" (1:4). He asked for the Swiss Mission, but there was one insurmountable difficulty— the post had already been promised to someone else. So Grant (again, via Morton) offered him the Mexican Mission. "I was bewildered by the proposition," John wrote. "Now I was tendered the highest and most difficult mission on the American hemisphere" (1:4–5). He was inclined to reject the offer, but after Grant went ahead and forwarded his name to the Senate as his nominee to serve as Envoy Extraordinary and Minister Plenipotentiary to Mexico, he agreed to accept it. He began his service on June 16, 1873.

The Mexican Mission proved to be the most extensive of John's overseas diplomatic posts. He was minister to Mexico from 1873 to 1880, which was the longest any American had served in that position to that point. While holding that post, John successfully advocated for US recognition of the Porfirio Díaz regime. President Rutherford B. Hayes nominated him to the Russian Mission without his solicitation, but he had no real desire to leave Mexico. John loved Mexico and thoroughly enjoyed his work there. "I left Mexico with many regrets and with a feeling of sadness at the separation from so many dear friends to whom we had become greatly attached, and from a Government which had been uniformly courteous and considerate of my personal relations" (1:141).

When the Fosters arrived in Russia, Alexander II was the ruling czar. Alexander had liberated the serfs in 1856, but by 1880 he was deeply unpopular and had survived five assassination attempts. The empress died on June 3, right as the Fosters were getting settled in St. Petersburg, and Alexander was assassinated on March 13, 1881. As a result, John wrote, "my duties during

31

that time were chiefly in attending imperial funerals and services for the repose of the dead!" (1:170–71).

By the late summer of 1881, John was ready to return home. He wanted his children to have an American education, and he also hoped to improve his financial situation—a prospect far from likely in the diplomatic service of the 1880s. He resigned on November 1, 1881, and moved his family to Washington. He purchased a house at 1405 I Street—the house in which his grandson Foster would be born just over six years later.

John intended to open his own law firm and spend the rest of his life practicing law in Washington, but by this time he had established a broad and collegial network in government service. His private life proved to be short. Over the next eleven years, John served as minister to Spain and negotiated Alaskan boundary questions between Russia and the United States. When James Blaine resigned as secretary of state in the Benjamin Harrison administration after falling ill to Bright's disease, John filled out the last eight months of his term, from June 29, 1892, to February 23, 1893. His most significant act as secretary of state was to produce the treaty draft for Hawaiian annexation. While the islands were not annexed in 1893 due to opposition from the incoming Grover Cleveland administration, John was gratified to see this finally occur in 1898. Citing concerns that another imperial power might have seized Hawaii, like Japan or Great Britain, he was relieved that the United States took possession of the islands. "We could not allow any other Power to occupy the Islands . . . neither could we with safety to our Pacific Coast territory permit their occupation by any great military power," John wrote. "I count it an honor and a useful service to my country to have borne some part in their annexation to the United States" (2:175).

Perhaps John's most consequential work in diplomatic service was accomplished while he was a freelancer. Most likely owing to his representation of persecuted Chinese laborers in Wyoming during the 1880s, the Qing government called on John to consult with its officials as they sued for peace with Japan during the First Sino-Japanese War in 1895. The resulting Treaty of Shimonoseki was partly a product of John's consultation with Viceroy Li Hung Chang, the chief Chinese negotiator. When a would-be assassin shot Li in the face on a narrow street after the third meeting of the conference (March 24, 1895), John saw an opportunity for the Chinese delegation to gain goodwill among the Japanese, and he counseled Li to exercise restraint. Claiming credit for a diplomatic victory, John wrote, "I found [the viceroy] inclined to be resentful about the attack. . . . I told him his suffering would be for his country's good . . . and that in my opinion the attack would turn out for the benefit of China, as Japan would be less exacting in its terms" (2:132–33). The Japanese had initially rejected a proposal for an immediate twenty-one-day cease-fire. After the assassination attempt, the Japanese, who were in a position to dictate all terms for peace, consented to the cease-fire, which provided "substantial evidence of the sincere sympathy of the Japanese," according to John (2:136).

John had two other opportunities to provide counsel to Li to the benefit of the Chinese position. First, when the Japanese provided Li with a harsh first treaty draft, John planned a carefully crafted response that focused on three issues—territory, indemnities, and commercial rights. John again claimed a diplomatic victory when Japan responded with a new treaty draft, in which it gave up many of its earlier demands. "These concessions made by Japan were a great relief to the Viceroy, and materially softened the terms, severe as they still were," John wrote (2:139).

Second, John served as Li's emissary to the Chinese foreign ministry when it came time to submit the treaty draft to the Qing government for ratification. John argued that if the government rejected the treaty, they would not be rejecting Li but the emperor. After all, said John, "every word of it had been telegraphed to Peking before signing, and, with the advice of the Cabinet, the Emperor had authorized its signature." To repudiate the treaty now would result in disgrace and the certain renewal of hostilities, which could only result in total Japanese victory (2:149–50). John's characterization of his work on the treaty was self-serving, but nevertheless, he was at the center of one of the most important diplomatic events in late nineteenth-century East Asian history. He also earned the abiding gratitude and trust of the Chinese government.

After John's work with the treaty was concluded, Li asked him to stay on as a consultant on an indefinite basis. Government reform was desperately needed, and Li had confidence in John's abilities to guide those interested in doing so. John gave as many reasons to decline as he could think of, but Li "gave me to understand that I should receive such compensation as would overcome these objections." John's final answer to Li's entreaties brought a decisive end to the conversation. John explained to Li that he had undertaken to spend time with seven-year-old Foster on the Ontario shore. "I had made an engagement with and a promise to my seven-year-old grandson, that I would come home in time to go a-fishing with him that summer, and that it would destroy all his esteem and confidence in me, if I failed in my promise!" As John told the story, Li immediately understood and insisted that John keep his commitment. When John got back home and went "a-fishing" with Foster, John photographed the boy with a muskellunge almost as large as himself. He sent the photo back to Li, and Li placed the photo in a personal album (2:156–57).

Many years later, when Foster was secretary of state, he was asked about why he wanted to be secretary. He brought up his grandfather, noting that he had been an officer in the Civil War and witnessed firsthand the brutality of armed conflict. "He had a terrible hatred of war," Foster said of him. "I acquired that feeling I think more than anything else. It wasn't so much [that I wanted] just to be Secretary of State but it was to be in a position where you could perhaps do something to do away with this terrible practice of nations fighting."[31] It is true that, in later years, Foster often wavered between being strikingly unsentimental about the memory of the most important figures of his life and being openly emotional about them. But their intellectual and emotional proximity to Foster is evident consistently in the warp and woof of his life.

Foster's mother, Edith (1863–1941), was, as her children often put it, "reared at the foot of kings."[32] Growing up with a father like John introduced her to tremendous experiences, yet she demonstrated a realistic awareness of her unique privilege and perspective. Prior to her marriage at age twenty-four, Edith lived and was educated in Indiana, Mexico, Russia, Spain, Paris, and Washington. In the context of her international upbringing, Edith had what she described as her first significant religious experience, came to be deeply affected by the outdoors, learned compassion for the poor, gained awareness of political and religious movements that shaped other cultures, and learned to deal with loneliness and the deaths of two of her younger siblings. She bore witness to some of the most momentous occasions in world history. She attended the funeral of Czar Alexander II of Russia, throwing a handful of sand into his grave after the coffin had been lowered. She anxiously mused on the surrealism of the 1881 shooting of the

American president James A. Garfield, whom her father knew personally. "I [was] horrified to think that such a thing could happen in *our* country," she wrote, and that it corresponded so closely in time—just a matter of three months—to the assassination of the Russian czar.[33] And she was present in the gallery of the House of Representatives on April 2, 1917, to listen to Woodrow Wilson ask Congress to declare war on Germany and enter World War I on the side of the Allies—"a thrilling occasion," she said in her memoir. She knew firsthand what it was like to dine with emperors in their palaces, yet she was naturally comfortable and patient in parochial settings like Watertown and Auburn, with people who were unassuming, simple, often uneducated, and frequently petty.

Edith first learned and cultivated a lifelong love of the outdoors while growing up in Mexico City between her ninth and fifteenth birthdays. "Mexico has left the deepest impression on my memory," she wrote in 1934. "I love to think of my years there." The Fosters lived on the third floor of a building occupied on the first floor by the Bank of England at 3 Calle de Lerdo. She would stand on the roof above their apartment and watch the sunsets over the mountains, "coloring their snowy tops a brilliant pink which gradually died away to dim blue," she wrote. "I used to walk up and down the great stretch of roof, my eyes fixed on the mountains, and, if I were alone, recite pieces of poetry." She and her parents would go out on horseback in the early mornings to the ancient palace at Chapultepec—the site of a major battle between American and Mexican forces, which occurred only about thirty years earlier during the Mexican-American War in 1847. Her later reflections on her youth in Mexico were dominated by, as she put it, "beautiful mountains and sunsets, delightful mornings on horseback and excursions which we frequently made into the country round about."[34]

When she was fifteen, Edith's parents sent her back to the States to go to school. The thought of being sent away from her family was shattering to her, and the horror of it was accentuated by the experience of being put on a steamer to sail away by herself. She remembered that she did not absorb the reality of what was happening to her until, while her father accompanied her to her stateroom, they encountered a little dog that John said reminded him of their dog at home. Then, utter despair hit her, the notion of "leaving my home, my family, everything I loved. . . . I went into my stateroom . . . and there I stayed for three or four days until we dropped anchor in the harbor of Havana." She was despondent, and her writing about the experience decades later seemed to have brought back her anguish. "There is something so inevitable about a steamer, other modes of conveyance can be stopped, but a steamship sails on and on to its far off haven," Edith wrote. "I have had some sorrows and disappointments in my life in the many years since then, but I have never suffered the hopeless misery I did then." Striking indeed it is for her to have described her anxiety in this way, realizing that she had lost two sisters, a baby brother, her mother and father, and her husband by the time she wrote this statement reflecting on leaving Mexico.

Still, in the agony of abject loneliness coupled with her suffering of the unique misery of seasickness, she came to a sudden realization that ignited her faith. While in port in Havana, she knelt to pray the Lord's Prayer, opened with "Our Father," and then suddenly stopped. "For the first time in my life I realized that God was my father." She realized that despite all her years of going to church, of reading and memorizing Scripture, of singing hymns, that religion meant little to her until this moment. "Now God meant something to me," she said. "He was my Father. I had touched reality. It was my first religious experience."

While in Russia, Edith was struck by the yawning gulf between the magnificently rich and grindingly poor. The upper classes spent the winters attending elaborate and luxurious parties that began at midnight and lasted into the early daylight hours. Russia was the site of the most vibrant social life among the world's diplomats, and Edith was struck by the sights, sounds, and tastes of that life. "The jewels worn by the ladies of rank were very wonderful, ropes of pearls and diamond tiaras and dresses spangled with real jewels." But she was also struck by the state of the lower classes of Russia. "Terrible poverty on one hand, greatest luxury on the other. The finest culture, side by side with the densest ignorance." She regretted that her exposure to Russia and Russians was confined to the very rich. "It was a disappointment to me that we could only come into contact with the highest class of Russians. Even our servants were Italian or Finnish," none of them native Russians, she wrote. Since French was the language of the elite, Edith was astounded that many of the younger members of Russia's upper class were actually proud of the fact that they could not speak Russian.

The Fosters were present in Russia during a remarkable but short-lived evangelistic revival sponsored by Colonel W. A. Pashkoff. The revival began after a group of Russian ladies had traveled to Switzerland and attended evangelistic meetings there led by an English nobleman, Granville Waldegrave, third Baron of Radstock. They invited Lord Radstock to come to St. Petersburg, which he did, and then his evangelistic preaching was continued by Russians. Pashkoff, an officer in the Imperial Guards, opened his palace on the Nevsky Prospekt to hold revival meetings for what had the makings of a major Protestant awakening. "We came to know Col. Pashkoff . . . very well," Edith wrote. The meetings at his palace "were attended by hundreds, even as many as one thousand crowding the rooms at times." Edith remained in Russia long enough to see and regret the police break up and ban the meetings and also to send Pashkoff into exile after the assassination of Alexander II.[35]

In the spring of 1881, Edith enrolled at a Protestant girls' school in Paris at 85 Rue de la Pompe. She attended school there for nearly three months with thirteen other students, among them the granddaughter of Victor Hugo. While in school, Edith recorded in her diary one evening that she had met a certain "Mr. Dunis" at a dinner hosted by some American friends living in Paris. She had actually misheard his name and learned later that it was "Dulles," not "Dunis." After this initial meeting, Edith reported that another American friend, a "Miss Cornwall," was convinced that "Mr. Dulles" and Edith were made for one another, and began inviting them frequently to teas where they would have further opportunities to get acquainted. "I had no thought of men at that time, and although 'Mr. Dulles' was very attentive all summer, I never thought he was interested in me." Allen Macy had, in fact, become very interested in Edith. He had been studying theology at Leipzig and Göttingen and had recently finished a trip to Palestine. Allen Macy was beginning his tenure as pastor of Trumbull Avenue Presbyterian Church in Detroit, and when Edith left Paris to move into her new home in Washington on I Street, he sent her a telegram. Edith's father suspiciously asked her, "What does that mean?" She hardly knew what to say.

That December, 1881, Edith's baby brother came down with typhoid fever and died after barely one year of life. Alexander, whom the family nicknamed "Sasha" because of his Russian birth, was born on December 2, 1880, and died on December 4, 1881. It was the only time she ever saw her father cry. The old war veteran, witness to hundreds of men blown away in one of the bloodiest battles in American history, sobbed like a child after the baby's funeral, burying his face in his hands and saying, "I cannot bear it." This was the first person Edith lost to death to whom she was close. Edith's older sister Alice had died in 1868 at age eight when Edith was only five. And little Mary Parke, or "Parkie," who had been born in Mexico City, died at ten years of age in 1888 a few months after Edith gave birth to Foster. "I have never felt death in that same hopeless way since," Edith wrote of losing baby Sasha.

But the rest of the winter of 1880–1881, Edith saw more and more of Allen, who frequently traveled to Washington to visit her. After taking her to hear a lecture by Henry Ward Beecher, he abruptly asked her to marry him. "If he had turned and placed a pistol at my head I could not have been more surprised," Edith said of her shock. At the time, she felt nothing more than friendship for this man who was nine years her senior. Edith's father would not give his blessing to any thought of engagement until at least a year had passed. They continued to see one another and correspond rather drily, calling one another "Mr. Dulles" and "Miss Foster."

When Edith's father received his commission to the Spanish Mission in 1883 and the family was off on another move to Europe, Edith wrote Allen Macy to break up with him. She was not convinced that he was husband material, nor was she altogether sure what it meant to love someone. While in Madrid, she had what appears to be her first romantic crush. She became infatuated with a Spanish doctor who was teaching her how to play the guitar. When her parents forbade her to have any further contact with him, Edith wrote, "I sent him off, but imagined myself ill-treated for some time."

But the next winter, 1884–1885, Edith returned to Washington and began seeing Allen Macy once again. By the end of the summer of 1885, Edith reported, she knew she loved him, especially when he dropped on her a veiled threat of going back to Detroit and never seeing her again. They were married on January 13, 1886, at New York Avenue Presbyterian Church. Allen Macy's father, John Welsh, officiated at the ceremony.

At the end of the memoir that Edith wrote in her sixty-ninth year, she gave some words of advice as she looked back on her long and active life. She counseled her grandchildren to cultivate four particular traits—a love of nature, a love of reading, a love of solitude, and fearlessness. Her son

Foster demonstrated these traits from his youth in his own ways, both at play and at work. She wrote to Foster after hearing him give a radio address in 1937 to tell him of her pride in what he had set out to become. "I want . . . to tell you how much I appreciate what you are doing in the cause of Peace and Religion. I remember that after graduation [in 1908], when you told me that you were going into the law and not the ministry, that you said you thought you could do just as much good in that field, and you are proving it. . . . I know the temptation to selfishness in the busy New York life and it makes me very happy that you are willing to sacrifice something for the real needs of the world."[36]

Edith closed her memoir with these words—"as we go fearlessly on our way through life enjoying the world around us . . . we come to know 'Another' who reveals Himself in the beauty of nature, in the thoughts of the great writers, in the depths of our own souls, and we are never alone. Life, death, and the great Forever are His, and we are His. (If this sounds like a sermon, remember I lived with a preacher for over forty years.)"[37]

That preacher was born in 1854 and died in 1930. Allen Macy came from a long tradition of Presbyterian ministers, theologians, and missionaries, but he was a theological liberal in the tradition of F. D. E. Schleiermacher, Albrecht Ritschl, and Adolf von Harnack. Allen Macy's brother, John Welsh II, was a fundamentalist who warned Foster against evolution, but Allen Macy enthusiastically embraced Darwin's theories.[38] Despite his quiet and introspective personality, Allen Macy maintained a deeply devotional and pious life and cultivated an atmosphere of piety at home and at church.

Allen was ordained in 1881 and served the Trumbull Avenue church in Detroit from 1881 to 1887. Representatives from First Presbyterian Church (FPC) of Watertown came to hear Allen Macy preach at his church in 1887 and were impressed. On November 17, 1887, Allen Macy was installed as pastor of the Watertown church. This was an old church, founded in 1803, shortly after the first white settlers arrived. Caleb Burnham, one of the first settlers in the area, erected a barn across from Sandy Creek. Ebenezer Lazelle, a missionary from New England, asked Burnham for the use of his barn to hold services. Thirteen people came to the service in Burnham's barn on June 3, 1803.[39] By 1887 when Allen Macy took the pastorate of the church, it dominated the landscape with its fine steeple and helped form the culture of the town through its ministries. Allen Macy's seventeen-year ministry was marked by a commitment to preaching, local mission work, and to building renovations at the old church.

Allen Macy's theological and philosophical convictions come through most clearly in the monograph he completed in 1907, *The True Church*. In that work, he sought to address the issue of church authority—"to be better able to answer sophistical questions such as 'who has authority to give sacred bread.'" Allen Macy's argument, sustained over three hundred pages of text, was that, broadly considered, there were two mutually exclusive theologies of the church. One was authoritarian, coercive, and dogmatic; the other was voluntary, free, and ethical. The first theology he described as "catholic" and included the Roman Catholic, Greek Orthodox, Chaldean, Coptic, Syrian, and Gregorian traditions. The second theology he styled "evangelic." He included the Lutheran and Reformed traditions in this group. For Allen Macy, those traditions that were catholic were false churches because they "limited Christian liberty and corrupted Christian service."[40] Those evangelic traditions were the true church because they respected human freedom and refused to exert force to compel belief.[41]

For Allen, intellectual freedom and the freedom to fulfill one's duty to Christ's ethical command were of prime importance for the church and for the individual. In fact, to be a legitimate church of Jesus Christ, a tradition had to have a high view of human freedom and resist all forms of compulsion. He wrote, "A unity which is maintained by *any* force whether physical or mental or so-called moral, is not unity, but uniformity. All genuine Christians, and therefore all true churches are one in certain respects, both freely and voluntarily."[42] What defined this unity was a common and immediate relationship with Jesus Christ, and a bond of love between the church's members that was modeled by Christ. That love would be expressed actively, naturally, and sincerely through the individual's sense of duty toward others. As Paul described in Ephesians 4:5, for the true church "there is one Lord, one faith, one baptism."[43] Allen Macy's emphases on the ethical over the dogmatic and individual freedom over institutional coercion were central characteristics of his preaching. From his youth, Foster accepted these features from his father, and later sought his father's advice on how to put these principles to use, especially as a young lawyer in the

1920s in the context of the liberal/fundamentalist controversies within the Presbyterian church.

It is striking that Foster adopted a similar dualism of two mutually exclusive ideas about authority and human personhood in the context of Cold War tensions during the 1950s. After 1949, with the fall of Nationalist China to the Communists, the Soviet Union detonating its own atomic bomb, and the invasion by North Korea of South Korea, Foster came to articulate world politics in terms of an essential conflict of two competing faiths, one authoritarian and coercive and the other democratic and free. For example, in a speech Foster gave to the Young Women's Christian Association in 1955, he contrasted two views on the meaning of "peace." He said the West's definition of peace "implies the inner tranquility which comes to those who are enabled to pursue happiness and develop their God-given possibilities of body, mind, and soul." In contrast, the Communists defined peace as "a state of enforced conformity where all men think alike, believe alike, and act in accordance with a pattern imposed by their rulers."[44] It is possible, even likely, that Foster never read his father's book, given his lack of interest in theology. But even if he never read the book, he did sit for three sermons each Sunday in the fourth pew on the right aisle near the pulpit from which his father preached for sixteen years. Foster's own sermonizing as secretary of state about the weakness of materialistic, godless Communism and the strength of America's righteousness and spiritual fiber bears conspicuous commonality with his father's ecclesiastical dualism.

From his infancy, Foster's elders raised him and his four siblings in a close-knit environment steeped in piety, nature, and devotion to customs. Watertown in the last decade of the 1800s was a thriving and picturesque place. Most people in town walked to take care of errands or to go to church or school, or rode in horse-drawn wagons. In winter, many folks drove in sleighs. Washington Street, on which FPC has stood since 1821, was lined with hundred-foot elm trees in the days when the Reverend Dr. Dulles was pastor; it stood just outside of the town center.[45] The Dulleses lived in the parsonage on Clinton Street until 1897, when they built a house of their own after their fifth child, Nataline, was born.

They had several pets—two ponies, several King Charles spaniels, and a cat named Sir Tibby of the Glen.[46] The children took vigorous baths in cold water and carried their Bibles to church, as well as some of their allowance money for the weekly collection. After church, the family would go home and prepare for Sunday dinner, which consisted of the same routine each week. "The dinner was almost always roast chicken, mashed potatoes, sometimes spinach, and *always* ice cream with chocolate or maple sauce," Foster's sister Eleanor recalled.[47] They would discuss the sermon, play games, sing hymns, and read together. Allen Macy and Edith both loved poetry, and William Wordsworth's poetry in particular. Eleanor wrote that the same Sunday routine week after week was not harsh or dull but comforting, emanating a sensation of home and constancy. "The emotion of those [Sunday] evenings was so poignant that even now I cannot accept easily the surge of nostalgia, the longing for those love-filled moments with my family," Eleanor wrote, some seventy-six years removed from her life in Watertown.[48]

In 1894, John built the first family cottage at Henderson on the Lake Ontario shore. They called it Underbluff, and it was the house in which the Dulleses and the Fosters lived together for three to four months every summer. Robert Lansing, John's son-in-law and husband to Edith's sister Eleanor, who served Woodrow Wilson as secretary of state, first took John to fish in Henderson, and he loved it so much that he purchased the lot on which he later built Underbluff. Other cottages followed—Linden Lodge, Greyledge, and Hillside were built and owned by other Dulleses and Seymours and Lansings.[49] Foster would go with Grandfather Foster to fish on the lake at eight in the morning and come home around six at night every day during the summers except Sunday. Allen, Foster's brother, also went—they would catch black bass, rock bass, and perch—although they threw the rock bass back. When they had caught numerous fish, they would land on the beach of one of the many islands out in the lake. They would cook their fish over open fires, along with corn, potatoes, and coffee. Conversation topics would be international affairs, or the wind and weather, or the fish. Often, Grandfather Foster would invite Uncle Bert (Robert Lansing) and numerous friends on other occasions to join Foster and Allen Macy on these outings. One of the people who went on the Dulles fishing outings was Bernard Baruch, adviser to President Wilson, who would prove to be one of Foster's closest friends and most valuable mentors.[50]

Into this world was John Foster Dulles born and raised—a Presbyterian world, a world steeped in international and patriotic tradition, a world in which family, poetry, reading, sailing, fishing, nature, service, and piety were built into the patterns of everyday living. How was it that a small-town boy growing up in an obscure corner of the nation, far from the centers of culture, power, and industry, could rise to become the most powerful figure of international diplomacy in the world of the 1950s alongside President Dwight Eisenhower? And how did his Presbyterian upbringing inform that figure's worldview when he occupied that lofty place of great power and privilege—the secretary of state's office in the US State Department building at Foggy Bottom? The answers to those questions are varied, complex, sometimes mysterious, and always debatable. But without reference to John Watson Foster, Allen Macy Dulles, and Edith Foster Dulles, it is not possible to understand satisfactorily John Foster Dulles the man and what he would represent in a world buffeted by war.

2

"His Character Is Straightforward and Sweet"
(1888–1912)

> He has fine acquisitive powers, and such things as interest
> him he very promptly takes hold of and retains. . . . He is rev-
> erential to a striking degree. . . . His logical acumen betokens
> a career as a thinker, for now he reasons with a clearness far
> beyond his age. . . . He loves a joke intensely and sees one
> without any explanation.
>
> —Allen Macy Dulles about Foster
> on his fifth birthday[1]

On March 11, 1888, the severest winter storm that anyone living in the
nation's capital could remember hit the city with Jovian force. A low-
pressure system from the south merged with a blast of cold air coming
down from Canada, and the "Blizzard of '88" paralyzed the region from
New England to the District of Columbia. The morning and early afternoon
of that day saw copious rains descend on Washington, such that the sewers
backed up and the streets began to flood. But by late afternoon, the rain had
turned to snow. Trees and overhead telegraph wires and their supporting
poles collapsed and crisscrossed the streets. What electricity existed in the
city also went down, and a fire broke out at police headquarters. By midnight, the entire city had gone completely dark. Because of the downed
wires and trees, both rail travel and telegraph communications were rendered impossible. The *Evening Star* described Washington as "completely
isolated all day."[2]

Surrounded by the howling winds and blowing snow outdoors, a family inside the house at 1405 I Street, NW, was welcoming its newest member into the world. Edith Dulles was staying with her parents. She had recently given birth to her first child, a boy, born on February 25. Edith and Allen Macy decided to name the boy after her father, John Foster.

Edith and Allen Macy had come down to Washington in late January so that Edith could be near her parents when the baby was born. It was a good thing they had done so. Two days before Foster's birth, Allen Macy left Washington to go back to Detroit, back to Trumbull Avenue Presbyterian Church, where he had served as pastor for the past several years. During the last years of his pastorate there, Allen Macy had been the chief fund-raiser for a new church building. Groundbreaking for the new building had taken place in October 1886, and the building was now finished. And though Allen Macy had already taken the pastorate at First Presbyterian of Watertown, he was obliged to preach at the new building dedication in Detroit. On top of that, Edith fell ill with puerperal fever after Foster's birth, and she was bedridden for the next two months. She would later write, "it was not until my birthday, April 25, that I was able to come downstairs."[3] But by the middle of spring, Allen Macy and Edith had taken their firstborn son back to their new home in Watertown, to the parsonage on Clinton Street. Uncle Joe came up from Princeton and baptized Foster in the green marble baptismal font the Lansing family had donated to the church in 1879 (which is still in use by the church to this day). Foster was baptized on June 1, 1888. Edith wrote, "he did not cry, but sucked his two fingers and looked about the church."[4] From very early, Allen Macy and Edith called the boy "Foster" to honor Edith's father and his family's heritage.

Establishing Lifelong Patterns

From his birth in 1888 to his engagement at age twenty-three to Janet Pomeroy Avery in 1911, Foster's upbringing, education, and relationships established patterns that endured until his death in 1959. At some times in his life the grooves of those patterns ran deeper than at other times, but he never completely broke away from them. His career as a lawyer, a churchman, and a diplomat emerged out of the paradigms of his experiences from childhood through young adulthood in Watertown, Washington, Princeton, and Europe.

The religious patterns Foster's family and church relations impressed on his mind formed a durable moral and pietistic frame of reference. Intellectually, Foster developed an analytical mind early in his life and built a base of knowledge in history, philosophy, rhetoric, and the law. He did so beginning in his teens. Experientially, his parents and grandparents opened a window for Foster into the larger world through travel to France, Switzerland, England, and Spain. They also served as the impetus for Foster to cultivate a love of the Great Lakes, especially Ontario and its islands, and for sailing and fishing. Finally, Foster developed indispensable skills in navigating the labyrinthine courses and thin-skinned personalities of high society, particularly while attending the Second Hague Peace Conference of 1907 with Grandfather Foster and during his law school years in Washington, when he rubbed elbows with a plethora of notables, including President William Howard Taft's family, US senators, Supreme Court justices, and business leaders at various teas, dinners, lunches, and balls. These religious, intellectual, experiential, environmental, and social patterns were well worn and well established during Foster's early years. They characterized—albeit to varying extents—the scope of his temperament, career, and relationships.

Foster's personality as a toddler gave early indications of characteristics that would make him famous in later life. It was obvious by the time he was five years old that he was pious, strong willed, intelligent, and possessed of an infectious and uproarious laugh. His mother and father doted on him, recording some of the most significant events of the first seven years of his young life in a diary that served as a baby book. One of his favorite songs as a toddler was "Jesus, Tender Shepherd, Hear Me." He scrupulously observed regular prayer times with the family. When Foster was two years of age, Edith described him as "very particular about the blessing, will not eat without it. . . . He generally is also very particular about morning prayers."[5] By his seventh birthday, Allen Macy noted with clear satisfaction that Foster had memorized Psalms 1, 19, 23, 24, 46, 100, and 103 along with several hymns, such as "The Son of God Goes Forth to War," "Onward, Christian Soldiers," "Stand Up, Stand Up for Jesus," "Jesus, Lover of My Soul," and "Glory to Thee, My God." In Foster's baby book, Allen Macy wrote, "his character is straight-forward and sweet. He is good at church and Sunday School."[6]

Edith and Allen Macy also noted that Foster could be stubborn. They took him to church for the first time on Christmas Day 1890 when he was nearly three, but "he didn't want to part with his money to put it in the collection." He was so animated in his tightfistedness that Edith took him out of the sanctuary, apparently for a spanking. And yet, his sense of justice was also clear at this tender age, because Allen Macy noticed that Foster associated the posture of prayer with righteousness and humility—"when at night he is angry and will not go to bed, he will not say his prayers, but when he is willing to pray, then he is also quiet." Allen Macy's conclusion to this observation was that Foster's "conscience is keen for right and wrong"[7]—a remarkably prescient observation.

Foster was just over a year old when he took his first trip to Henderson. By the time he was two, Edith described him as a "great chatterbox," talking "from morning till night"—another famous Dulles trait. But he learned early on that fishing was no time for conversation—his first fishing trip with Grandfather Foster occurred in June 1890, and he went fishing every day (except Sunday). Edith reported that Foster "would hold out his stick most patiently, perfectly delighted when we occasionally gave him a minnow."[8] By his fifth birthday, Foster already was developing a noticeably muscular frame and wanted to be big and strong "like Samson."[9]

Foster took his first trip (of many) to the White House on March 15, 1892. The occasion was the fifth birthday of President Benjamin Harrison's grandson, Benjamin Harrison McKee. Grandfather Foster was close to President Harrison. He became secretary of state under Harrison just three months later. Edith saved a clipping from the *Evening Star* describing the event as a "charming . . . state banquet. . . . There is no doubt but that they had all the fun."[10] John Philip Sousa was in attendance, leading the Marine Band as it stomped out marches for the children, and Edith wrote that the Marines' music and bearing, with their red uniforms and gold lace, entranced Foster.[11]

As Foster grew up, along came more Dulles children—Margaret was born on April 25, 1889 (on her mother's twenty-fifth birthday); Allen on April 7, 1893; Eleanor on June 1, 1895; and finally Nataline on January 22, 1898. Because of the age differences, Foster was closer as a brother to Margaret and Allen growing up. He was more of a father figure to Eleanor and Nataline. Nataline, nine years younger than her brother, remembered him taking her to the circus for her tenth birthday. "That was a tremendous event in my life, being taken to the circus by my older brother," she reflected nearly sixty years later.[12]

Each of the children attended the public schools in Watertown, but Edith and Allen Macy thought the public schools were poor in quality. They augmented their children's public education with tutors and private schooling. The Dulles offspring also possessed the unique experience of being pastor's children, so their religious education was particularly advanced. And since both Edith and Allen Macy shared a lively affection for classical literature, all the children grew up reading extensively in Shakespeare, Wordsworth, Milton, Longfellow, Tennyson, Browning, Dickens, Scott, and other masters. Foster did not have much formal training in grammar as a youngster, but by the time he graduated from Watertown High School, he knew Greek and Latin well enough to parse English verbs. He easily passed the English, Latin, and Greek sections on his Princeton entrance exams, receiving a conditional pass only on Greek composition.[13] "My father felt that one acquired education through association with great men of the past," Margaret said. "So that rather than study English grammar, we were just supposed to be exposed to great writing."[14] Indeed, in an essay Foster wrote early in his freshman year at Princeton (peppered with misspellings), he confessed, "It is hard to write five hundred words on ones preperation [sic] in English when one has not spent five hundred minutes preparing it." Still, Foster took comfort in the fact that "my knowledge of grammatical rules . . . consists chiefly in what I have learned from Latin and Greek."[15]

Growing up in the household of a pastor meant that the better part of any given Sunday was spent in church. This was certainly true for Foster—he usually attended three church services along with Sunday school. Each morning, all the children were loudly summoned to a bath of cold water by a gong that Allen Macy rang. Short prayers were said prior to breakfast, and a hymn or two were sung, accompanied by Edith on the piano. During the summers in Henderson, the Dulleses attended the Methodist church in the village, walking the three miles from the shore to the church most Sundays. Whether it was in Watertown or in Henderson, Sunday dinners were a regular ritual. After dinner, everyone would get together and sing hymns, talk about the sermon and Bible lessons, and recite Scripture verses from memory.[16] Foster and Allen would sometimes join the Sunday evening sessions with their pet crow perched on one of their shoulders, to the great delight of their younger sisters.[17]

Fishing Trips and Studies Abroad

Foster and Allen became close friends in their childhood years as their father and grandfather introduced them to fishing. Allen described the brothers' fishing trips on Lake Ontario as "very serious business." Besides their father and grandfather, Foster and Allen had another mentor in Will Stevens, a local man and lifelong friend of the family who taught them the ways of the fish and the lake. "Great fellow," Allen said, "great influence on both of us." Foster and Allen would compete against one another for the most fish caught (below the legal limit of thirty-two) or the largest fish. They would also make small sailboats with penknives, no longer than about a foot, and race those little handcrafted vessels in the water off the little beach at Underbluff. When heading out early in the morning for a day of fishing, they would choose their fishing ground based on the direction of the wind. They had a quaint poem they put to a tune and sang—

> When the wind is in the north,
> Then the fisherman goeth not forth.
> When the wind is in the east,
> Then the fishes bite the least.
> When the wind is in the south,
> It blows the bait in the fishes' mouth.
> When the wind is in the west,
> Then the fishes bite the best.[18]

Will Stevens taught the boys that fish were creatures of habit, and if you learned their habits you could catch them easily. He also taught Foster most of what he knew early on about sailing. His father, grandfather, and uncle were skilled fishermen, but no one in the family knew anything about sailing. Will taught Foster how to navigate *No. 5* on the unpredictable lake without relying on a motor. "We started out with nothing but sailboats," Allen said. "And if the wind died down you jolly well rowed home. Sometimes we'd go ten, fifteen miles away."[19] Eleanor loved Will and credited him with impressing on Foster the virtue of avoiding idle chatter. "Will never used four words if two would suffice." Foster himself became a man of few words in one-on-one conversations. While observing her brother interact with colleagues at the State Department, Eleanor was struck by how much Foster reminded her of Will. Will died in February 1958, just over a year before Foster, at the wise old age of ninety-eight.[20]

Foster was a boy who loved adventure, who reveled in a physical challenge even if that challenge was quite dangerous. And he loved animals, particularly birds. As a child, Foster had an impressive collection of birds' eggs that he had gathered by climbing up trees and locating the nests. He was adamant that one must only take one egg, and if there was only one egg in the nest, one must leave it alone. The story of his climbing to the top of a maple tree at Henderson to collect a crow's egg, and then bringing it down in his mouth, was one of his sisters' favorite stories to tell.[21] He also loved the physical challenge of swimming, and he set a goal for himself to swim across Henderson Bay, two miles in length. "He practiced until he knew what his strength was," Eleanor wrote. He made the swim in open water with Allen Macy following alongside in a rowboat. With each challenge he undertook, whether it was sailing, swimming, fishing, or climbing, "he took full account of the facts and then applied his experience and skill to achieving his goal."[22]

Not only was young Foster adventurous, he was also calm, cool, and collected in times of stress. Eleanor related the story of a sailing expedition on *No. 5*, when the boat almost went down in Lake Ontario during a storm. Eleanor had invited her friend Mary to join her and her brothers on a nice outing on the lake, but the weather turned on them. Mary was definitely not "salty"—Eleanor described her as a "landlubber." During the storm, Allen was at the bilge pump, Foster at the tiller, and Eleanor was controlling the sail ("at the sheet") and bailing. To give Eleanor a break, Mary took the bucket, but "as soon as the boat heaved she let the bucket go overboard." Foster saw what happened but said nothing. Eventually, Foster got the boat safely under the lee of an island. Once they were safe, Mary asked Foster, "If the boat had sunk, when would we have been rescued?" Foster coolly replied, "Tomorrow."[23] Foster's imperturbability was another well-known trait in his later years, one that he demonstrated on many occasions.

The year that Foster graduated from high school, 1903, Grandfather Foster sent Edith, Foster, and Margaret on a European trip so that the children could learn French. Reflecting upon that trip over thirty years later, Edith wrote, "I have made a good many trips to Europe, but I am sure that the trip I made in 1903 with Foster and Margaret was in many ways the most enjoyable of all." When Edith told the children that they were headed to Europe, they were ecstatic—all except Allen, of course, who wanted to go but had to stay home for being too young. "How Foster and Margaret reveled in the numerous plans of steamships and enjoyed making out routes of travel. . . . It was the first touch of foreign life the children had ever seen and they were wild with excitement."[24] Given all of Edith's experiences overseas as the child of a diplomat, one can understand why she would be so thrilled to see this European adventure through her children's eyes.

Edith, Foster, and Margaret left Boston March 28 on the SS *Commonwealth* and arrived in the Azores on April 3, after a journey over rough seas. They proceeded on the *Commonwealth* to Gibraltar, Genoa, and Naples, disembarking on April 11. Their destination was Lausanne, Switzerland, and Edith's goal was to find a family "who might be willing to take [them] for the summer" as boarders and teach the children conversational French. But Edith did not have any contacts in Lausanne, so she had to literally knock on doors and introduce herself and her children and make her request house by house. They searched Lausanne for a week, and finally arrived at the home of M. and Mdm. Bischoff and their son Henri on the Rue de la Petite Vuachère. M. Bischoff was an artist, and their home looked out over Lake Geneva and the Alps. For two months, Foster studied Greek and French and Margaret attended riding school. In July, Allen Macy and Uncle Joe joined them, and Foster fulfilled his one great desire while in Switzerland—to climb the Breithorn, a 13,600-foot peak in the Alps, with his father. After visits to Paris and London, the family went home together on the SS *Canada*, embarking for America on September 3.[25] Foster took to French quite well during the short time he resided in Europe. By the next year, he had earned a pass in first-year French and a conditional pass in second-year French on his Princeton entrance exam.[26]

Returning home, Foster spent the next academic year after graduating high school studying under a private tutor.[27] The years of his childhood passed as he lived and flourished in Watertown with his parents and siblings. He sporadically spent time living with his grandparents in Washington, and always spent the summers with his entire family at Henderson. All the Dulles children described their parents as being formal and predictable, but also fun loving and encouraging of their adventurous streak. They were the first people in Watertown to own skis. Sunday dinners were legendary for the variety of food and the fact that they were usually about three hours in length. Foster ate more than anyone else—"the raw tomatoes, and raw onions and the soup and the steak, or chops, potatoes and ear after ear of corn, and then fish, and maybe cucumbers . . . maybe another vegetable, and then two or three kinds of pie [followed by] doughnuts and coffee," Eleanor remembered watching Foster eat in wonder at the size of his appetite.[28]

Birthdays and anniversaries were celebrated with much enthusiasm, and Christmases were particularly memorable. After Edith's sister Eleanor met and married Robert Lansing (the Lansings were an old and prominent Watertown family), the children opened Christmas stockings three separate times—at home, at "Aunt's" (as the children called their Aunt Eleanor), and at the Lansing house, which was located across the street from the Clinton Street parsonage. And when the family was not together for Christmas, ties were still maintained through letters. Grandfather Foster wrote a lengthy letter to Foster on his second Christmas, describing in great detail all the presents at the house in Washington. He closed his letter by admonishing him to "kiss sister [Margaret] oh so many times for me, and don't let her forget Grandpapa," perhaps in the spirit of his own dying father's last request.[29] The family also scrupulously attended church services every Christmas Day, and the children delivered presents to the poor throughout the town. Edith and the children regularly made around two hundred presents each year to distribute.[30]

At Henderson, the family always looked forward to Fourth of July celebrations. On the back porch, which looked out directly over the lake, the children lit Roman candles, sparklers, and firecrackers with delight and laughter. After dark, they made paper balloons that could carry candles. They would make and light several of these flying contraptions, and they would sail off high over the lake. The children watched them as they drifted off, and they were visible for miles.[31]

After Allen Macy left Watertown's FPC for a teaching post at Auburn Seminary in 1904, Foster and Margaret would invite large numbers of their friends over to their new house on South Street in Auburn for overnight house parties that apparently lasted for several days. Foster would lead the boys out on what Eleanor described as "the grandfather of the panty raid." The boys managed to get various articles of clothing from the girls' trunks and string them up on high branches in the trees "and then tried to appear very innocent." Later, the girls would get their revenge, taking the boys' socks and ties and stringing them up on the trees and bushes. Foster loved practical jokes and teasing, and these kinds of things went on frequently during Foster's childhood—"all very normal and not too exciting, but still it was good fun," Eleanor said many years later.[32]

Foster took his first trip to Main Duck Island in 1902 when he was fourteen. Main Duck is about twenty nautical miles west of Henderson. The island is a bit under a thousand acres, characterized by forests, ponds, extensive meadows, smooth stone beaches, high bluffs, and crystal clear, placid waters in the bays on its leeward side. And in those days, game was plentiful. Deer would cross over from the mainland to the island on the frozen lake during winters and remain on the island in spring and summer till the ice formed again on the lake. A lighthouse operated on the island by the Canadian government from 1913 to 1977 on its western tip. In 1902, however, there was no lighthouse and the island was a First Peoples reservation.

Main Duck has a curious history. In 1905, a colorful local fisherman named Claude W. Cole (who enjoyed being called "King Cole") acquired the island. During Prohibition, Cole was a rumrunner, and Main Duck was his base of operations. Cole told tales about a French ship that wrecked off Main Duck shortly after the French and Indian War, and that the soldiers and crew who survived brought the seamen's pay chest full of gold coins to the island and buried it. A historian named Willis Metcalf reported in 1934 that the seven graves of the castaways had always been visible, and that a boulder near where Foster later built his cabin bore an inscription with the date of either 1764 or 1769. When Foster first visited the island with his family in 1902, a fishing colony existed there that transported its catches to the mainland.[33] After Foster received the catboat *No. 5*, he frequently sailed out to Main Duck and its neighboring Yorkshire Island with Allen, sometimes with Eleanor and Nataline, and often with friends from Princeton. From his earliest days sailing on the lake in the old catboat, Main Duck Island was always the place of Foster's dearest affection, more than any place he visited in the world.

Off to Princeton

Princeton University ran deep in the Dulles family tradition. When Foster graduated high school, it was only natural that he follow in the footsteps of his forebears. He entered the Princeton class of 1908 as a lad of only sixteen. He was the second-youngest member of a class numbering 148, in a student body of 1,286 as of October 1904.[34] Records of Foster's undergraduate years at Princeton are somewhat sparse. Scholars have noted that not much is known or understood about his life there, and even the John Foster Dulles Oral History Collection at Princeton reveals that many of his classmates did not remember him.[35] Still, his activities at Princeton have produced several interesting paradoxes.

For example, it is well known that Foster did not join any of Princeton's famed eating clubs but instead took his meals with a close circle of friends. This is quite true, but this close circle of friends invented their own club, named it the "Aldaric," and designed their own cap.[36] And in 1932, Foster ended up joining the eating club Cottage on Prospect Avenue in Princeton.[37] Foster was not athletic, but he did play tennis and tried out for other sporting activities on campus. During the second month of his freshman year, he tried out for the Cane Spree—a Princeton intramural sporting tradition among freshmen and sophomores dating to the 1860s involving fighting with canes. Although some of his classmates confessed to not remembering him, others raved about him and claimed he was loved and admired by everyone in the class of 1908.[38] His friend Everard "Pat" Miller claimed that Foster was naturally brilliant, did not need to study hard, and thus was not a "poler" or a "greasy grind"—Princeton colloquialisms for a stuffy, serious bookworm.[39] But another close friend, Edward Shedd, claimed that he studied especially hard and was in fact known by friends as a "poler."[40] Foster was a serious student, exceedingly devoted to his classes, was always in his room at 10 p.m. to study, and was selected as valedictorian of his class. But he was involved in extracurricular activities—he was a member of the chess team, the tennis team, and the prestigious Whig Society, the storied debate team that competed with teams from the other Ivies and also with its Princeton rival, the Clio Society, founded in 1765 alongside Whig. He was outgoing and gregarious around his friends, but he also kept certain exploits secret from them—such as the time he surreptitiously climbed to the top of Nassau Hall to remove the bell clapper, a feat he shared only with his sisters Margaret and Eleanor.[41] He apparently had a uniquely upsetting social difficulty his first year (which is unknown) and believed that he had gone to Princeton too young. Still, he adjusted well and found a home there. This is evidenced by his attending the Second Hague Conference of 1907 as a nineteen-year-old, winning a number of academic prizes, and making lifelong friends with his professors (his logic professor, John Grier Hibben, later became Princeton's president). Foster was an active alumnus after graduation, and he was invited back to Princeton's campus to speak on three occasions—in 1936, 1946, and 1952.[42]

Foster lived at 27 Mercer Street during his freshman year, and then moved into 163 Stafford Little Hall his sophomore year.[43] He lived in Stafford Little for the remainder of his time at Princeton, and ate every meal with the same eighteen men for four years.[44] Early in his Princeton career, he wrote a paper on whether Abraham Lincoln deserved to be counted a better president than George Washington. He probably wrote this essay in preparation for a Whig Society debate, and the essay is an interesting case study in his intellectual development. The essay demonstrates Foster to be literate about Lincoln's biography because, in it, he took Lincoln's historical complexity into account. He also quoted James Russell Lowell's tribute to Lincoln at the conclusion of his essay, revealing a precocious and sophisticated ability to call on classic American literature to clinch an argument: "Sagacious, patient, dreading praise, not blame / New birth of our new soil, the first American."[45] But since he only briefly mentioned Washington in the first lines of the essay, it is a textbook case of special pleading, not too unusual for a young undergraduate attempting his first foray into college-level writing.

But by Foster's senior year, his intellectual acumen had developed to an impressive degree. He majored in philosophy and made regular appearances on the honor roll, joining that august company every semester while at Princeton (except the second semester of junior year, when he was at The Hague). He won the MacLean Prize, a junior class prize with a cash award of $100 given to a member of either Whig or Clio for the best speech.[46] He also won the Dickinson Prize, an honor founded in 1782 that came with a cash prize of sixty dollars. This award was for his junior paper, entitled "The Theory of Judgement," a paper on epistemology.

Among his many challenging courses, Foster took Woodrow Wilson's course in elements of jurisprudence. According to the course description, Wilson taught "an exposition of jurisprudence as an organic whole, exhibiting the nature of its subject matter, its relationship to cognate branches of study, the inter-relationships of its several parts to each other, and their proper function and aim."[47] Foster scored a one—the highest grade attainable—and Wilson remained an important and influential figure for years afterward.

Foster's grades, while always high, improved steadily from freshman to senior year. He had six twos, one three, one four (in Hygiene, of all things!), and the rest ones in his first year, averaging a 1.64 for the year. But by graduation, Foster had improved to an overall average of 1.08 for the full four years, received highest honors in his major of philosophy, and was inducted into Phi Beta Kappa.

Perhaps the most notable accomplishments of Foster's Princeton career occurred during his junior and senior years. As noted, in 1907, Grandfather Foster invited his grandson to attend the Second Hague Conference, meeting that summer. At first, Foster served as his grandfather's secretary, but he was later invited to serve as the secretary to the Chinese delegation. And in 1908, Foster built upon his junior paper to write his senior thesis—a critical analysis of William James's pragmatic epistemology with the same title as his junior paper, "The Theory of Judgement." For this paper, Foster won the Chancellor Green Mental Science Fellowship. The prize came with a $600 honorarium, which he used to study under the famed French pragmatist at the Sorbonne, Henri Bergson, from 1908 to 1909.

First, attending the Hague Conference: the unique nature of this experience for a nineteen-year-old hardly needs to be mentioned. What words are there to describe how amazing this opportunity must have been for a junior in college? Foster kept a diary of his time at The Hague from June 12 to August 15, 1907. Most of the entries describe a myriad of social engagements— teas, lunches, dinners, and dancing. He made several friends, and his diary contains their contact information. But he also collected all the calling cards and social invitations he received as secretary to the Chinese delegation. He put these memorabilia into a large scrapbook, which contained a vast array of beautiful engravings.[48] Upon returning to America, his Princeton chums all gathered around the scrapbook to see the collection and congratulate

Foster. Everard Miller recalled "how we boys, when we gathered around looking at his album—our eyes just fairly popped out!"[49]

Foster's diary does not specify what his specific duties were at the conference—his entries refer mostly to the dates and times he was present at its meetings. But he did have one claim to fame, and he related the story years later at a New York Bar Association lunch in 1931. Foster told his audience that no one had thought to establish any sort of protocol for the order by which the delegations were to be ranked. Rank was an important function, because it determined how the proceedings of the conference would be ordered. A delegation receiving calls from another delegation was senior in rank to that which was doing the calling. Thus, the possibility of the conference dissolving due to ruffled pride and thin skin was high. To compound the problem, no one apparently was creative or decisive enough to propose a plan and carry it out, and there were two hundred delegates in all. So Foster, the young diplomat, hatched an idea. He proposed that the secretaries of each delegation should visit all the hotels where the other delegations were staying, and leave calling cards from the delegations they represented all in one afternoon. And to accomplish this expeditiously, the secretaries should all travel by automobile. "In this way, the conference was able to get off to an orderly start and the World War deferred for nearly seven years," Foster joked.[50] In his diary, he noted that he and a colleague personally delivered 1,200 calling cards by automobile the day before the conference began. The calling cards he delivered were those belonging to the three delegates representing China, including his grandfather, as well as his own.[51] Foster's experience at The Hague was the first one in diplomacy of his long career. He was hooked, and the experience of attending this conference was a major factor in his later decision to become a "Christian lawyer" like his grandfather.

If Foster's secretaryship at The Hague set him on a lifelong path of diplomacy, it is also possible that his senior thesis marked the beginning of a lifelong interest in philosophy and ethics. The first ten pages of "Theory of Judgement" are missing, but since the paper is sixty-three pages in length, it remains possible to pinpoint his argument and follow his rationale. The work was a critical analysis of pragmatic epistemology, and in it Foster maintained a continuous engagement with William James, John Dewey, Immanuel Kant, G. W. F. Hegel, Friedrich Schiller, Arthur Schopenhauer, and others.

Foster began his study by considering the difference between rationalism and pragmatism. He identified several problems with how the American pragmatists James and Dewey differentiated pragmatism from rationalism. Neither of these thinkers, said Foster, dealt with the problem of reconciling the unchanging ideal with the changing reality. And these thinkers also did not consider the implications of the power of human thought to achieve something for the good of humanity, other than the mere passive acquisition of knowledge. "The reconciliation of this ideal end with a changing reality must be solved by the pragmatist," Foster asserted. But, "to be continually changing reality without improving or bettering it in any way seems not only irrational but unpragmatic."[52] Foster continued his critique by walking his audience through seven specific epistemological, ontological, religious, and ethical problems faced by Jamesian pragmatism. How did the pragmatist attain epistemological satisfaction? How could a pragmatist believe in God? How did a pragmatist handle the potential of the individual losing faith? Was pragmatism dependent on a correspondence or a coherence theory of truth? How did pragmatism simultaneously draw from, and protest against, both theories? Why did pragmatists reject certain hypotheses that appear to be consistent with their understanding of truth? What posture should pragmatists have toward epistemic and religious authority? Foster concluded his essay by arguing that while "pragmatism is a protest against rationalism," it should not totally reject the authority of reason. For Foster, if pragmatism was defined too broadly, it was meaningless, but if it was understood too narrowly, it was inadequate as a tool for understanding the nature and possibility of knowledge. Pragmatists should acknowledge the validity of feeling as a basis for truth, but "reason must be left the ultimate judge of truth, though it may well be that feeling and will verify the decisions of reason."[53] In other words, for Foster a pragmatist should embrace a broad enough definition of knowledge to include subjectivity but balance those epistemic sources with a rationalism that adjudicates tensions between subjectivity and objectivity.

Foster's senior thesis represents an intellectual journey of a thousand miles from his essay on Lincoln and Washington in terms of logical structure, critical thought, historical complexity, and defense of a thesis. His senior thesis was the crowning achievement of his Princeton career and set his mind toward a lifetime of thinking about actively working to achieve the common good, the constant conflict between the dynamic and the static, and the danger and futility of defending the status quo in the face of inevitable change.

And what of his religious activities while at Princeton? Where did Foster attend church, and did he exhibit any interest in going into the ministry? Not much is known about Foster's spiritual life, but his friend Pat Miller said that they were drawn to one another because they were both sons and grandsons of pastors and missionaries. And Pat admired Foster for what he regarded as a strong moral character—Pat called him "a Christian man from the heart of his soul."[54] But Foster did not seem to be involved in any religious activities while at Princeton and apparently showed no interest in going into the ministry.

Instead, Foster was interested in politics, history, and philosophy (his major). To Pat, "he was quite clearly headed for international law."[55] Still, while Foster was at Princeton, he had a high regard for religion's utilitarian value. Eleanor described Foster's attitude in this way: "[religion] was the force for good; and if it's a force for good, and if you want to do good, you associate yourself with it."[56] As a senior at Princeton, Foster believed religion was a force for good. Foster accepted the Kantian understanding of knowledge formation, that our minds actively create knowledge rather than passively receive it. Proceeding from this assumption, Foster asserted that "mere change of reality unless it is changed for the better is useless; indeed, worse than useless, for we have expended energy with no results."[57] To him, religion benefited from pragmatism because pragmatism rescued religion from blind rationalism. Moreover, pragmatism demonstrated religion to have real use in the shaping of reality, both practically and theoretically. If Eleanor was right, and Foster believed that the church was a force for good in 1908, then that conviction was consistent with his larger understanding of the nature of reality and the way in which one knew and interacted with it. So, while Foster had shed the piety of his early youth, he had not given up on religion, at least in the abstract. The cooling of Foster's pious fervor during his young adulthood is apparent, particularly during the early 1930s when he stopped attending church regularly, but so is his enduring theological and biblical frame of reference, which was the product of his deeply religious upbringing.

Foster gave the valedictory address at Princeton's commencement exercises on June 10, 1908. Weeks later, on August 18, Foster sailed to Europe on the SS *New Amsterdam* in order to embark on a year of study under Bergson at the Sorbonne. Edith and Allen Macy joined him, as did Margaret, Allen, and Nataline (Eleanor remained at school, living with the Fosters in Washington). The family lived with their old friends in Lausanne, the Bischoffs, for two months, then moved to 82 Avenue de Breteuil in Paris. Foster attended lectures at the Sorbonne, and he also spent about a month in Madrid to brush up on his Spanish.[58] He kept a diary in French and recorded lengthy passages on international fishing rights, but in it he noted very few details of his life and activities in Paris.[59] Nataline and Allen got quality time in with their brother: Nataline was a child of ten and eleven in Paris, and she got to know and admire Foster while in Paris. And Allen and Foster climbed the Diablerets Massif together, a Swiss mountain 10,350 feet in elevation.[60]

Foster met one person while in Paris who would prove later to make a singularly important difference in his life, but he did not realize it at the time. Her name was Janet Avery.

Upon returning to the United States in the spring of 1909, Foster matriculated at George Washington Law School in Washington. His grandparents had built a new four-story redbrick house at 1323 Eighteenth Street, NW, and Foster lived with them while he pursued his studies. He completed his three-year course of study in two years and maintained the highest grade average in the history of the institution to that time. But since he did not complete the required three-year residency, he was not granted a diploma—at least not in 1912, which was the year he was to graduate. The school finally granted him a diploma backdated to 1912 while he was serving as secretary of state.[61]

Foster's diary of his years in law school conveys a glamorous, youthful, privileged world of a brilliant young man cultivating and expanding a rich network of the wealthy and the powerful. It also demonstrates that Foster was enjoying his life as an eligible bachelor, and that the field of potential spouses was broad and pleasing. From 1909 to 1911, Foster flitted about Washington going from luncheons and teas here to dinners and dancing there. He was also at the center of his grandparents' entertaining at their spacious home. His grandmother "presided like a duchess over the tea table at five o'clock" while Grandfather Foster hosted the power players in Washington—senators and congressmen, Supreme Court justices, ambassadors, and cabinet officials. "The women with their sequins and plumes and the men with their decorations and sashes were dashing and romantic," Eleanor wrote as she described the formal dinners at the Fosters' house.[62]

Early Career and a Happy Rediscovery

While Foster was reading Frederick Pollack, Francis Marion Burdick, and Melville Madison Bigelow on tort law, he was also courting the daughters of the most influential people in the capital. He was frequently in the company of Frances Noyes, the daughter of Frank Brett Noyes, one of the founders of the Associated Press and president of the *Evening Star.* Dora Clover was another close friend—her father was Rear Admiral Richardson Clover, and her grandfather was Senator John Franklin Miller of California. In January 1911, Foster met Harriet Anderson, niece to President and Mrs. Taft. Young Foster was smitten by her. He succinctly described her in the margin of his diary: "Stunner!"[63]

The most prominent of all the young ladies Foster befriended while in law school was Helen Taft, President and Mrs. Taft's daughter. Foster's diary is replete with references to her, and it appears that Foster's interest in her went beyond friendship.[64] Not only did Foster accompany Helen to several functions, he also attended numerous dinners and balls held in her honor, such as her coming-out party on January 14, 1911, and a dinner held for her hosted by Oliver Wendell Holmes on February 1 of the same year. But after February 5, Foster's references to Helen cease for some unknown reason.[65]

Besides having the fun of courting young ladies and cutting the rug at dances and balls, Foster spent much of his time building a professional network. He joined Phi Delta Phi, a legal fraternity in 1910, and attended meetings of the American Peace Society and the Carnegie Endowment for International Peace. He cultivated a lasting friendship with his old logic professor John Grier Hibben, who followed Woodrow Wilson as president of Princeton in 1912 after Wilson's departure to serve as governor of New Jersey in 1910. Foster and the Hibben family were frequent companions over the years, and Professor Hibben spent two days with Foster in Washington at the end of 1910. Foster was a frequent guest at the White House, and he built relationships with the vice president, the interior secretary, the secretary of commerce and labor, and the chief justice of the United States, among others. For a young man in his early twenties, raised as a pastor's son in the north country of New York, Foster seems to have made himself quite at home alongside the members of high society. Some of the relationships Foster made during these years, such as with Robert Taft, the future senator from Ohio and paragon figure for many postwar conservatives, lasted for decades. He acquired a taste for being near money and power at the highest level, and he enjoyed it immensely.[66]

One curious diary entry is dated February 18, 1911. On this date, Foster traveled to New York City to "see Mr. Sullivan at Sullivan & Cromwell."[67] Algernon Sydney Sullivan and William Nelson Cromwell had established the powerful Wall Street law firm in 1879. They were, in some ways, a strange combination. Sullivan, much older than Cromwell, was an anticorporation trial lawyer. Cromwell was one of the first of the new breed of corporate lawyers, an animal birthed out of post–Civil War industrial America. Legal scholar Erik M. Jensen described Cromwell as "a master strategist" and "one of the originators of the 'law factory,' making it possible to routinize much of the legal service provided to corporate clients."[68] Sullivan died in 1887 (which makes one wonder why Foster wrote that he was going to see Sullivan), and by the time Foster was completing his legal studies and looking for work, Cromwell was the elder statesman of the firm. He had spent most of his career enriching himself and making his firm one of the most powerful in the nation by situating it as a power broker between business and government. Between 1896 and 1903, Cromwell represented what became known as the New Panama Canal Company, which had acquired the interests of Ferdinand de Lesseps, who had set out and failed to construct a canal across Nicaragua. Through relationships and contacts that Cromwell had built in the American government, as well as contacts in Colombia and Panama, Cromwell engineered a shift in the canal's route, from Nicaragua to Panama. While Foster was learning the craft and payoffs of network building, Cromwell had already become the master. Cromwell described how he grew the firm through political networking: "In the course of . . . more than 30 years, the firm of Sullivan & Cromwell had . . . come to know, and be in a position to influence, a considerable number of public men in political life, in financial circles, and on the press, and all these influences and relations were of great and decisive utility, and of valuable assistance."[69] In the craft of networking, Foster, the young and impressionable law student, was perfectly situated to sit at Cromwell's feet.

Foster had been searching for jobs at major Wall Street firms during his years in law school but had come up short again and again. In the eyes of the prestigious Manhattan law firms, a degree from George Washington could not hold a candle to one earned at Yale or Harvard. Still, having an influential international lawyer for a doting grandfather who had also served as secretary of state helped Foster immensely in the situation, especially in the relatively small legal world of 1911. Grandfather Foster had known and worked alongside Sullivan in Indiana, before he formed Sullivan and Cromwell. He appealed to Cromwell, asking him to meet with and advise young Foster. What emerged from this meeting was a fifty-dollar-a-month job as a clerk, a job that Foster did not relish. But Grandfather Foster, anxious for his grandson to remember his place and not look a gift horse in the mouth, encouraged him to take the long view and not get distracted by the toil and obscurity of starting at the bottom. "You must not allow yourself to tire of the druggery [sic] of the office—that is what new clerks have to go through, I suppose." And reminiscent of the words he used to describe his own father, Matthew, Grandfather Foster reminded his grandson, "Was it the Apostle Paul . . . who impressed upon us to 'despise not the day of small things'?"[70] While Foster admitted in his diary that he initially preferred to work at the law firm of Spooner and Cotton, he began an enormously lucrative and influential career for himself at Sullivan and Cromwell, one that lasted until 1949.[71]

Around the same time that Foster was preparing to pass the bar and secure a career, he rediscovered Janet Avery, the girl he had met in Paris while studying at the Sorbonne in 1908. Foster had become acquainted with several beautiful and wealthy young women since his time in Paris, but none compared to Janet in his eyes. Janet was an Auburn girl. Her family lived close to the Dulleses, whose house was at 67 South Street, just north of town. Exactly when Foster and Janet became reacquainted is not clear, but by the spring of 1911 they definitely had begun seeing each other. Foster was in Auburn at this time, preparing to take the New York bar exam in Rochester. Janet caught his eye while he was in Auburn—"Foster always liked objets d'art," Eleanor said. She was attractive, quiet, and studious, fluent in French and deeply read in French literature, having gone to school in Paris. Foster was taken with what he saw as her irresistible charm, quiet and reflective demeanor, and serious intellectual interests. "You can imagine him in Auburn, working hard, and then he sees this girl with whom he can talk about Paris, the world, and literature and philosophy, and who is good to look at," said Eleanor.[72] Foster, displaying his characteristic confidence and calm, took his bar exam in Rochester and finished only as much of it as he needed in order to pass. With an hour yet to go before the end of the exam, he left Rochester, hurried to Auburn, and asked Janet to go on a picnic with him. He proposed marriage, and she accepted. Dulles biographer Townsend Hoopes called this audacious act Foster's "first application of brinkmanship."[73]

Both the Dulleses and the Averys were surprised at the brevity of the courtship and the suddenness of the engagement. Allen Macy and Edith were concerned at first that Foster was spending too much time with Janet when he was supposed to be studying. The Averys were worried that they knew next to nothing about Foster, and that he had not been brought up in Auburn. Foster's father was offended by the Averys' concern, exclaiming, "Well, the idea of anybody not realizing what Foster is like!"[74] Still, the engagement became official, whether the families were ready for it or not.

Janet and Foster were married on June 26, 1912. Their forty-seven-year marriage was legendary for its affection and stability. Even Hoopes, no admirer of Foster Dulles, describes the marriage as a "genuine love match," and family, friends, and colleagues—even Foster's enemies—gave Foster and Janet a great deal of credit for nurturing a deep and sincere love and care for one another.[75] Foster was protective of Janet to a fault, so much so that he once threatened to throw Eleanor out of their house for interrupting Janet one morning as she was getting dressed. Eleanor was living with Foster and Janet during the early thirties in New York while writing her book on international banking, and Eleanor would visit with Janet in her bedroom before going out to study at the library. "Foster came to me one day, and he said to me, 'If you ever speak to Janet while she's brushing her hair, you will have to leave this house immediately!'"[76] Hoopes wrote that Foster and Janet were entirely happy being together, and were so devoted to one another that they neglected their children. It is true that Foster was more comfortable with Janet than with any other human being, and took immense delight in her for the rest of his life. In 1957, as they were getting ready for a formal dinner with Queen Elizabeth II, Janet came down the stairs in a blue-gray satin dress. When Foster saw her, he said, "This is a queen—my queen."[77]

Foster came of age in two worlds. One world was steeped in north country New York provincialism. The other was the sophisticated and glittering world of Washington society. One was shaped by the patterns of strict religious routine and education. The other followed the contours of privileged culture. One was simple in its proximity to natural splendor and the rhythms of seasonal change observed in a myriad of ways in the natural world of Henderson. The other was complex in its proximity to power, wealth, and prestige in Washington and Europe. Piety, family devotion, reading, sailing, fishing, and swimming marked Foster's Watertown/ Henderson life. But his life in Washington and his travels abroad opened up vistas beyond the simple existence of the Presbyterian parsonage and the cottage by the lake. Foster grew into what he became because he was able to move comfortably in both worlds. He did not see those worlds as mutually opposed to one another, as if the provincial and the cosmopolitan were at war with one another. He lived in both, was a product of both, and took both on their own terms throughout his life. To understand Foster as a human being, it is necessary to account for these two worlds of which he was a product.

Foster's religious life during his early years was defined by his experiences in church on Sunday mornings, the times around the dinner table discussing the notes he took from his father's sermons, the memorized Bible verses and hymns recited on the porch on Sunday evenings. These experiences were deeply ingrained in Foster's personality. He did not continue all these religious traditions in his own family, at least not consistently. Nor did he exhibit much interest in reading theology or forming doctrinal convictions. He was not a fundamentalist—he was not raised a fundamentalist, and he never gave much thought to doctrine. And by the time he arrived at Princeton, the piety of his early years had largely disappeared. He still attended church regularly, especially during his law school years. And in the early years of his marriage and career, he was a lay leader in his congregation. But he was a young man who had convinced himself that utility was of prime importance, and if an idea or an institution was not contributing solutions to real problems in the world, then that idea or institution was not only useless, it was meaningless. Foster's Princeton years marked the beginning of the development of a hard line between the world of piety, church, and religion and the world of law, diplomacy, and business. For the next chapter in Foster's life, he would live as though these two worlds were important in their own right, but as if they had no relationship to one another. Thus, until 1937, he would gradually come to believe that faith did not, could not, speak meaningfully or usefully to the world.

Still, a religious frame of reference emerged from Foster's youth and continued to shape him. This frame of reference endured for the duration of Foster's life, even though his commitment to his faith came and went. But it was not religion alone that formed the structure of this frame of reference. A love of nature and of ideas was part of this structure, and a love of power, wealth, and the associations that increased that power and wealth was also part of that structure. Foster's complexity can be traced to his earliest years, and the interaction of his loves in his thought and action animated his personality and decisions in later years—decisions that would have momentous consequences in American religious and international life for much of the twentieth century.

3

"Does the Ark Need the Sustaining Hand of Uzza?"
(1912–1926)

> The ideal procedure for satisfying oneself as to the spiritual
> beliefs of another is a conversation of a most intimate char-
> acter, in an atmosphere of sympathy, with a total absence of
> formality and restraint.

> —John Foster Dulles[1]

At the young age of thirty, Foster sailed from New York to join the
American delegation at the Versailles Peace Conference, the meeting
that was to conclude the most appalling war in anyone's memory. The First
World War lasted from July 1914 to November 1918. Traveling across the
Atlantic in December of 1918, he found an envelope containing a letter
from his mother. On the back of the sealed envelope was written an inscription—"Read when out at sea."[2] Upon opening the letter, Foster found
a heartfelt plea from a proud but concerned mother.

Since leaving home in 1904, Foster's religious life had been sporadic. He
did not attend church regularly while at Princeton, although he was more
faithful in attendance while living with his grandparents in Washington
during law school. Since he was fifteen, Foster had traveled to Europe, enjoyed a sophisticated education, rubbed elbows with America's ruling class,
studied cutting-edge ideas, and joined one of the most prestigious law firms
in the nation. He did not pause much to reflect on his religion. In fact, he
confided to his father in 1918 that he had begun to have doubts about his
Christian faith. Edith wrote to Foster that she was not particularly worried

about him, but she still hoped he might spend some time thinking about his relationship to God during the long days in transit across the Atlantic. After all, he was on his way to take part in the most momentous international conference since the Congress of Vienna in 1815.

In her letter, Edith confessed to Foster that she no longer believed some of the things she had taught him when he was a child—perhaps to demonstrate some solidarity with his own skepticism. But despite her struggles with doubt, she said she held on to the universal fatherhood of God and the ethical example of Christ. In a moment of introspection, she told her son, "as I try to live the life that a child of God should live, I feel the need of a perfect life to guide me, a life lived here under our conditions and so the life of Christ becomes a necessity to me." Her understanding of the meaning of Christ's life and teaching was consistent with the liberal preaching she had heard from Allen Macy over the decades. But then, perhaps reflecting on the deaths of two sisters and a baby brother long ago—and the death of her father the previous year in 1917—she touched on a personal note. "While I have lost much," Edith wrote, "God, Christ, and duty mean more and more to me. I hope it is so with you, too. Lovingly, Mother."[3]

While there is no record of Foster ever responding to her letter, Edith need not have been too concerned that her son was truly losing his faith. For one thing, Foster kept this letter for the rest of his life, and that fact gives some indication that he cherished his mother's words. Foster Dulles kept his inner life to himself, despite whatever external piety he showed. And he did take his religion seriously even though he understood its meaning and application differently at different times in his life. He had grown up in a liberal Protestant environment and was trained in pragmatist theories of epistemology. His elders raised him to stress the external and practical outworking of Christian responsibility and morality as prior to the cultivation of inward religious affections. In his formal education at Princeton and at the Sorbonne, he had accepted a metaphysic that emphasized change over stasis in time. Foster held firmly to convictions informed by his understandings of truth, ethics, and reality. During the early years of his career, he thoughtfully applied those convictions in three specific contexts—war, international relations, and the fundamentalist-modernist controversy raging in the Presbyterian denomination during the mid-1920s.

The fundamentalist-modernist controversy was the one major theological dispute in which Foster became engaged, although less for the theology and more for the pragmatics. This controversy, as it took place in the Presbyterian denomination in the 1920s, provided a forum in which his actions had lasting importance to the American Protestant environment in the early twentieth century. In the first days of Foster's involvement in the controversy, the elder Dulles wrote Foster several letters to fire him up for the struggles. At one point in the spring of 1924, Allen Macy wrote to Foster, likening fundamentalists to the biblical figure Uzzah: "Cannot Fundamentalists win through the truth, without persecution and prosecution? Does the Ark need the sustaining hand of Uzza?"[4] The elder Dulles—a committed modernist—and his son were of one mind on the controversy. While Foster operated largely out of the spotlight in the great debates shaking up Presbyterian churches between 1924 and 1926, his role was decisive in helping to set the denomination on a course away from fundamentalism. While battling fundamentalists, Foster was also reflecting on his experience at Versailles. He began developing his ideas on war and internationalism beginning in 1921 in terms of what he saw as the practical effects of Christianity and what he saw as the duty of a Christian nation in a world rent by war.

Life and Career in Brief

It is beyond the scope of this study to cover Foster's legal and diplomatic career in detail. Several biographers have described the complex features of Foster's activities. Still, an overview is necessary to provide some context for his burgeoning ideas on war, internationalism, and the church.[5] Foster was hired at Sullivan and Cromwell in 1911 and was commissioned a captain in the army shortly after the United States entered World War I. He reached the rank of major a few days before the armistice. By 1919 he had become a partner in the firm, and by 1926, he was promoted to managing partner. His activities representing the interests of his firm overlapped with those representing the interests of his nation. He worked for the State Department and the War Trade Board, and served on the Reparations Commission at Versailles. These involvements gave him increased prestige at Sullivan and Cromwell, as well as a growing network of influential friends and an expanding list of clients for the firm, which financially enriched him.

Foster also volunteered his time and legal services to the interests of his church and his denomination. Beginning in the early twenties, Foster served as ruling elder at Park Avenue Presbyterian Church, pastored by his Princeton classmate Tertius van Dyke. He was a trusted figure in the congregation. In 1922, Foster spoke on the necessity of tithing faithfully to the church, resulting in an increased number of parishioners committing themselves to the church's financial health. "I am greatly indebted to you for your fine address in the church yesterday," van Dyke wrote Foster. "Anyone who could take offense at anything you said on the delicate subject of church finances is certainly a pathological case."[6] And anyone who has ever gone before a congregation to preach on money can appreciate the value of van Dyke's compliment.

It was also during this time that Foster and Janet saw the births of their children—John in 1913, Lillias in 1914, and Avery in 1918. After Foster returned from Paris in the fall of 1919, the family moved from a house they owned in Washington to a small apartment in New York. The building, which no longer exists, was located at Eighty-Eighth Street and Madison Avenue. Lillias described it as a small place. She also remembered from her early childhood that her father would become so absorbed in his daily morning paper that he'd forget his toast and burn it to a crisp, then consume it with exaggerated relish to the delight of the children. "He always maintained that he just loved to eat this charcoal that came out," she said. By 1923, the Dulleses moved out of the apartment and into their house at 72 East Ninety-First Street. Avery recalled that Sundays were special days. Headed to church, Foster dressed in a suit and a top hat and carried a cane. The family would return home to Sunday dinner and the singing of hymns, as in the old days of Foster's youth in Watertown. Foster also loved to lead in singing children's songs during the week (these were never sung on Sundays). Jingles like "A Bicycle Built for Two," "Oh My Darling, Clementine," and "Oh Dunderbeck" were all in Foster's old Princeton songbook, and they rang throughout the house.

> Oh Dunderbeck! Oh Dunderbeck! How could you be so mean!
> To ever have invented the sausage-meat machine;
> Now all the rats and pussycats will nevermore be seen;

> They've all been ground to sausages in Dunderbeck's
> machine.[7]

The early years of Foster's career were busy. As Dulles biographer Ronald Pruessen writes, Foster was "a well-traveled and well-connected young man. He was intelligent, he was willing to work hard, and in relatively short order, success came."[8]

This period of Foster's career represents a link between his past and his future. Specifically, contacts he had in the 1910s and '20s with his uncle Robert Lansing, his former professor Woodrow Wilson, and his old Princeton chum Tertius van Dyke served as connections to Foster's past. His legal and diplomatic work in Central America, early involvement in the framing of the American posture toward Soviet Russia, contributions to the issue of war reparations against Germany, and the legal counsel he provided during the Presbyterian controversy each anticipated future efforts that marked his legal, political, and diplomatic career from the 1930s to the end of his life.

Robert Lansing, Foster's Uncle Bert, graduated from Amherst College in 1886 and married Eleanor Foster, Edith's sister, in 1890. He got his start in the diplomatic field working on arbitration in the Bering Sea Commission in 1892. He also served as counsel on the Alaskan Boundary Tribunal (1903), the Hague Tribunal for Arbitration of the North Atlantic Fisheries (1910), and the Anglo-American Commission (1911). Additionally, in 1911 he settled disputes regarding the harvesting of seal fur between the United States, Japan, Britain, and Russia. He served as counsel in the State Department beginning in 1914, and after William Jennings Bryan's resignation as secretary of state in 1915, President Wilson tapped Lansing to succeed Bryan in that office. He led the State Department from 1915 to 1920.

Lansing's ties to Wilson provided Foster with the necessary admittance to a Democratic administration, the first since Grover Cleveland's ended in 1897. While Foster's most significant benefactor, Grandfather Foster, had been a power player in American diplomacy in the late nineteenth and early twentieth centuries, he was a Republican. Grandfather Foster helped him secure his position at Sullivan and Cromwell, and from there, Foster became connected to Latin American issues via American and French bankers. As early as January 1913, Lansing wrote Foster to see if he might be interested in working with the American and British Claims Arbitration Agency in Washington for as long as a year. Uncle Bert wrote, "If I receive a favorable reply from you, I shall be in a position to present the matter to the Secretary and ask for your appointment."[9] Foster was tempted by the offer but had to beg off after being discouraged by his superiors at Sullivan and Cromwell, namely, Royal Victor, the firm's managing partner. "It did not seem . . . to Mr. Victor that it would be advisable for me to absent myself entirely from my work here for a year at this time when I am just beginning to get more intimately in touch with the work of the office and with its clients."[10]

Notwithstanding this demurral, Foster went to Lansing in 1916 on behalf of his friend Emiliano Chamorro in his candidacy for the presidency of Nicaragua. The same year he also prevailed upon Lansing to send two navy destroyers to Cuba to protect the interests of his clients in the midst of political unrest. And as America and Germany were drifting closer to war in 1917, Foster honored a request from Lansing to go to Panama, Costa Rica, and Nicaragua to secure from those countries assurances that they would either be pro-Allied neutrals or enter the war as Allied belligerents. Lansing knew his nephew was well suited for this mission, since Sullivan and Cromwell was the official counsel to the Panamanian government. Foster found Latin America friendly to the Allied cause and the Panama Canal safe from any pro-German mischief. Shortly after Wilson delivered his war message to Congress on April 2, 1917, Panama and Cuba both declared war on Germany, largely due to Foster's ministrations.[11] Uncle Bert could not have been more proud of his nephew. "Mr. Dulles was entirely successful in his Panama mission," Lansing wrote after the war. "The day after the United States entered the war, both [Panama and Cuba] proclaimed a state of war with the German Empire."[12]

When he returned to the United States in May of 1917, Foster went straight to Washington and served in the State Department as special counsel for Central American affairs. After a brief stint in that role, he applied for admission to Officers' Training Camp for combat service. His application to be trained as an officer was rejected for having poor eyesight, so he decided to enlist. But on September 5, 1917, Foster was commissioned a captain in the Signal Officers Reserve Corps, a noncombat role. In February 1918 he was recommissioned in the regular army, and the next month was assigned to the War Trade Board to serve as liaison between it and the General Staff in the War Department. The following July, he reapplied for combat service "to report to the commanding officer Central Artillery Officer's Training School, Camp Taylor, Kentucky."[13] He was again rejected but became assistant to the chairman of the War Trade Board, Vance McCormick. On November 9, 1918, two days before the end of the war, Foster was promoted to the rank of major. He was honorably discharged six weeks later on December 18, 1918. Pruessen attributes Foster's rapid rise in the army to "several mutually reinforcing factors: awareness of Dulles's previous experience with financial and commercial matters at a prestigious law firm, day-to-day recognition of his basic abilities, and a dollop of appreciation for the fact that he was the nephew of the Secretary of State."[14]

At the War Trade Board, Foster's duty was to ensure proper coordination with the War Department. This entailed ensuring the enforcement of the blockade against Germany, securing smooth shipments of necessities between the Allied nations, and negotiating with Spain for the purchase of raw materials for American forces. Foster was a key figure in the requisitioning of Dutch ships that lay in American ports, adding 354,478 tons of shipping capacity to the United States.[15] A committee was also formed to explore possibilities for an economic aid package to Russia, but the rise of the Bolsheviks complicated those plans. Foster was the treasurer of this committee, named the Russian Bureau, Inc. He became directly involved in the Wilson administration's efforts to undermine Bolshevik power by overseeing the dispatch of $5 million in economic aid to anti-Bolshevik forces in Siberia (via Vladivostok) in the form of clothing and clothing materials, food, machinery (for agriculture, lumbering, mining, trapping, and mechanical repair), and general hardware, including household utensils. Foster drafted the memorandum directing the War Trade Board to adopt this program, and President Wilson signed it on October 1, 1918.[16]

When Foster learned that Wilson would be personally leading the American peace delegation at Versailles, he went at once to see Uncle Bert to ask him for an appointment. He undoubtedly expected to find Lansing amenable to the prospect, but Lansing rebuffed his request. Lansing was against Wilson's plan to lead the delegation, believing that Wilson's idealism would be laughable alongside the *realpolitik* of the victorious British and French, who wanted nothing more than to see Germany humiliated.

Wilson, in turn, was suspicious of Lansing, believing that he wanted the spotlight for himself. Aware of this tension existing between himself and Wilson, Lansing thought it unwise to propose including his nephew on the American Peace Delegation. Undeterred, Foster turned to another senior figure and family friend, Bernard Baruch, head of the War Industries Board and a member of the delegation. Baruch was fond of Foster and impressed with his competence. Baruch asked Foster to be his assistant, and from that time to Foster's death, they remained close colleagues and warm friends.

Baruch became the principal American on the Reparations Commission, and Foster started out as a legal adviser. But it was not long before Foster took on greater responsibilities, becoming a full-fledged member of the Reparations Commission. He earned Wilson's attention in short order, as he engaged with other senior members of the delegation like Thomas Lamont and Norman Davis. Wilson regularly included Foster in high-level meetings, and the two were in general agreement that reparations against Germany should be adjusted according to what the Germans could actually pay, rather than serving to destroy the German economy. Where they disagreed was on whether to include pensions in the total amount the Germans were to pay in reparations, and this became a troublesome point of contention between Foster and the professor-president.

Shortly after Prince Max of Baden—the German head of state after the abdication of Kaiser Wilhelm II—expressed to Wilson a willingness to negotiate a peace with the Allies on the basis of the Fourteen Points in October 1918, Wilson followed up with a list of additional conditions. These additional conditions, with the Fourteen Points as a basis, became known as the Pre-Armistice Agreement. One condition was that reparation payments would come from "Germany for all damage done to the civilian population of the Allies and their property, by the aggression of Germany by land, by sea, and from the air."[17] The Germans acquiesced. Famously, at the eleventh hour of the eleventh day of the eleventh month of 1918, the armistice went into effect and the guns fell silent after four years of carnage. World War I was over, but Germany was unprepared for the aftermath. It would be held solely responsible for the war by the victorious Allies.

While the Germans were counting on the peace negotiations to follow the grooves of the Pre-Armistice Agreement, the British and the French wanted to see Germany pay for every conceivable cost of the war. With his eyes on the German economy, British First Lord of the Admiralty Eric Geddes famously said, "We shall squeeze the orange until the pips squeak."[18] Both Wilson and Foster believed this would be a breach of the Pre-Armistice Agreement. In February 1919, Wilson cabled Lansing to tell him, "I feel that we are bound in honor to decline to agree to the inclusion of war costs in the reparation demanded. The time to think of this was before the conditions of peace were communicated to the enemy originally. We should dissent and dissent publicly if necessary not on the ground of the intrinsic injustice of it but on the ground that it is clearly inconsistent with what we deliberately led the enemy to expect and can not now honorably alter simply because we have the power."[19]

But just weeks later, being convinced by a proposal from Field Marshal Jan Smuts of South Africa,[20] Wilson began to broaden his understanding of the meaning of "war costs" to go beyond "damage done to the civilian population" to include payment of pensions compensating for "deprivation of the civilian population of the services and earning capacity of persons who were called to the colors and then were perhaps killed or wounded." Foster, perceiving a critical compromise on the issue of limiting the scale and scope of reparations, tried to argue to the president that his position supporting pensions was illogical. He did so in the presence of Baruch, Davis, and Lamont. His point was that there was no logical distinction between the financial loss of one breadwinning soldier in a family through the draft and the loss of another soldier from a different family who might have to pay for his own accouterments with which to fight. For Foster, this was a slippery slope. If such pensions were to be included in overall reparations costs, then there would be no limit whatsoever to what Germany would have to pay, and thus the American commitment to keep reparations in check would be futile. Foster tried to diplomatically describe the president's reaction to his appeals in minutes he kept of the meeting in a mild and formal tone—"the President stated that he did not feel bound by considerations of logic, and . . . it was a proper subject of reparation under the agreed terms of peace."[21] In reality, Wilson blew up at his former Princeton student. He cried, "Logic! Logic! I don't give a damn for logic. I am going to include pensions."[22] Wilson got his way, and the reparation costs were set at about $32 billion—a staggering amount. It was still much lower than initial British and French proposals, but they were placated after Foster and

Davis drafted Article 231 of the Versailles Treaty (the infamous "war guilt clause") and convinced them to accept the clause in lieu of higher reparation figures. Article 231 later became one of the major background causes for the Second World War, and Foster's role in the drafting of the war guilt clause is an inescapable part of his legacy.[23]

Despite this awkward confrontation between Wilson and Foster, Wilson's confidence in Foster remained high. Foster was scheduled to leave Paris in early June, but the president asked him to stay and continue to "handle the very important and difficult matters with which you have become so familiar and which you have so materially assisted in handling." Wilson added, "My request is justified by the confidence we have all learned to feel in your judgment and ability."[24] Foster was elated. He immediately enclosed the letter in a note to Janet, saying, "Here is a copy of the President's letter—pretty nice!"[25] He was tasked to serve as economic and financial adviser to the peace commissioners and continue to work on crafting reparations proposals and settling economic issues surrounding the treaties with Austria and Bulgaria. He also joined the Supreme Economic Council and the Provisional Reparation Commission, which undertook to apply specific reparation clauses of the Versailles Treaty (which was signed on June 28, 1919).[26]

Upon returning to the United States in September of 1919, Foster immediately resumed his legal work in New York with Sullivan and Cromwell. Since his departure in the spring of 1917, Foster had grown from being a middling lawyer to an internationally recognized expert on global economics as well as a presidential adviser. And for the first time, Foster began thinking about how to craft a peaceful world order with the United States as one of the indispensable players. Still, upon returning to New York, he devoted himself entirely to his legal clients and became a full-time international business attorney. His clients included corporations and banks all over the United States, Latin America, and Europe, whose financial interests were scattered all over the world. Prior to the Wall Street crash of 1929, Foster managed a number of loans to nations and international entities approaching the value of $1 billion.[27] By 1926, Foster was promoted to managing partner of Sullivan and Cromwell after Royal Victor's sudden death. He was only thirty-eight, and he held this position until 1949.

And yet Foster found time for church and the fundamentalist-modernist controversy that erupted in the Presbyterian denomination in 1922. As indicated previously, van Dyke occasionally asked Foster to address the congregation on a variety of topics, including a 1925 request to preach on "the Christian conscience on international relations."[28] While Foster confessed to being "appaled [*sic*] at the prospect" of preaching, he went ahead with it and henceforth spoke from pulpits throughout his life.[29] Foster continued on as an elder of Park Avenue Presbyterian until 1928. He resigned after moving out of New York City to the rural Cold Spring Harbor on Long Island. While he did not join a church on Long Island (preferring golf, tennis, and sailing on Sunday mornings), he briefly renewed his eldership at Park Avenue to help with its merger with Brick Presbyterian Church in 1937. Once the merger was complete, he resigned again over the strenuous objections of his friend and partner in the fundamentalist-modernist controversy, Brick's pastor, William Pierson Merrill.[30]

In 1921, Foster began a long association with the Federal Council of Churches, accepting an invitation from FCC president Robert E. Speer to serve on the council's newly formed Commission on International Justice and Goodwill. Two years later, Foster began service with the National Conference on the Christian Way of Life. He also was a member of the Universal Christian Conference on Life and Work, an entity created by the Presbyterian General Assembly. In 1924, he joined the Committee to Study War, which was formed by the Presbytery of New York.[31] And that same year, women's voting rights and peace activist Carrie Chapman Catt invited him to lecture on economics and war at the 1925 Conference on the Cause and Cure of War. This was an ecumenical conference sponsored by nine women's organizations, including the League of Women Voters (which Catt founded in 1920), the Federation of Women's Boards of Foreign Missions in North America, the National Council of Jewish Women, the National Women's Christian Temperance Union, and the Young Women's Christian Association, to name a few. Foster's newfound stature in the legal and diplomatic fields situated him well to lend an influential voice to the church, in Presbyterian circles and beyond, in terms of how it viewed itself and how it conceived of its mission in a world of growing complexity and insecurity.

Formulation of Ideas on War and Internationalism and Engagement with the Presbyterian Controversy

At first glance, it may seem that Foster's vision for engagement with the world and his contributions to Presbyterian identity are disconnected. How did the morality of war, the necessity of international economic cooperation, and the conservative-liberal divide relate to one another? The glue that brought these apparently disparate issues together for Foster was Christian duty. As a liberal Presbyterian layman, he saw himself as responsible to use his knowledge and experience to the benefit of others, and he believed it was the church's mission to engage with and shape cultural norms. Thus, he thought it necessary to articulate a Christian ethic of war on behalf of his denomination because he had a role in crafting the post–World War I peace. He considered it the duty of the United States, a Christian nation blessed with power and prestige, to cast a vision for economic relationships between nations that promoted mutual prosperity and prevented future war. And he considered it his duty to his church and denomination to get involved in the fundamentalist-modernist controversy. In his mind, the fundamentalists were attempting to impose an unconstitutional, authoritarian rule upon the churches. To Foster, striving for order, justice, freedom, and community was incumbent upon Christian individuals, churches, and nations, no matter the controversy.

War and Internationalism

Foster had been home from Paris for a little over a year, and the experience of serving on the Reparations Commission was still fresh in his mind. Herbert Hoover had just taken office as secretary of commerce, and Foster sent a note congratulating him. A couple of weeks later, Foster sent Hoover a copy of a memorandum he wrote, "The Importance to the United States of the Economic Provisions of the Treaty of Versailles." In that memorandum, which Foster explained was for popular consumption, he argued that war was, at bottom, an interruption in "executor engagements, both public and private." The role of a peace treaty was to restore those engagements and correct the interruptions, not simply by reestablishing the *status quo ante bellum* but by envisioning and enacting a new postwar order that promoted smooth resumption of free exchange between parties that had been at war but were now at peace.[32]

Foster's early ideas about war and peace were rudimentary in the early 1920s. Pruessen characterized Foster as one who "always demonstrated the angular vision that came with a perch in a Wall Street tower."[33] He left Versailles optimistic but became more dejected as the mood in the United States turned toward isolationism and against the League of Nations. Foster thought that American interests were the world's interests, and when American interests advanced, the whole world benefited. He could mix conservatism with idealism, arguing that wars were inevitable but there were ways in which war could be made virtually obsolete. He expressed wariness at nationalism and human lust for power but also believed that the peoples of the world could cultivate a spirit of cooperation that would make world peace attainable. During this period, Foster also took the first steps in attributing the causes of war and failure of internationalism to the perennial conflict between those who embraced change and those who desired the status quo. This was one of Foster's dominant themes in later years. For Foster in the early 1920s, war and internationalism were usually inseparable. Whenever he spoke of war, he made reference to the need for a basis of international agreement, even during periods of irreconcilable conflict between nations. It was because of his participation at Versailles that he began thinking seriously about world order for the first time.

Perhaps the first speech Foster gave on the subject of war and internationalism after returning from Paris was at an Armistice Day gathering at Bronxville, New York, in November 1921. The Washington Conference, called by Secretary of State Charles Evans Hughes in order to prevent a new naval arms race by limiting naval armaments, was getting under way, and Foster wanted his audience to understand that a new spirit of internationalism was the key to preventing future wars. Foster thought that the Washington Conference was a step in the right direction, but only if international cooperation was the basis of the meeting. Foster expressed optimism that the world was tired of war. "Germany . . . has been crushed. It is no longer a menace for the future. . . . The spirit of militarism has been destroyed in the German people." To him, Great Britain was more interested in commercial pursuits than in militarism. The only concerns Foster had were for France and Japan, which he conceded were wary of both a vengeful Germany and a potentially aggressive United States. Still, "we may generalize by saying there is a universal longing for peace and for limitation of armament such as never before existed." And while there were indeed problem spots in the world, they were not insurmountable should international collaboration be implemented.[34]

One dynamic that Foster observed in his speech was that, when nations were allied together in time of war, their determination to achieve victory at great sacrifice was consummate. He looked to specific examples of how the Allies cooperated during World War I to defeat the Central Powers, even to their own economic detriment. Both the blockade of Germany and the imposing of emergency shipping regulations by the Inter-Allied Maritime Council had negative effects on each Allied nation's economy—yet the goal was victory, and every other consideration was thrust aside in pursuit of that all-important goal. The creation of an Allied Supreme Command during World War I, with French marshal Ferdinand Foch taking command of all Allied troops on the western front, meant that non-French nations had to entrust their soldiers' lives to a foreign commander. But the act resulted in increased efficiency and made winning the war with Germany more attainable. Nations should not wait for the emergency of war to make such sacrifices for the international good, Foster believed. The pursuit and maintenance of peace must be established as a goal worth sacrifice. "It is as difficult to maintain peace as it is to win a war, and we can never maintain peace unless the peoples of all the leading nations compel their leaders to recognize that they regard the maintenance of peace as a result as important to be attained as was victory during time of war."[35] The idea that peace must be waged just like war would find expression in Foster's career many more times in the years to come.

Foster was interested in the popular post–World War I idea of outlawing war. The idea of banning war had been discussed at least since 1910 when Andrew Carnegie established the Carnegie Endowment for International Peace, which was dedicated to advancing the concept. Grandfather Foster was one of the founding trustees, and Foster attended meetings with his grandfather while a student in law school. Since World War I was so devastating, the idea gained enough traction internationally to result in the Kellogg-Briand Pact of 1928.[36] Foster prepared a brief paper on the subject, probably as early as 1922, in which he doubted the possibility of effectively banning war. "Such a view is far too superficial and while the motives of those who advocate this simple remedy are doubtless the best, yet it can hardly be expected that their efforts will produce any practical result."[37] Wars prior to the First World War, he noted, only affected limited populations and only among the belligerent nations. With modern war, however, no nation could remain immune to war's destructive effects. Even neutrals would suffer because nations in the twentieth century had become interdependent to an unprecedented extent.

Foster suggested that while outlawing war was unrealistic, war was not the only necessary remedy for settling irreconcilable differences between nations. He brought up the alternatives of negotiation and arbitration but argued that these methods historically fell short. If negotiation was possible, then war was unlikely anyway. And arbitration efforts were time consuming and terribly complex, and had historically only been helpful when competing interests were minor. No, the best way for nations to settle irreconcilable differences over major competing interests, according to Foster, was in an international court modeled on the United States Supreme Court. Foster wrote, "those who are seeking processes of settlement other than war should insist upon experimenting at least, with a permanent International Court of general jurisdiction. It would also be natural that such a demand should first and most insistently be formulated by the United States, since we ourselves have established the greatest international court which the world has known, and have seen it operated with extraordinary success. I refer, of course, to the Supreme Court of the United States."[38] When Foster referred to the Supreme Court as "international," he was thinking about the relationships between the original colonies and, subsequently, between the states of the early republic. In those days, the states had competing interests and often were in conflict with one another. From its founding, Foster noted, the Supreme Court had maintained peace between them by offering a forum for litigation, and even though the Court had no authority or method for enforcement, the states had generally accepted its decisions.

Such a model, Foster recalled, was proposed in The Hague Conferences of 1899 and 1907. He also referenced the new Permanent Court of International Justice, which was beginning to hear cases in 1922. He was deeply critical of those isolationists in the United States who were blindly opposed to the League of Nations and offered "red herring" arguments to justify their antagonism. War, Foster argued, might be natural to humans. But with international cooperation in setting up a forum for the nonviolent litigation of disputes, perhaps war could be rare. American leadership and the American example were indispensable in providing such an alternative to war.[39]

Foster was entirely convinced of the necessity of American leadership in the prevention of war and the building of a peaceful world order. He also urged internationalism as a method for pursuing national self-interest rightly understood. Simply put, Foster argued that nations needed one another. Speaking before the Foreign Policy Association in December 1921, Foster called for an international economic conference modeled on the Washington Conference that had recently concluded. Isolationists recoiled at the thought of international engagement, but this was foolhardy because nations depended on one another for economic prosperity. Foster painted a stark picture of how economic depression in Europe affected the American economy. At the end of the war, American economic power was thriving at unprecedented levels and increasing, but soon policymakers got complacent. Prosperity, Foster said, "went a little to our heads. . . . It led our Government to the decision that we should refrain from any international discussion of economic and financial problems. We had everything; the others had nothing. What was there to discuss?"[40]

But complacency was having deleterious effects on the American economy. Foreign branches of American banks had closed, manufacturing was off its high levels, unemployment was on the rise, and trade was slowing. "Why has all this occurred?" Foster asked. "For a time all that we touched seemed to turn to gold. Yet like King Midas, we are now faced with starvation."[41] Foster wrote that the problem was that the European governments discarded the gold standard and turned to paper, resulting in high inflation and the inability of Europe to buy from America. What was needed was a restoration of the gold standard in order to establish a common standard of value across the world that would stabilize the European economy and international trading networks. But none of this was possible without an economic conference. The Washington Conference had been called out of a sense of urgency to prevent a naval arms race in the Pacific. Something similar was just as urgent to stabilize the world economy. Americans should mix their idealism with a dose of realism, taking self-interest into account as they advanced the good of the world. "The world is an economic whole," said Foster, "and any nation which intelligently advances its own interests cannot but thereby better the conditions of the world as a whole."[42]

A year later, Foster was prepared to go a step further in using the concept of national self-interest rightly understood to advance internationalism. In September 1922, Foster wrote an essay in *Foreign Affairs* in which he argued that the United States should not merely readjust interest payments on Allied debts but forgive whatever portion the debtors were unable to pay. If European nations were obsessed with paying off debts owed to America, there would be no way they could expand their economies and thus "make good the losses of war."[43] In a similar argument Foster made to Hoover in 1921, he wrote that the world needed a restoration of economic conditions in which normal exchange of goods could take place for its own sake. The United States, Foster asserted, had a unique opportunity to set the terms of those conditions through bold leadership. The United States would not realize any of the money lent to the Allies during the war anyway. "It will cost us merely so much of the Allied debts as would in any event be uncollectable," he said.[44] The alternative for America was to let things drift, selfishly demanding repayment of debts it would never see and abandoning Europe to its fate.

As the decade of the 1920s advanced, Foster received more and more recognition as an expert on economics and international affairs. He was also receiving recognition from prominent Presbyterians. In 1924, he was asked to sit on the New York Presbytery's Committee on War alongside Presbyterian ministers Anthony H. Evans, John A. Erickson, Mebane Ramsay, and layman Harold A. Hatch, a textile manufacturing executive with Deering, Milliken & Co. in New York City. In this capacity, he contributed to a report produced by the committee and offered a paper in response to Hatch.

The committee's report called for the outlawing of war and for "the hastening of the day when nations shall learn war no more."[45] Due to the moral authority the United States possessed at the armistice, the report concluded that it was America's duty to lead the world in this effort. A conference on international disarmament, a popular referendum on war "except in case of threatened invasion," and immediate American involvement in the Permanent Court of International Justice were also part of the committee's agenda. For the committee, war and the gospel of Christ were mutually exclusive.[46]

Hatch condemned all forms of war as anti-Christian, but Foster took issue with the idea that war per se was evil, and thus contrary to the spirit of Christianity. With this response, Foster also distanced himself from the committee's general conclusion that war should be outlawed. Christ, Foster wrote, never condemned war as an absolute evil. "He taught that right and wrong are not characteristic of acts and manifestations. It is only to the inner human spirit of the doer that such adjectives as good and evil, Christian and unchristian, are properly applicable," Foster argued. Furthermore, Foster said that war was only one possible method of coercion. Economic and diplomatic pressure in the form of isolating a nation could also be used as an effective mode of coercion. Foster could find no "moral difference between thus imposing, by non-intercourse, our will upon others, and the immediate dispatch of a military expedition to oust the unwelcome Government."[47] The same effects could be achieved through less violent means than war, and there might or might not be evil intentions associated with those means.

Still, Foster believed that "every man should strive for a warless world."[48] War was violent and usually conducted in a spirit of hate, and so war was usually unchristian. But the answer to the problem of war was not to outlaw it. Rather, it was to pursue disarmament along with some means of settling disputes between nations. Foster here advocated for American participation in the World Court. His primary point was that America was duty bound to take the primary role of leadership on the questions of war, disarmament, and international cooperation. "Will the Christians of America advocate that their country assume that role? We face no foe in any quarter. . . . This I submit as a program worthy of the followers of Christ."[49] Again, American indispensability, Christian duty, self-interested actions taken pragmatically in the interest of the common good—each of these themes began to occur regularly in Foster's thoughts on war and internationalism at the beginning of the 1920s.

One other prominent theme emerging in Foster's thought was the interaction between change and stasis. Foster had begun thinking of the inevitability of change as early as his junior year at Princeton, and he later developed a philosophy based on pragmatism in his senior thesis. In early

1925, at the Conference on the Cause and Cure of War, Foster tested out some early ideas on dynamic change and stasis in his talk on economics as an impetus to war.

The conference was held in the Hall of Nations at the Washington Hotel between January 18 and 24, 1925. As organizing chairman, Catt's overall goal was to unify the women's organizations represented around an anti-war message so that they would "serve as missionaries to . . . the remotest crossroads." In her invitation to Foster, Catt expressed frustration at the way the high ideals of the Versailles conference had stalled and come to naught. Catt wrote, "the disorganization of the peace forces is discouraging and these women are determined to know and act."[50] She invited Foster to speak on the topic of economic rivalries, and Foster agreed. In his response to Catt, Foster said that economic factors were not the primary cause of most wars, but economic interests principally contributed to national power and prestige. "I do believe that economic and business considerations often lead to the setting up of so-called 'strong' governments which are apt to involve nations in war."[51] Foster's title was "Economic Motives and How They Lead to War."

The lineup for the conference consisted of many respected figures from the time, including Major General John F. O'Ryan ("Can War Be Abolished?"), General Henry Tureman Allen ("America's Attitude toward Armament"), Judge Florence Allen (Ohio Supreme Court judge, "Women and War"), Mary E. Woolley (president of Mount Holyoke College, "Education and International Understanding"), Frank J. Goodnow (president of Johns Hopkins University, "Relations between East and West"), and Anna Garlin Spencer (Unitarian minister, "Women's Organizations as a Contribution to International Understanding"). President Calvin Coolidge was on hand to open the conference.[52] Discussions on causes of war centered on over-population, mass migration, national insecurity, imperialism, and human psychology. Beatrice Hinkle, a psychologist, argued that in one generation war could be abolished, and women had the unique opportunity to "force men to find new means of solving this chief problem of civilization."[53] The cure for war could be found in such solutions as arbitration, the World Court, codification of international law, international cooperation through the League of Nations, fighting human trafficking of women and children, advancements in medical technology, the teaching of history, encouraging missionary efforts, and freedom of the press.[54]

Foster's talk was part of a series of lectures on economics as a cause of war. Edward M. Earle, professor of history at Columbia University, spoke on imperial rivalries. William Smith Culbertson of the US Tariff Commission spoke on competition for markets and raw materials. When Foster rose to speak, he argued that the greatest cause of war was the almost irresistible desire to protect wealth rather than to attain wealth. The attainment of wealth entailed contractual relationships, so nations became dependent on one another as they grew wealthier. Problems arose when self-interest rightly understood turned into pure selfishness. Rulers of nations looked to maintain their economic power and conservatively "seek to resist any change which threatens the position which they have acquired."[55] Alliances between the ruling classes and strong governments resulted in isolation and the maintaining of the status quo. Such governments tended to be reactionary because they were threatened by economic and social change. Foster said, "an external war may be and often is the last thing which would be desired by those who desire a 'strong government.' But if you once get a government with fighting qualities, you cannot, if you would, confine its employment of those qualities to the field of internal social struggles."[56] Change was inevitable, according to Foster, and futile efforts to resist change led to disruption, chaos, and war.

The thesis of inevitability of change over stasis became a central feature of Foster's religious beliefs, and it appeared again and again in his thought for the rest of his life. The concept, as Foster saw it, was rooted in reality, the nature of truth and knowledge, and ethics. Diplomatic historian Bevan Sewall argued that American pragmatism, as it relates to the concept of dynamic change, is the primary means by which we come to understand Foster's approach to religion and faith. Sewall wrote that Foster "did have a long-standing commitment to some of [pragmatism's] core principles: the idea that beneficial change could be achieved through an individual's actions and beliefs; that progress could be secured by adopting a trial-and-error approach to problem solving; and that sweeping ideological positions should, if possible, be avoided."[57] While it may be a stretch to regard pragmatism as the sole means of understanding Foster's religious posture, there is no doubt that it was a significant tool in Foster's intellectual toolbox.

The Presbyterian Controversy

On May 21, 1922, a young Baptist minister named Harry Emerson Fosdick rose to preach from the pulpit of the venerable "Old First," the First Presbyterian Church in Manhattan. Fosdick was a guest preacher at Old First, but he had filled the pulpit every week for several years and the congregation considered him the de facto minister. Fosdick was a mesmerizing speaker with a razor wit and was the most famous liberal preacher in America. After that day, his fame only increased.

He was a 1904 graduate of, and later a professor at, Union Theological Seminary and, as Fosdick described himself, was "strongly influenced"[58] by social gospel luminary Walter Rauschenbusch. In 1917, in a fit of overweening jingoism, Fosdick wrote a book in support of America's intervention in World War I called *The Challenge of the Present Crisis*, which he later regretted. He went to Europe as an itinerant preacher to the soldiers under the auspices of the YMCA, and his experiences ministering to troops at the front sullied his view of war. After returning to his post at Union in 1918, Fosdick was invited to preach at Old First as a supply preacher but then was offered the position of a permanent guest preacher to serve under the ministry of George Alexander. Fosdick accepted and remained at that post until 1924, when he resigned under dark clouds largely of his own making.[59]

The sermon he preached that spring morning was entitled "Shall the Fundamentalists Win?" The "fundamentalists" represented those conservatives in Protestantism seeking to recover aspects of historic orthodoxy that were being questioned after the popularization of Darwin's evolutionary writings and the rise of critical methods of biblical interpretation during the second part of the 1800s. Basing his remarks on Acts 5:38–39, Fosdick attacked the fundamentalists for wishing to drive liberals out of the Presbyterian and Baptist denominations. He saw fundamentalists as being threatened by "new knowledge . . . about the physical universe . . . human history . . . and other religions."[60] He took issue with them for holding to the inerrancy of Scripture, the virgin birth and substitutionary atonement of Christ, and the personal return of Christ in glory as essential to the Christian faith. For fundamentalists to assert that one could not be a Christian and deny these essentials, Fosdick argued, would be the equivalent of establishing "a doctrinal tribunal more rigid than the pope's."[61] Thirty years later, Fosdick contended that his sermon was meant to be conciliatory, "a plea for tolerance, for a church inclusive enough to take in both liberals and conservatives without either trying to drive the other out."[62] If so, he was fooling himself.

Ivy Lee, a fellow liberal Presbyterian and pioneer in public relations, asked Fosdick if he would consent to having his sermon printed and distributed for a mass audience. Fosdick agreed, and 130,000 copies were produced with funding from John D. Rockefeller Jr. It appeared under the new title, "The New Knowledge and the Christian Faith"—Rockefeller's idea and ultimately fruitless attempt at tact.[63] But this attack on historic Christian orthodoxy was seen by conservative Presbyterians as an alarming threat to the theological integrity of the church and a betrayal of the pastoral office.

Almost immediately after Fosdick delivered his sermon, Clarence Macartney, fundamentalist pastor of Arch Street Presbyterian Church in Philadelphia, preached a rebuttal sermon entitled "Shall Unbelief Win?" The sermon was printed in the *Presbyterian*, and by the following October, under Macartney's leadership, the Presbytery of Philadelphia adopted an overture to the General Assembly, that is, a request from a lower governing body to a higher one that particular action be taken. The Philadelphia Overture, specifically naming Fosdick and referencing the section of his sermon in which he attacked the doctrine of the virgin birth, held that such skepticism was contrary to the teaching of the Presbyterian church and "the Church catholic in all ages." Thus, the overture called for the General Assembly to admonish the Presbytery of New York. It did so to secure doctrinal orthodoxy in the First Presbyterian Church on the basis of the doctrinal deliverances to the General Assembly of 1910 and 1916, which had endorsed five specific theological affirmations. These included (1) inspiration and inerrancy of the Bible, (2) the virgin birth, (3) substitutionary atonement, (4) the bodily resurrection and ascension, and (5) the historicity of miracles. These so-called Five Points were to be binding for any and all candidates seeking licensure to the ministry.[64] The 1923 General Assembly, meeting in Indianapolis, endorsed the Philadelphia Overture, thanks to the guidance of Macartney and the oratory of William Jennings Bryan, the former secretary of state and Democratic nominee for president in 1896, 1900, and 1908. Bryan, the most sensational orator of the day, died five days after his greatest battle on behalf of the fundamentalist cause in the Scopes trial of 1925. By a vote of 439 to 359, the General Assembly directed the New York Presbytery to report back to the 1924 meeting as to how it would bring Old First into conformity with the Westminster Confession and the Five Points over the course of the following year.

George Marsden, in his study of the controversy, noted that 1923 was the high-water mark of fundamentalism in the Presbyterian denomination. "Even the secular liberal press . . . was defecting," Marsden wrote. The *Nation* and the *New Republic* both saw the logic in the fundamentalist position, that if the modernists wanted to jettison key points of orthodoxy, they were free do so but were not free to remain Presbyterians.[65] Still, the modernist party was alarmed at the action taken by the General Assembly because they saw it as an abridgment of freedom of thought and expression. In response, Robert Hastings Nichols, a professor at Auburn Theological Seminary (and colleague of Allen Macy Dulles), and Henry Sloane Coffin, president of Union Theological Seminary, drafted a statement objecting to the 1923 General Assembly's action. The statement, known as the Auburn Affirmation, had collected its first 150 signers by December 26, 1923, including John Grier Hibben, president of Princeton University, William Pierson Merrill of the Brick Presbyterian Church, and Foster's pastor and friend, Tertius van Dyke of the Park Avenue Presbyterian Church. The Affirmation stated that the Confession and the Bible were the only doctrinal standards, and furthermore, the Confession "does not require [ministers'] assent to the very words of the Confession, or to all of its teachings, or to interpretations of the Confession by individuals or church courts." Its signers stood against the Five Points as a legitimate rule for orthodoxy and asserted "liberty of thought and teaching."[66]

Less than one month later, in January 1924, the Presbytery of New York offered a report in compliance with the directive of the General Assembly, demonstrating the actions it intended to take regarding Fosdick's sermon and the orthodoxy of Old First. The elders of First Church reported to the investigating committee that they were satisfied that Fosdick's thought and preaching were entirely within orthodox bounds as prescribed by the Confession, and the presbytery concurred. Not only that, but the presbytery reported "its confident expectation that our brother of another denomination [that is, Fosdick, a Baptist] who enjoys the freedom of that pulpit will carry on his work in good conscience."[67]

The Affirmation and the New York Presbytery's report had the effect of throwing gasoline on a fire. Twenty-one New York elders promptly filed a protest against the report, citing among other things that Fosdick unabashedly described himself as a liberal and that the presbytery had no direct jurisdiction over a guest preacher from another denomination.[68] This protest was followed by a formal complaint against the report addressed to the stated clerk of the New York Presbytery to be offered at the 1924 General Assembly. The complaint asserted three points. First, the New York Presbytery failed to carry out its directive. Second, the presbytery's report was supposed to be unbiased and comprehensive. But since the presbytery heeded the opinions of Old First's elders and that of Fosdick himself, the complainants charged, "it was not." Third, the complainants quoted from Fosdick's writings and sermons as far back as 1915 and found them wanting. Fosdick's teachings, they protested, "have not been, and are not now, evangelical."[69]

This background is necessary to grasp the environment Foster entered in the spring of 1924. To simplify complicated circumstances, there were three phases to Foster's involvement in the controversy between 1924 and 1926. Although Foster was deeply engaged in the Fosdick case, he stayed with the controversy even after that case had been resolved. In phase one (1924), Foster defended Fosdick's ministry at Old First; in phase two (1925), he defended the licensure of a young Henry P. Van Dusen, future president of Union Theological Seminary; in phase three (1925–1926), he defended the membership in the New York Presbytery of Rev. Carlos Fuller and the licensure of Cameron Parker Hall. In sum, phase one was a partial victory for Foster, phase two was a defeat, and phase three, a complete victory.

Phase One

On April 15, 1924, H. G. Mendenhall, stated clerk of the Presbytery of New York, informed Foster that the presbytery had elected him to serve as a commissioner at the General Assembly in Grand Rapids, Michigan, in June.[70] Foster was enthusiastic about attending. He immediately wrote to his closest Princeton friend, Bill Finney, a physician at the Mayo Institute in Rochester, Minnesota. "I do not know just where Grand Rapids is," Foster confessed, "but I imagine it is somewhere in your general locality. Can't you come over and assist us in breaking lances with [William Jennings] Bryan on behalf of the modernists?"[71] Rochester is nowhere near Grand Rapids, but Foster was clearly in a fighting spirit, and his legal acumen was somewhat sharper than his knowledge of upper Midwest geography.

Two weeks after Foster's election as commissioner, Nichols wrote to Foster asking him for his legal opinion on whether or not the General Assembly had the authority to enforce doctrinal uniformity. As a codrafter and signatory to the Auburn Affirmation, Nichols was preparing to defend the Affirmation at the General Assembly and argue that under the Presbyterian form of government, only the presbyteries had such authority. Foster concurred. From the beginning of his involvement in the controversy, Foster was a central figure on the modernist side, working to steer the contest in a *constitutional* direction and away from a *doctrinal* direction. Foster directed a legal, rather than a theological, strategy aimed at shifting the initiative of the controversy to the modernists and putting the fundamentalists on the defensive. In other words, the fundamentalists would no longer have a lock on logical arguments. As Foster put it, "if the majority of the [General] Assembly wish to impose interpretations of the Westminster Confession, which in effect, make new tests of orthodoxy, and if they wish thereby to eliminate a large body of the church [that is, the modernists], they must certainly go about their task in a constitutional manner and submit to the Presbyteries the new tests of orthodoxy which they propose to impose."[72]

Foster joined George Alexander, William Pierson Merrill, and George P. Agnew to represent the New York Presbytery defending Fosdick to the Permanent Judicial Commission at the General Assembly. As the only attorney among the presbytery's representatives, Foster served as legal counsel. The Judicial Commission was established by the General Assembly (which in 1924 comprised about nine hundred people) as a court of fifteen to hear preliminary arguments in church disputes. Once the commission ruled on a case, the General Assembly would vote on whether to adopt the decision or send it back for review. Up to that time, the General Assembly had always accepted the commission's rulings. Whatever the commission would rule in the Fosdick case was expected to be adopted by the Assembly.[73]

There were two tasks for the commission—to render a decision on the status of the New York Presbytery's report on Fosdick and to decide whether the General Assembly could impose the Five Points on the churches. In the first issue, the goal for the modernists was to prevent the commission from ordering the presbytery to fire Fosdick from Old First. This was partially achieved—the commission stated in its report, "we do not mean that the First Presbyterian Church of New York must of necessity be deprived of the services of Dr. Fosdick, which they so much desire." So far, so good for the modernists. But the commission also regarded Fosdick's relationship to Old First as "wholly without precedent" and "an anomaly" since he was not a Presbyterian and had been filling the pulpit of Old First as a permanent guest for several years. The solution the commission proposed was for the church to invite Fosdick to become a Presbyterian, and then hire him as their full-time pastor.[74]

This appeared to be a satisfactory resolution. Fosdick, however, suspected that if he became a Presbyterian, the fundamentalists would be watching him like a hawk. "Once within the regular ranks of the Presbyterian ministry I could be tried for heresy the first time I uttered a liberal conviction," Fosdick wrote to his reading audience decades later in his autobiography.[75] But at the time, the self-styled, broad-minded liberal warily confided to his secretary in private, "there must be some '[n-word] in the fence.'—and I shall await the real news before beginning to think about it."[76] Fosdick resigned his post at Old First in October 1924.

As to the commission's decision on the Philadelphia Overture and the Five Points, Foster could claim greater success. Reveling in his role as counsel to the New York Presbytery, Foster wrote to his father, "I was in the thick of the fight. . . . I was almost daily engaged in controversy with [William Jennings] Bryan, all of which was most interesting."[77] Timothy Pfeiffer, another of Foster's Princeton classmates, recalled, "Foster made mincemeat out of Bryan from the point of view of logical statement and reasoning."[78] The commission ruled that it was "unconstitutional" for the General Assembly to enforce compliance with the Five Points, and Foster regarded this as "the decision . . . of the greater importance."[79] He turned out to be right, and he worked to solidify this victory in the Presbyterian denomination for the next two years.

Phase Two

The next two phases of Foster's engagement with the modernists involved disputes over the New York Presbytery's recognizing the legitimacy of ministers or ministerial candidates who would not affirm the virgin birth. Phase two involved the case of the licensure of Henry P. Van Dusen, future president of Union Theological Seminary. In March 1925, Coffin and Nichols invited Foster to help write the legal brief defending the presbytery in sustaining Van Dusen's licensure. Since Foster's success at the 1924 Assembly in the matter of the Overture, Coffin did not think it would be too much trouble—"the case is absolutely simple if we can get the judicial commission to maintain its attitude of last year."[80]

Timothy Pfeiffer and Foster wrote the draft of the brief defending the presbytery and the Synod of New York in Van Dusen's case. Their argument was that Van Dusen never affirmed the virgin birth, but neither did he explicitly deny it. Furthermore, Van Dusen affirmed the deity of Christ and the Holy Spirit, substitutionary atonement, the doctrine of the Trinity, the Bible as the word of God, and personal immortality after death. Most importantly, the New York Presbytery's constitutional authority to license was original under the form of government, and the General Assembly did not have the power to enforce belief in the Five Points. The brief filed by the modernists stated, "the Constitution, not theology, is the source from which the validity of this assertion must be traced. The theological soundness of the doctrinal deliverances of 1910 and 1916 [the Five Points] is not in issue. Whether sound or unsound, the attempt to make them or any other doctrinal deliverances of the General Assembly a part of the Church's fundamental law, would be, if successful, a complete reversal of historic Presbyterianism and would eventuate in Church anarchy. This is not heresy; it is orthodox constitutionalism."[81] The Judicial Commission at the 1925 General Assembly decided against Foster and the modernists in the Van Dusen case. While the commission's 1924 decision stood—the Assembly could not establish the Five Points as a general test for orthodoxy in the churches—it did rule that the Assembly had the authority to apply the Five Points as a test when it came to licensing candidates for the ministry.

Phase Three

While in process of defending Van Dusen, Mendenhall, Coffin, and William Adams Brown invited Foster to defend two other candidates in yet another complaint filed by the fundamentalists.[82] In this case, the New York Presbytery allowed Rev. Carlos Fuller to join its membership and also licensed Cameron Parker Hall to preach, despite neither having affirmed biblical inspiration, the historicity of miracles, the virgin birth, or bodily resurrection. That December, Coffin asked Foster to write the brief in defense of the presbytery, and Foster nearly declined. He said, "I had not realized that appointment on the Committee would involve me in writing briefs in these two cases."[83] Foster reluctantly agreed to prepare the brief, and it turned out to be the most masterful stroke of his entire involvement in the controversy.

In reviewing the fundamentalist complaint regarding Fuller and Hall, along with the material from their examinations, Foster found that the record showed no doctrinal affirmations or denials whatsoever. All the record showed was that Fuller and Hall had been examined, that the Committee on Examination was "satisfied as to the candidates' beliefs," and that "this view was accepted by a majority of the Presbytery."[84] Given these circumstances, the presbytery deserved the benefit of the doubt, and thus could not be held to be in error in the cases of Fuller and Hall. Furthermore, the only way to really know what a candidate believed was to have a personal interview with that candidate. This the Committee of Examination did, and the presbytery accepted the committee's evaluation and satisfaction. But, said Foster, if some authoritative statement of faith was a basis for a candidate's cross-examination, then "he should, as in a civil trial, have the benefit of counsel," who could facilitate responses that were in accordance with the statement of faith whether the candidate was sincere or not. "Such a procedure is unthinkable," wrote Foster. "It would totally destroy the spiritual element in induction into our ministry and substitute a purely ritualistic perspective."[85] He closed his argument by appealing, once again, to the strength and reliability of constitutional procedure and the dangers of legalism and ecclesiastical tyranny.

The Synod of New York found in favor of Foster's brief in January 1926. The 1926 General Assembly accepted the synod's decision. Foster's successful argument merged with a general trend in the Presbyterian Church in the USA toward modernism, resulting in the defection of the fundamentalists to Westminster Seminary and the Orthodox Presbyterian Church, largely under the leadership of J. Gresham Machen.

Foster became the toast of the modernist camp. Voices were raised in gratitude to Foster for his victory. Tertius van Dyke wrote, "you have hit the nail on the head as it never yet has been struck. . . . Your paragraph on the word 'satisfaction' is a masterpiece. . . . I have never before seen assembled such an argument as you here present."[86] Brown described the brief as "the best statement of the issue which I have seen anywhere."[87] Coffin said, "you have done an extraordinarily difficult and delicate task with supreme skill. I was filled with admiration." Four days later he wrote, "I simply marvel each time at the success with which you have accomplished a very difficult task."[88] Ten months later, Coffin wrote Foster after the Judicial Committee concurred with Foster's defense: "The decision of the Judicial Commission is a great triumph for you. . . . I cannot thank you enough nor tell you how sincerely I admire the masterly way in which you prepared that brief."[89]

The controversy did not end with the synod's decision, but Foster saw his victory as a timely opportunity to bow out. In January 1926, Mendenhall sent Foster a request to take up yet another fundamentalist complaint against the New York Presbytery, but Foster declined. Still, Foster had made his mark on the controversy and had attracted the attention not only of modernists but also of fundamentalists. James E. Bennett, one of the fundamentalist complainants in the Van Dusen case, continually peppered Foster with pugnacious letters throughout 1926. Foster tried ignoring him, but eventually he had to ask Bennett to leave him alone—"I have your letter of May 6th and have received a number of preceding communications. In view of the uniformly intemperate character of these I should prefer not to receive any more."[90] Foster had done his duty, as he saw it, for his church and denomination. His greatest contribution was to put the Presbyterian church on a path of skepticism of historic orthodoxy, and of emphasis on social concerns animated in part by the ecumenical movement, of which Foster became a key player.

This period of Foster's life, from 1912 to 1926, represents the start of his legal and diplomatic career, the formation of his worldview, and the establishment of a personal and professional network that proved critical to his decades-long rise in influence to the end of his life. We see the beginning of patterns of thought informed by his religion, which itself was animated by pragmatism, duty, and order. Foster's ideas on the relevance of religion in general and the church in particular matured over the course of the next several years, and the effects of that development had consequences for the shape of the modern world.

4

"Work, for the Night Is Coming"
(1927–1939)

There can be no salvation until we have set right the funda-
mentals. The urgent task of the Church is to restore God as
the object of human veneration and to recreate in man a sense
of duty to fellow man.

—John Foster Dulles[1]

During the summer of 1935, Foster took his wife Janet, his children John
and Lillias, his brother Allen, and his friends Bob Hart and Ferdinand
("Ferd") Eberstadt on a monthlong cruise down the St. Lawrence River and
into the Gulf of St. Lawrence from Clayton, New York, to Charlottetown,
Prince Edward Island. They took the cruise in Foster's forty-foot yawl, the
Menemsha, which he acquired in 1927. The *Menemsha* was a fine, if somewhat spartan, sailing vessel—reliable, sturdy, broad of beam, and capable
of exacting conditions in both saltwater and freshwater. Foster and other
members of the crew carefully kept a daily log on the cruise, from July 21
to August 17, that contains details of a sailing excursion that, on the one
hand, was luxurious and enchanting and, on the other hand, harrowing
and exhausting. Foster reveled in hard sailing—his sister Eleanor called
him a "full canvas sailor."[2] The log describes being nearly run down by an
ocean liner one morning at 4 a.m.; of struggling against five-knot currents,
strong winds, and heavy seas; of shivering cold; and of reeling and pitching
in four-foot waves with the spray drenching Lillias and Janet on the bow
while they took photographs. The log also recorded the gaff rig breaking;

the toilet clogging; "seas running freely over both leeward and windward deck and foredeck, and also coming over the stern"; and a failure of the backstay and shroud supporting the mast, threatening disaster. "We make temporary repairs of the backstay and proceed under jib, jigger, and motor, the jib and jigger alone giving her fast headway, so that the motor races as we slide down the big seas," Foster wrote.[3]

But the trip offered incomparable pleasures: of fishing for salmon on Anticosti Island in the Gulf of St. Lawrence; of lying on deck wondering at the northern lights, of staying up all night gazing at the full moon; of views of high mountains and timber on the shore; of rising early to the welcome of warm sunrises and still waters; of swimming in coves; of sailing swiftly attended by white porpoises diving and splashing alongside; of the exhilaration of running twenty miles a day and more under sail, and of collapsing into bunks and falling into deep sleep following eighteen- and twenty-hour days of punishing exertions against the elements. Breakfasts were often hasty and basic, and lunches were absolutely nonexistent. But Foster never scrimped on dinners. The entry for July 24 reads, "Marvelous dinner—cocktails and pate de foie gras, steak, fresh mushrooms, potatoes, fresh corn, sour cherry tart, ale, cheese, and brandy. Beautiful sunset and nearly full moon makes it hard to go below."[4]

The years between 1933 and 1940 were Foster's most active period of sailing on *Menemsha*. With friends and family, Foster skippered the vessel on explorations of Nova Scotia, the Bay of Fundy, Lakes Superior and Huron, and the Gulf of St. Lawrence. *Menemsha* was a fine craft, but Foster did not want the bells and whistles found on luxury boats. He preferred "simple gear, without many winches or gadgets," Eleanor wrote. He had no electric depth finders and no radio. Foster believed that the point of sailing was to rely on one's own resources as much as possible and to escape the trappings of civilization in order to face the beauty and challenges of the natural and untamed world. Eleanor described Foster as fearless yet responsible; undaunted by threatening elements but also not careless with people's lives. "He rarely changed his plan of sailing because of a rising wind or high seas. . . . He kept morale high even when the going was tough and the effort exhausting."[5] Foster's experiences in the outdoors were, to him, sacramental representations of his experiences as a churchman, lawyer, and diplomat.

His life was marked by a consistent love for, and draw toward, the outdoors.

Any treatment of Foster Dulles has to account for this central characteristic of his that began in his earliest years and continued until the final months of his life. Going outdoors for Foster was much more than a vacation, a time away from the pressures of a full career. The irresistible pull that the natural world exerted on Foster represented something much deeper than a chance to "get away." The outdoors and the experiences he enjoyed there were signs offering practical wisdom for living and were a reflection of how he perceived his place in the world. "He would make analogies between things in nature and things in sailing and things which were in the sphere of diplomacy and international finance, or whatever he was working on," Avery said.[6] Both his contemporaries and his biographers marvel at Foster as an enigma. His life and work can be interpreted through the lenses of liberal Protestantism, family heritage, WASP privilege, pragmatist philosophy, and early twentieth-century politics and economics. But the natural world centered on Lake Ontario and its environs is indispensable to grasping the man and his mission.

Roswell Barnes, one of Foster's closest friends, remembered his keen sense of Christian duty in the cause of "righteousness" but described it not as a burden but as a joy. In describing his feeling of obligation, Barnes said Foster undertook every activity in work and play with profound seriousness not only because of Christian duty but also because he loved facing the challenges presented. In other words, for Foster, Christian duty emerged from a blend of divine calling and the joy of facing a great challenge. Barnes said, "he had a sense of moral obligation . . . but this was almost fun for him. . . . I learned that he was working somewhat the way a man plays a game. Very hard." Foster's tirelessness and energy were legendary, noticed by everyone around him, including his detractors, and these traits were a source of inspiration for his admirers. He believed he had been born in a momentous time of world history, and that God had given him serious work to do in service of his nation and the church. Furthermore, Foster believed he had been blessed to live in a created order that offered practical tools for understanding divinely ordained responsibilities. Barnes said Foster's approach to his work and his approach to play were inspired by both a powerful sense of vocation and a boyish delight in all that the world offered. "He takes everything seriously," Barnes said. Speaking of work and play, Barnes continued: "He works at it so hard because he is having a good time. He was just at home in it."[7] For Foster, the natural world of tossing waves, howling winds, quiet sunsets, and cold swims was not necessarily exclusive to the world of war, peace, and change.

The period from 1927 to 1939 offered Foster a host of challenges, with the onset of the Great Depression, the coming of a new world war, and the question of the role the churches should play in whatever world followed. Foster knew, as a new war approached between 1937 and 1939, that the churches would be indispensable in framing a postwar world, even if it had to be crafted out of a Nazi victory. In the late 1920s and into the '30s, Foster began to emerge from merely a Wall Street finance and international lawyer to a world-renowned ecumenical churchman. Nineteen thirty-seven was the year in which Foster experienced the most significant religious turning point in his life, in which he came to see himself as divinely called to usher the Christian church onto the world stage. The church had to make the decisive difference in the most pressing issues facing humanity. His struggles against the natural elements, as Avery insisted, provided Foster with key analogies for understanding those challenges. And the words of one of his favorite hymns, which he learned around his mother's piano as a boy, took on a new meaning for him in the face of looming threats to world order from German fascism and Japanese imperialism.

> Work, for the night is coming,
> Under the sunset skies;
> While their bright tints are glowing,
> Work, for the daylight flies.
> Work till the last beam fadeth,
> Fadeth to shine no more;
> Work, while the night is dark'ning,
> When man's work is o'er.

Context for Foster's Intellectual and Religious Development

At the end of his life, Foster considered his work during the 1930s and '40s as representative of the most creative years of his life. It was an uncertain time, to be sure. The Great Depression was under way, and war clouds were gathering in Europe and in Asia. Those war clouds would break forth a storm by the end of the decade such as the world had never seen. By 1940, the unthinkable had occurred—German armies conquered France in a mere six weeks, a feat she failed to accomplish in four years between 1914 and 1918. During these grave crises, Foster came into his own as a serious thinker. By 1939, he had established himself in the highest circles of international diplomacy and lay Christian leadership through his writing and speaking. The turning point of his career came in 1937 after attending the Oxford Conference on Church, Community, and State. Foster had already enjoyed the reputation of an international finance expert since the Versailles Conference, but beginning in the mid-1930s, he found his voice. From 1935—and really 1937—he became a major theorist on war and peace, world order, and the role of religion in international politics.

The major theme characterizing his writing and speaking beginning in 1935 was the necessity for orderly and peaceful change. Foster wrote about war and internationalism during the 1920s while his experiences in Paris were still fresh in his mind. He circled around to his Princeton training in philosophy, and also to his days studying under Bergson at the Sorbonne in 1908–1909, in articulating the concept of the inevitability of change, which beginning in 1934 dominated his thinking. It is also no accident that he found this concept corroborating itself in the natural world. Avery spoke of how Foster applied pragmatist principles while contending against the natural elements while sailing. In predicting weather patterns on Lake Ontario, Foster never took too much comfort in calm conditions because to do so exposed oneself to complacency. Once complacency had set in, the dynamic forces of wind and storm could blast upon the unprepared mariner to overturn placid conditions. They would set up a new set of realities with which to contend. Recalling his youth, Avery also said his father taught him how to forge progress out of capricious change. To Foster, change was inevitable, but human intelligence crafted progress from change through the application of creativity. Foster believed that, if this principle were true, one would find it normative not only in human interactions but also in nature. Avery put it like this:

> I remember one instruction which he gave me when I was trying to pull a backstay against the wind. We were going about, tacking back and forth, and I was trying to tighten it up, and I was pulling it directly.

And he explained to me that it was impossible to pull directly against the force of the wind because the wind was much stronger than I was. He said, the thing to do was to take one loop around the cleat and then to pull indirectly on an angle. If I wasn't pulling directly against the wind in this way, I could help to make some progress, even though I was not as strong as the wind. And, there again, I think, was the principle which he applied in circumstances of practical life—that he wouldn't directly oppose a hostile force which was strong, but he would try to find some indirect way of opposing it and making progress against it. So, we used to have great fun navigating and things like that.[8]

In 1927, Foster was in his first full year as managing partner at Sullivan and Cromwell. After having advocated for the need for American economic engagement with Europe based on the idea that Europe's financial destiny was directly tied to America's, Foster was feeling optimistic about the future. Between 1924 and 1929, the United States was banker to the world, engaged in what Pruessen calls "the most extensive financial foray into the international arena that Americans had ever taken in peacetime."[9] As his banker clients were lending millions to nations in Central America and Europe, they were also loaning money to Germany to help them meet their reparations obligations more quickly after the Dawes Plan was finalized in 1924. The Dawes Plan seemed to be the answer to the gnawing problems of Germany's inability to pay the reparations agreed upon at Versailles in the face of growing French impatience with Germany. In 1923, France and Belgium seized the Ruhr Valley, which produced the lion's share of Germany's coal and iron, in an outburst aimed at speeding up reparations payments in the form of goods and in answering what they saw as German abuse of the Versailles Treaty. Occupation of the Ruhr resulted in further economic destabilization in Europe and led the Americans and the British to propose a way to relieve the reparations burden on the Germans. Bankers under the leadership of Rufus C. Dawes made provisions for reduction of reparations payments and loans to Germany to facilitate more rapid and reliable payments. Another international crisis seemed to have been averted.[10]

For Foster, the upshot of these apparently improving conditions was that bankers seemed to be more reliable than politicians at figuring out solutions to difficult problems. In a 1928 address to the Foreign Policy Association,

Foster pointed out that the French politicians ignored the bankers' pleas to alleviate German reparations, and instead occupied the Ruhr Valley. After it became obvious that the occupation was a fiasco, Foster said, "the politicians came back to the bankers and said, 'After all, perhaps we need your help. Won't you tell us now on what conditions you will loan money to Germany?'" Foster went on to describe the resulting Dawes Plan as "the bankers' . . . drastic answer" demanding that "the occupation of the Ruhr must be ended and Germany's economy liberated." Foster was ecstatic over the Dawes Plan, so much so that he believed it to be the source of a German economic "revival." He regarded it as "unprecedented, I think, in the whole history of the world."[11] It was America's responsibility, and her responsibility alone, to come to Europe's aid after the bloodletting of World War I, according to Foster. By the eve of the 1929 crash, Foster believed that American bankers had led the way in securing a future of economic promise for Europe and, consequently, for America, too.

As a Wall Street lawyer and businessman, Foster was extremely successful. He was the lead partner at a major international law firm that included twenty partners and eighty lawyers during the 1920s and 1930s, and he sat on boards of fifteen different organizations.[12] He was thus poised to accomplish some personal goals. Most immediately, he began looking into purchasing his beloved Main Duck Island around the same time as moving his family to Cold Spring Harbor in 1928. In the fall of that year, he reached out to a Toronto attorney named Britton Osler to find out who owned Main Duck, and if the island might be for sale. Prohibition was the law of the land, and Foster wrote, "lest you should think that I am planning to establish a rum-running base . . . I find the island a good locality for sailing and might be interested, if the price were reasonable, in buying all or part of the island and putting up a rough camp there."[13] Osler inquired at the Registrar of Deeds in Picton, Ontario, and discovered that Claude Cole had owned the island since 1905. In the summer of 1929, Foster made contact with Cole, who operated a fishing business (and a rum-running operation!) from Main Duck and Cape Vincent, New York, a town close to Watertown. They actually met face-to-face on Main Duck. Standing on a smooth pebble beach on the island, Cole agreed to sell Main Duck to Foster for $25,000. Just weeks before the October 29, 1929, stock market crash, Foster sent Cole a formal offer to buy for that price. But Cole's son, Cecil, abruptly intervened with his father and stopped the deal. Despite this, Foster secured from Cole the promise of first refusal in case he ever decided to sell.[14]

A few months passed, and in February 1930 Cole reached out to Foster at his Wall Street office. He wanted to send Foster "some liturture" and expressed his desire "to see more of You & Yours this comming season & I want to impress on Your mind You & Your friends are very welcomb visotors & want You to feel at home at any & al times."[15] Clearly, Cole was trying to keep in touch with Foster because he was keen on selling Main Duck and getting some ready cash. By 1933, Cole offered to sell to Foster again, but by that time, the Depression was definitely making its impression. Cole asked for $50,000 this time, emphasizing the lucrative nature of the fishing business he ran on the island and the physical improvements he had made since 1929. Foster countered with a $20,000 offer, writing to Cole that "at the present time conditions are very far from normal. There are big estates on Long Island which cost anywhere from $150,000 to $200,000 which can to-day be bought for $25,000. Money to-day is relatively so much more valuable and buys so much more than it did in 1929."[16] Cole refused the offer, and the matter between them was dropped for another four years.

Foster's statements offer a glimpse into his mind concerning the economic situation after 1929. His attitude toward the Depression was marked by dread. In 1929 and throughout the 1930s, Foster's main clients were major corporations and banks with interests predominating in central and eastern Europe. Looking back on those years, we of today might be tempted to wonder what worried Foster. After all, his presence graced not a single breadline. He remained in his position of privilege and power for the duration of the economic crisis. But "he was never content to look only at his bank balance," as Pruessen observed. For one thing, Sullivan and Cromwell was feeling the pinch. In 1928, American bankers were offering $1 billion in international loans; by 1931, that figure had dropped almost 80 percent to $191 million. Payments for outstanding loans were not forthcoming—the Banque Adam in Paris went under, as did the Credit Anstalt in Vienna. Banks fell like dominoes in Hungary, Czechoslovakia, Germany, Romania, and Poland. Britain went off the gold standard in the fall of 1931, which resulted in a 50 percent devaluation of the pound. Twenty-five other countries went off gold in

1931, leading to a decline of American exports from $3.8 billion in 1930 to $2.4 billion in 1931.[17]

Foster remained a dedicated internationalist throughout the 1930s, convinced that the nations of the world were interdependent. He always resisted economic isolationism, protectionism exemplified by the Smoot-Hawley tariff of 1930, and restrictive immigration policies. The economic crisis of the Depression pointed to the necessity of more economic engagement with the world, freer trade policies, and less manipulation of currencies—in short, the United States should not pull back from the world but should join with other nations to recover from the financial disasters of the years since the end of World War I. For the United States to isolate itself meant the exacerbation of the world economic crisis, which, in turn, would have the ultimate result of disrupting the world order and threatening another global conflagration, this time more destructive than the last one.

The world of the 1930s became more and more dangerous as the years progressed. In November 1919, the United States Senate rejected the Versailles Treaty and refused to join the League of Nations, in a sharp rebuke to President Wilson. The failure of the United States to join the League of Nations doomed that venture from the start. But America did initiate efforts at disarmament, particularly by calling the 1922 Washington Conference, which resulted in limiting naval tonnage between the United States, Britain, Japan, France, and Italy to a ratio of 5:5:3:1.67:1.67. Three separate treaties limiting armaments and colonial expansion came out of the Washington Conference. Additionally, in 1928 American secretary of state Frank B. Kellogg proposed a treaty outlawing war. French foreign minister Aristide Briand endorsed Kellogg's proposal and incorporated further language, resulting in the Kellogg-Briand Pact, also known as the Pact of Paris. The United States Senate, in a burst of idealism, ratified it 85–1, and twenty-two other nations, including Germany, also adopted it.

European powers made efforts at fulfilling the Versailles Treaty, such as the Locarno Treaty of 1925, which attempted to secure the boundaries between France, Belgium, and Germany, to be guaranteed by Britain and Italy. It was supposed to soften tensions between the French and the Germans, particularly after the occupation of the Ruhr, which had disastrous effects on French-German relations. Foster saw that the problem with the Washington Conference treaties and the Locarno Treaty was that neither allowed for any flexibility but attempted to establish a 1922 and 1925 reality, respectively, for all time. The problem with Kellogg-Briand was that it proved to be nothing more than a sentimental pipe dream. Such treaties were bound to fail, and Foster would remind his readers of these failures in his later writings.

The Versailles Treaty also failed with regard to the future of German and Ottoman overseas territories, which were lost after the war. Wilson had hoped that these former German and Ottoman holdings would pass under a trusteeship called mandates. Lands in Africa, the Middle East, and the Pacific were to be held in trust by, not annexed to, Britain, France, Japan, the Union of South Africa, Australia, and New Zealand. The League of Nations was supposed to supervise the mandate system to make sure that processes were in place that put the territories on the path to self-government. In practice the Allied powers treated the mandates as annexed territories and drew boundaries arbitrarily, with no regard for the interests of indigenous people.

Unrealistic boundary determinations, static treaty arrangements, hypocritical treatment of colonial peoples, and the failure of the United States to join the League—in conjunction with German reparations, the Allied debt crisis, and the international financial crisis initiated by the collapse of the American economy in 1929—all came together to bring about the failure of the liberal projects in central Europe and destabilization of the Far East. Japan, Germany, and Italy took seven major steps between 1931 and 1939 toward a new world war:

- In 1931, the Japanese invaded Manchuria and set up a puppet state called Manchukuo, and withdrew from the League two years later in 1933.
- In 1933, Adolf Hitler became chancellor of Germany and led German withdrawal from the League. In 1935, Hitler flouted the Versailles Treaty by openly rearming Germany, and in 1936, German forces reoccupied the Rhineland, an act also in violation of Versailles.
- In 1935, Italy invaded Ethiopia, which was an independent nation and a member of the League of Nations. The League condemned the action, but Britain and France balked at intervening militarily on Ethiopia's behalf.

- In 1936, the Spanish Civil War broke out between profascist forces aided by Germany and Italy and pro-Communist forces aided by the Soviet Union. The profascist forces under Franco prevailed by 1939 because of special training and material aid provided by Germany and Italy. Also in 1936, Hitler and Mussolini concluded the Rome-Berlin Axis agreement.
- In 1938, Germany annexed Austria in direct violation of the Versailles Treaty. Austria had been created by the League.
- Also in 1938, Germany annexed the Sudetenland in Czechoslovakia, the only successful democratic country created at Versailles. British prime minister Neville Chamberlain and French premier Edouard Daladier facilitated this annexation through the infamous policy of appeasement at Munich in September 1938. By the spring of 1939, Hitler had taken the rest of Czechoslovakia, without any repercussions from the League.
- In August 1939, Germany and the Soviet Union agreed to invade and partition Poland as part of the Molotov-Ribbentrop Pact. On September 1, Germany invaded Poland from the west, and on September 17, the Soviets invaded Poland from the east. The Soviets also invaded Estonia, Latvia, Lithuania, and Finland. Britain and France declared war on Germany on September 3.

Through Foster's many European contacts, his travels to Europe, and his staying abreast of events, it was easy for him to see the dangers of another world war as early as 1931. He had written his musings on war and the need for international cooperation in the early 1920s, but the ideas he articulated from 1934 to 1939 were distinct from his earlier writings by their rapid development, intricacy, pertinence, and creativity. They were arresting in their defenses of Germany, Italy, and Japan and criticisms of Britain and France. Most noticeable of all was how his ideas matured from purely economic, diplomatic, and philosophical arguments to arguments justified by and applied from religious bases. While many of Foster's ideas from this period were not new, he made a sudden turn to spiritual resources starting in 1937 in order to shape his theories on war and internationalism—and this was new for Foster. And he regularly and continually looked to spiritual resources in the solving of world problems from 1937 until his death in 1959.

In his writings during the 1930s, Foster drew inspiration from several sources. Most immediately, he feared a new global conflict and exercised his mind in coming up with ways to avert such a catastrophe. When it came to the nature of change, he reached back to his philosophical training at Princeton and the Sorbonne and additionally found practical application in nature. From his days at Princeton to his time in Paris, his admiration of Woodrow Wilson was undiluted, and Wilson was a muse of his ideas especially in the 1930s. He also drew from the practical lessons of capitalism that he learned firsthand on Wall Street as well as lessons from federalism, which he knew distinguished the American system of government. He looked to capitalism and federalism in proposing models for international prosperity and cooperation and the promotion of peace. In sum, Foster used these years to argue that change was inevitable; that peaceful change could and must be ordered through the creative application of intelligence and will; and that the church, drawing on spiritual resources, was indispensable to the securing and maintenance of peace.

Foster as World Order Theorist, 1934–1939

During the fall of 1934, Foster put pen to paper in an effort to apply the concept of change to a world that seemed almost reconciled to the inescapability of force and violence. "It is bewildering that the world should again be moving toward war," Foster wrote in an *Atlantic Monthly* article entitled "The Road to Peace," which ran a year later in October 1935.[18] Ever since his attendance at the 1907 Second Hague Conference with Grandfather Foster, world leaders had never spoken so much of peace, and yet war seemed to be the regularly accepted standard for settling disputes—a painful irony. As Foster said to Ellery Sedgwick, editor of the *Atlantic Monthly*, he had been thinking of "the problem of preserving peace" for a long time.[19] What really got him motivated to write in the mid-1930s was his realization that, while everyone seemed to long for peace and abhor war, few were thinking about the root causes of peace and war. Americans seemed to Foster not as interested in such thinking since the idealistic 1920s when Carrie Chapman Catt organized the Conference on the Cause and Cure of War. Nevertheless, it seemed to Foster that people needed a clearly stated, realistic definition of peace in order to know what they were looking for and how to obtain it.

"The Road to Peace" is a short article, but it is dense and imbued with an urgent tone. Foster saw that all were saying peace, peace, but there was no peace. The League Covenant, the Pact of Paris, the Locarno Treaty, the Washington Naval Treaty—all these monuments to peace had been established since 1919, but "in the face of this, we sense that we are inevitably moving on toward war."[20] Human nature tended to search for someone else to blame, and Americans were finding perfect candidates for the embodiment of the devil in Hitler, Mussolini, and the Japanese military chiefs. But rather than ask what went wrong, or who to blame, Americans ought instead to ask what were the fundamental causes of war, what constituted peace, and how could peace be attained. If the right questions were not asked, Foster wrote, "we are striking at shadows, leaving untouched the solid realities that cause them." What then was the reason for war? In a word, change. Change was inevitable, it was an undeniable fact of reality, and the peace efforts since 1919 had all tried to prevent change. So no one should have been surprised that war loomed. "Forces which are in the long run irresistible are temporarily dammed up. When they finally break through, they do so with violence," said Foster.[21] This simple reality, obscured by complex factors, demanded attention. Foster believed he had found the "true nature of the problem,"[22] and identifying the root problem was necessary if people really wanted to arrive at peace.

Foster conceded that it was a common human tendency to resist change, but such resistance really was futile and even undesirable. "Healthy life and growth" were impossible without change, so change should be accepted and welcomed. "No one expects that a hundred years from now the world will be as it is to-day," Foster said. Changes might occur gradually; their effects might not be noticeable until many years hence or they might occur as a "great shock." But changes over those hundred years would, with certainty, occur somehow. And if those changes broke like a storm with suddenness, violence, and confusion, it would be because people had sought to prevent the changes from occurring at all.[23] Understanding this vital truth about the way of things as they were was essential if war was to be avoided, or at least palliated in its effects.

After all, said Foster, history demonstrated that change was facilitated by force in international relations. Governments were instituted to both wield coercive force to support civil laws and oppose unlawful force. The societies that set up their governments faced material conditions that were in flux. As he explained, "wealth, power, and position constantly change. Fortunes made by economy, foresight, and industry are lost by profligacy, stupidity, and idleness." If governments tried to prevent such dynamic economic and social changes, the result would be violent revolution. Foster pointed to the French and Russian Revolutions to make this argument. But on the world stage, there was no sovereign that held nations to an objective legal norm. All nations wanted peace according to conditions that pleased them, and those conditions were in flux. Foster lamented that the only existing mechanism to keep the peace among nations was the treaty system, but treaties sought to establish conditions for peace that were static. What's more, terms of treaties could not be changed except through unanimous consent. Unanimous consent was an impossible standard because for treaties to be altered, one nation would have to consent to sacrificing its interests on behalf of another nation. But nations generally would not give up their interests voluntarily. They would have to be compelled to do so by force. To break these impasses, war resulted. "History clearly shows that it is force, or the threat of force, which principally accounts for the evolution of the world to its present state," said Foster (493).

Foster's understanding of how nations related to one another can be seen through the lens of how Thomas Hobbes articulated his theory of the state of nature in his 1651 treatise *Leviathan*. Prior to establishment of government and civil law, every individual is a law unto himself or herself. In this situation, there is freedom but no security. Every individual should seek peace, and if peace must be attained through force, then so be it. Thus, Hobbes defined the fundamental law of nature as "that every man, ought to endeavor Peace, as far as he has hope of obtaining it; and when he cannot obtain it, that he may seek, and use, all helps, and advantages of War." Its corollary is the right of nature: "By all means we can, to defend ourselves."[24] For Foster, this state of affairs was true for nations, which were sovereign powers living among themselves with no arbiter to justify or restrain their actions as they pursued their interests.

For Foster, the only way a peace plan could actually work is if it acknowledged two realities: inevitable change and the fact that no other alternative to force had ever been found. In considering those realities, a peace plan would have to be flexible enough to adapt to changing conditions, rather than establish fixed rules and conditions. This was Foster's problem with the Versailles Treaty. The victors of World War I—mainly France—wanted to monopolize their position of dominance to the exclusion of the defeated powers, mainly Germany. One way they sought permanent hegemony was through the League Covenant and, eventually, the Locarno pact, which made boundaries sacrosanct and inviolable, unless a nation voluntarily ceded its territorial rights to another.

The Washington Naval Agreement and the Pact of Paris were equally problematic. Foster worried that the Agreement would perpetuate the naval arms ratios among the five powers, and "if so, the treaty will be turned into a continuing instrument for the prevention of change" (494). To him, the Pact of Paris was totally unrealistic because it repudiated the use of force without any effective alternative. The language of the treaty only allowed for the use of "pacific means" in the pursuit of national interests. This nomenclature was far too vague, and as of yet, no one had any meaningful "pacific means" in mind that could bring results as decisively as force had historically done. In effect, Foster maintained, "the Pact would, thus, perpetuate the world as it is" (494). In sum, Foster argued that the primary means nations had used to effect peace, namely, treaties, ironically did more to establish conditions for future wars by seeking to maintain the status quo. Change, when it occurred, could only break upon the world violently under such conditions, resulting in successive wars that only increased in their destructive effects.

The principal case in point for this tragic irony was Hitler's policy of rearmament, which was in direct response to the Versailles Treaty, through which France sought to keep Germany in a permanent state of weakness and inferiority. By the early 1930s, Foster wrote, France and Britain should have begun making provisions for releasing Germany from its treaty obligations. "This was not done, with the result that Germany, by unilateral action, has now taken back her freedom of action," wrote Foster (495). Here, Foster identified a tragic dilemma. The German repudiation of Versailles was wholly unnecessary. Article 19 of the Covenant of the League of Nations allowed for change through a revision process supervised by the Permanent Court of International Justice. But Article 19 had never been tried because sovereign nations would have had to sacrifice some of their freedom of action for the good of the international community. "So long as the world is organized along national lines, it is, I think, impracticable to attain peace through the establishment of an international tribunal empowered to dictate momentous changes," wrote Foster (496–97).

The sovereignty system, with its "territorial rigidity," maintained concepts of peace that were understood solely in terms of any given nation's particular interests. It was also responsible for isolationism, protectionism, and the resulting hobbling of economic prosperity not only within the boundaries of each nation but also for the world. In 1935, Foster advocated for "economic fluidity" as the antidote to the rigidity of the sovereignty system—the free flow of goods, people, and capital "can bring about a large measure of international flux without shock to national boundaries" (499). The real path to peace could only be taken when nations recognized the inevitability of change and took steps to "assure orderly evolution" through "self-restraint and self-sacrifice" with regard to national interests. Foster believed that the only alternative to such a course of action was war (499).

As mentioned above, Foster seemed to be revisiting the pragmatism he had learned at Princeton and the Sorbonne. Writing in the early 1970s, historian Albert N. Keim said that "the core of Dulles's view of international affairs was an evolutionary Bergsonianism." However, no documentary connective tissue exists between Foster's writings on peaceful change and Bergson's thought, nor did Foster ever reference his own early writing on pragmatism and the effect of human intelligence on change. But Bergson clearly made an impression on Foster. Bergson believed that change was inevitable, and it was reflected in conflict between dynamism and stasis. When imbalance between dynamic and static forces occurred, war resulted. Keim wrote, "Dulles had quite clearly taken his distinguished teacher's ideas and made them his own."[25]

Reactions to Foster's article were overwhelmingly positive. When he submitted the draft of his article for consideration to the *Atlantic Monthly*, the editors enthusiastically accepted it and paid him $175 (over $3,000 in 2020). Foster ordered two hundred reprinted copies of the article, and he distributed it widely to his family, friends, and colleagues. Fan mail began rolling in. A month before the article ran, Foster received a letter from Edward Aswell of Harper & Brothers Publishers, who had been on the *Atlantic Monthly* editorial board that had accepted the piece when it was submitted. He had recently come to Harper and asked to stay in touch with

Foster. "The Road to Peace" ultimately developed into the book *War, Peace, and Change*—published by Harper & Brothers four years later in 1939.[26]

Other letters of praise came from curious sources. The Japanese, German, and Italian ambassadors were delighted with the piece. In gratitude, Japanese ambassador to the United States Hiroshi Saito sent Foster an autographed copy of a collection of his speeches entitled *Japan's Policies and Purposes*. Hans Luther, the German ambassador to the United States, praised Foster for demonstrating "a splendid sense of fairness and a fine understanding of the problems with which we are all faced." Mussolini's ambassador to the United States, Augusto Rosso, was also enthusiastic: "far from me the intention of being a flatterer, but I do want to say that I find your study a most interesting, far-reaching and enlightening one." He went on to say that he wished Foster had been in Geneva to lend his voice in defense of Italy's invasion of Ethiopia before the League of Nations, "somewhat along the lines of your article."[27] These favorable responses show the nature of Foster's posture toward German, Italian, and Japanese aggression in the early 1930s. He stopped short of endorsing their nationalistic actions, but he did believe they were dynamic powers acting much as the United States and Britain had as they expanded their territories in the nineteenth century. Foster repeatedly took up for Japan, Italy, and Germany in his writings during this period, and he continued to defend those nations' actions as late as 1939.

Closer to home, Foster received scores of positive responses from friends, colleagues, and family members. He heard from his boss, William Nelson Cromwell; the president of Princeton, Harold Dodds; the president of Rutgers, Robert C. Clothier; Associate Justice of the Supreme Court Harlan Stone; and Madeleine Scharf of the Daughters of the American Revolution, who requested reprints for mass distribution. D. C. Poole, the director of Princeton's School of Public and International Affairs, invited Foster to give a public lecture at the university, to be sponsored by the Stafford Little Foundation. And his mother, Edith, wrote him to say, "if more people would think clearly as you do, things would not be in such a mess."[28] The positive feedback Foster received in the weeks following publication of his article shows that many people agreed with him about the dangers of demonizing the Germans, Italians, and Japanese. Many Americans did not yet perceive how degenerate the Axis powers would prove to be.

The publication and reception of "The Road to Peace" gave Foster the affirmation he needed to keep writing on the subject. Between 1936 and 1939, he built on the themes from the essay in writings and speeches given both in the United States and in England. Over the next four years, he developed his views on the causes of war, the nature of change, and his program for peace. He also added new themes to substantiate his older arguments, which he amplified. And in 1937, he added the need for spiritual resources to his analysis of war and peace. Although Foster had begun writing on war and peace during the 1920s, "The Road to Peace" set him squarely on the path to becoming an internationally recognized expert on the topic.

In March 1936, Foster returned to his alma mater to give the Stafford Little lecture. He entitled his talk "Peaceful Change within the Society of Nations." Foster's content had developed more nuance and sophistication since the publication of "The Road to Peace" the previous fall. He continued to frame his ideas around the concept of inevitable change and dynamic forces but critiqued the sovereignty system more fully. Foster's admiration for Wilson was evident as he detailed Wilson's vision and blamed the British and French for failing to understand and apply his ideas. The solutions he offered were far more organized and detailed than in "The Road to Peace." Foster was on his way.

"Change is the ultimate fact," Foster argued. But change could only be directed toward beneficial ends by the application of human intelligence. Through planning and creativity, human beings could convert chaos and violence into growth and advancement. "We can impart to change an element of selectivity. Thus we attain what we are pleased to call 'progress' as distinct from pure 'change.'"[29] But to human intelligence must be added positive action for real progress to occur.

To Foster, war was the application of force, resulting in change most obviously to national borders. Borders were representative of the sovereignty system. Wilson's program was designed to create an international structure that allowed for peaceful diffusion of dynamic forces through elasticity of borders. "He, of all the political leaders, had shown the most statesman-like vision. . . . He had a duty and it was a duty to which he responded—more adequately than has, perhaps, been appreciated" (11). Under Wilson's plan, elasticity of borders would have been ensured through freedom of the seas; through the mandate system that would have internationalized colonies for the good of both indigenous peoples and the world; through free trade; and through boundary adjustments under the auspices of the World Court. The League of Nations, the crown jewel of Wilson's program, would have provided the operative mechanism—collective security. Had Wilson's vision been implemented, national borders would have been made less relevant and "war would have no further legitimate place" (13). As events occurred, nationalism returned to Europe and isolationism settled over the United States. And attempts at keeping the peace in the absence of Wilson's program were all doomed to failure.

Foster leveled a blistering criticism against the peace efforts of the 1920s, characterizing them under three headings: realist, intellectual, and sentimental. The realists, Foster said, "take no stock in anything but force." Realist peace efforts were predicated upon the concept of deterrence—build up an enormous force in order to monopolize power and ensure superiority permanently. "France is the principal exponent of this theory," according to Foster. The problem here was that the nation that France was trying to keep down, Germany, was in the process of violent explosion. "Germany bursts, one by one, the bands with which she was bound." However, by the time Foster gave this talk, France was already resigned to the coming of another war. "Realism" would fail (15–16).

Foster cast intellectualism as a program attempting to apply reason to the problem of war. Total war was so destructive, so deleterious to human progress, that its occurrence was unthinkable. Logical arguments against war were fine, Foster said, but "while [the proponent of intellectualism] stops to argue, he is engulfed by the forces to which he would deny existence." Thus, "intellectualism" was also doomed (18).

Finally, sentimentalism turned away from logic and reason to emotionalism in advocating against war and for peace. For Foster, the Pact of Paris represented all that was pointless about this category of peacemaking. And unfortunately, "the United States is the leading exponent of this school of thought." In the Pact of Paris, Foster said, we simply declared war to be illegal, which made sentimentalists believe war "will no longer be respectable and people will not indulge in it." Even the churches embraced this strategy (and Foster helped the Presbyterian church craft its positions—see previous chapter). But the problem with the sentimentalist method was that while emotion could be used against war, emotion could also be used convincingly in favor of war. How this played out could be seen in American history—witness the war fever in 1898, Foster said, as "we fought Spain as crusaders on behalf of oppressed Cubans." War fever thrived on the idea of a "cause" calling for the ultimate sacrifice. Sentimentalism turned against itself (18–19).

The problem with Wilson's program, Foster insisted, was not that it failed, but that it was never tried. But 1936 offered new opportunities to put Wilson's plan into effect. Weaken the sovereignty system by stabilizing currencies, open up free exchange of goods, and lift arbitrary restrictions on immigration, Foster urged. Furthermore, the League should carry out Article 19 of the Covenant and make treaties flexible as times and circumstances changed. Foster also introduced the concept of federalism in this speech, recalling how the state boundaries of the American union did not serve as barriers. They were open for the free flow of money, goods, and people—and yet, each state retained its sovereignty. Foster said that it was not too late to reform the mandate system to conform to its original vision, and freedom of the seas should continue to be enforced. "We would thus have changed the society of nations so that peaceful movement and change would be facilitated and so that national boundaries would no longer be rigid and forbidding barriers" (30).

"The Road to Peace" and "Peaceful Change" provide a sense of where Foster was headed in his theorizing on war and peace through 1936. But not even Foster was prepared for the decidedly religious course his ideas were about to take. In 1936, John H. Oldham, secretary of the Commission of Research of the Universal Christian Council, came to the United States from his native Britain to make preparations for the upcoming Oxford Conference on Church, Community, and State. The Oxford Conference was, as Keim described it, "the crest of the Ecumenical movement in the interwar years."[30] It was long in the making, and Oldham was searching for laymen who could contribute to the vision of the conference, which was summed up in the phrase "let the church be the church." In other words, as John Mackay, president of Princeton Theological Seminary, put it, "the Church's real problem is to *be* the Church—to be in its existence what it basically is in its essence."[31] Oldham intentionally sought laymen in order to find creative ways to apply Christian ethical teachings to international problems, and to break away from traditional formulas usually put forth by clergy. "The conference was going to be dealing with things that are somewhat out of the ordinary purview of ministers and theologians," said Samuel M. Cavert, general secretary of the Federal Council of Churches.[32] Oldham was well acquainted with Foster's work as part of the Presbyterian controversy during the early 1920s, and his thought on diplomacy and international relations. Cavert said that when Oldham met Foster, he was deeply "impressed . . . and he brought very strong urgings to bear on [him] to go to Oxford."[33] Foster prepared a paper to deliver in the section entitled "The Universal Church and a World of Nations," presided over by Mackay. Foster's paper was entitled "The Problem of Peace in a Dynamic World."

In this piece, Foster made an abrupt turn to spiritual resources as the key ingredient in solving the problem of international conflict. The talk contained Foster's familiar themes of the sovereignty system; the inevitability of change; critiques of isolationism; the model of American federalism; defenses of Germany, Italy, and Japan (which he compared to prisoners in solitary confinement); and the need to provide outlets for dynamic forces. But at the conclusion of the talk, Foster sharply asked, "What of the so-called 'Christian' nations? They boast of high ideals, but have they the spiritual fire with which to drive out the petty instincts which bind them to a system that spells their doom?" He transitioned to a critique of the intellectualist camp of peacemakers, but instead of advocating for the usual program of free interchange between nations, he closed by saying, "Reason can chart the course. It can point out what are the obstacles, the human weaknesses, that interpose. But to overcome these obstacles, *is the task of spiritual leadership.*"[34] This was the first time Foster included any reference to religion in any program of handling questions of war and peace.

Prior to traveling to Oxford, Foster did not have high expectations for the conference. Just before attending the Oxford Conference, which was held July 12–26, he attended the International Studies Conference in Paris. Its theme was "Peaceful Change," and its participants included political figures, academics, and lawyers. Foster was very disappointed. Reflecting on the failure of this conference to achieve anything meaningful, he said, "No attempt was made to arrive at any agreed report," even though the participants represented some of the best minds in Europe and America.[35]

Foster, accompanied by Janet, crossed the Channel into England. He hoped Oxford would be different, but he was losing hope in the ability of the churches to apply the ethical teachings of Christ to real problems. "Despite the fact that my beliefs are somewhat diluted," Foster wrote in 1938, "I have always assumed . . . that it was the Christian churches which could be looked to for the life of mankind. . . . But recently I had begun to doubt."[36] His skepticism was rooted in his observation that the churches were becoming steeped in affluence and high social standing. The churches had forgotten how to sacrifice and suffer. "Church membership had ceased to be synonymous with dangerous and difficult living for a high ideal."[37] Still, Foster was ready to give the conference a chance because the world situation in 1937 was becoming desperate, and he was open to new ideas from a familiar quarter—the church.

Foster's reaction to the conference was dramatic. Keim wrote that Foster "went to Oxford as an expert in international law. He returned to the United States as a churchman."[38] Instead of finding church leaders fighting and squabbling among themselves over futile and sentimental hopes for peace, he found them forging a unity out of their differences and casting a vision for peace consistent with his own. He found Christianity to be "more than a name—it was a vital living force."[39] He also found, to his surprise, that the churches had a unique contribution to offer the world as it moved closer to war: the idea of universality. Universality, for Foster, meant at least two things. First, it had an abstract meaning that was to become something very real, that is, the kingdom of God on Earth. Second, it had a practical meaning reflected in the participants of the Oxford Conference. Christian churches from all over the world were represented; "an important cross section of all mankind" was present at Oxford.[40] This was important, because at Oxford he found humanity rather than nations. These two features of universality reminded Foster of a concept he heard preached from his father's pulpit all his life growing up in Watertown—the liberal Protestant exhortation about the fatherhood of God and the brotherhood of man. Furthermore, Foster was impressed that the participants acknowledged that there were limits to how much churches could engage international problems. Church leaders were not to shape public policy, but they were to form the consciences of those in power who were responsible for those policies. Lastly, the participants were honest about their real differences, and yet, "no attempt was made to deal with or to eradicate such differences." Those present at Oxford recognized their differences but strove to emphasize their unity in finding solutions based on Christ's teachings. The Nazi persecution of the churches in Germany put differences in perspective, and yet it showed that Christians in the world still knew what it meant to sacrifice and suffer. Foster said of the persecuted German Christians, "it was demonstrated that the 'blood of the martyrs is the seed of the Church.'"[41]

Foster's participation in the Oxford Conference and his writing and speaking led to the most significant writing project he had undertaken to that time. All his work on the problems of war and peace culminated in the writing and publication of his 1939 book *War, Peace, and Change*. Joseph A. Brandt of Princeton University Press wanted to publish it, but Foster decided to go with Harper because that firm was able to produce it more quickly.[42] The book, though plodding, captures Foster's thoughts on why the world faced the problems it did at the end of the 1930s, and how peaceful solutions could be found in league with the indispensable work of the churches in providing spiritual resources toward that end. In fact, reviewers found much to admire about Foster's book but unsurprisingly criticized his appeal to religion as an answer to complex economic and political problems. Edward Corwin, McCormick Professor of Jurisprudence at Princeton, was one who scoffed at Foster's argument about the indispensability of the churches. Foster's close friend Lionel Curtis had corresponded with Corwin and reported his feedback to Foster. "From letters he has written to me I gather that his tendency would be to regard the whole religious approach as a myth."[43] Foster was not discouraged by such criticism. He replied, "I am afraid that the position in the States as regards reviewing is not on a very high level."[44]

What was Foster's religious answer to the problem of recurrent war in *War, Peace, and Change*? One of the themes Foster labored to develop was the problem of the personification of the nation. Populations tended to give personal characteristics to their nation, casting the nation in innocent and heroic terms and ultimately deifying it. As they did so, they vilified their enemies, casting those nations in personified demonic terms. They did this because the churches had lost their vitality and watered down their religion, and the people thus looked to something other than God to worship. The state filled the vacuum. Foster wrote, "the nation-deity concept is responsive primarily to the yearning of human beings for identification with some spiritually superior enemy."[45] The corollary to the nation-deity concept was the concept of a nation-devil—a national enemy that the people equated with pure evil, and one that required fundamental sacrifices to defeat. Foster had spoken of the problem of one nation vilifying another back in "The Road to Peace," noting that Germany, Italy, and Japan had been the victims of this characterization. He had developed the idea by 1939 around the dualism of nation-deity and nation-villain. His old friend Henry Sloane Coffin praised Foster for his succinct encapsulation of this aspect of religious nationalism in the coining of these terms.[46]

The religious answer was that the churches needed to recover their vitality by reinvigorating the ethical principles of Christ. This was the idea behind the Oxford Conference and its exhortation to "let the church be the church." Instead of venerating the nation, people needed a worthy recipient of their worship—God. And it was the church's responsibility to inculcate this devotion into the people. By extension, the churches needed to teach people that sacrifice for the nation was good, but sacrifice for other human beings was better. "Religious concepts remain potentially inspiring and able to create a spiritual unity which overrides national boundaries," Foster wrote. "Charitable, philanthropic and educational causes exist in large number."[47]

In the short period from 1935 to 1939, John Foster Dulles had won respect in the fields of business, law, academics, politics, diplomacy, and religion. Shortly after the appearance of *War, Peace, and Change*, Roswell Barnes, associate secretary of the Federal Council of Churches (FCC), wrote Foster to congratulate him. "Since reading your book I have been remarking to many friends, 'You must not miss John Foster Dulles' new book "War, Peace, and Change" which is in my opinion the most significant book in the field of international relations in recent years for our purpose.'"[48] Because of the quality of the book and the reach of Foster's audience, Barnes told Foster that he was nominating him for chairman of the FCC's Department of International Justice and Goodwill. Foster was the department members' first choice, Barnes said, because of his understanding of world affairs, his practical experience, and his status as a layman. Foster had gotten the attention of leaders in the FCC, and the course of his life for the next decade would be defined by his work with that body.

Still, it is important to emphasize once again: John Foster Dulles at this time was no pious, ascetic Christian. His religion, by his own admission, was "diluted." His understanding of what Christianity meant was limited to ethics. He was not theologically curious, and his doctrinal understanding of the faith was limited to moral law, God's providence, and human freedom and dignity. Theologian John Coleman Bennett, who had been a younger colleague of his father's at Auburn, described Foster's understanding of the faith as "limited." Foster's Christianity was a collection of beliefs that were "somewhat secularized Calvinism perhaps, and moralism, as we say—not much sense of the elements of grace in the Christian faith."[49] The irony was that Foster charged the churches with promoting religious nationalism by diluting Christianity, even though he admitted his own beliefs were also "diluted." Foster's failure to grasp an understanding of Christianity as an ethical program built upon a foundation of theological doctrines led him into a similar snare as he reacted against Soviet Communism in the 1950s. A stronger grounding in theological and philosophical principles would have given Foster more intellectual ballast as circumstances changed in the post–World War II world, and as he reacted to those changes.

Still, Foster's beliefs are best described as adhering to a tradition handed down from his forebears, applied in moral law, and practiced best in and through the institution of the church. As pragmatic and undogmatic as Foster's Christian belief might have been, it was sufficient to place Foster on a career trajectory that ultimately took him to the highest levels of both the ecumenical movement and international diplomacy.

5

"Everything Is Fine until You Relax"
(1940–1946)

During the years when it was possible to think calmly of these
matters, I resolved that I would constantly strive not to identify national self-interest with righteousness.

—John Foster Dulles[1]

Foster and Janet had three children. Lillias was their only daughter. Born
in 1914, she studied for the Presbyterian ministry, attending Union
Theological Seminary in New York from 1954 to 1958 under the presidency
of her father's friend, Henry P. Van Dusen. She also held degrees from Ben-
nington College and Columbia University. Lillias served on the pastoral
staff at Madison Avenue Presbyterian Church in New York from 1958 until
her retirement in 1969.

Lillias recounted an experience from her younger days that dispels
the myth of a humorless Foster Dulles. Foster could be quite zany around
people close to him. When Lillias was eighteen, she and a number of her
friends had a get-together for Pemberton ("Pem") Berman, a close Dulles
family friend. Lillias and her friends hosted Pem at a Manhattan restaurant
and, for some reason, elected not to invite Foster or Janet. Unbeknownst
to Lillias, a suitor of hers named Peter came to visit her at the Dulles home
and found Foster there alone. Foster invited Peter into his study and told
him that Lillias was away at a party. Peter was obviously a little hurt that
he hadn't been invited. Foster said, "Peter, I'll tell you what. I wasn't invited
either, but we're going to the party tonight." Foster provided tuxedos for

himself and Peter so they could dress up as waiters. They went downtown to the restaurant, slipped in, and began waiting on tables. Janet had returned home in the meantime, learned where Foster was, and proceeded downtown herself. She put on a maid's costume and came to the party so dressed. Foster and Janet thus went around the party in costume, to everyone's amusement. At some point during the festivities, Foster slipped away and stuffed a pillow under his shirt. He came back out among the partygoers, produced a carving knife, and slashed his midsection with it in a flamboyant act of hari-kari. Feathers went everywhere. Lillias was shocked. Foster thought it was hilarious.[2]

Foster and His Children

Foster enjoyed his children and was a devoted family man. He cultivated relationships with each of his children through activities and contexts that reflected his tastes, enjoyments, and humor. He also believed that he could teach his children lessons through simple things like games, betting on random uncertainties, and meal preparation. And of course, there was sailing. Foster took each of his children, John, Lillias, and Avery, on sailing trips. Lillias usually went on sailing adventures only when Janet was along. Janet enjoyed sailing, but she was not thrilled about sailing in tempestuous conditions, nor was she enthusiastic about the all-night cruises that Foster relished. Foster often took Lillias out for shorter weekend excursions with one or two friends.[3]

Foster gave each of his children a pocketknife to carry around because, he believed, one should always have a practical tool handy in times of need. He taught them how to use their pocketknives—to sharpen pencils, to whittle—and provided general tips on handling and caring for knives. He taught them how to tie knots, another practical skill. At various times and in unexpected places, Foster would look at the children and demand, "Pocketknife!" His rule was that they were to instantly produce their pocketknives to show him that they were indeed carrying them. Whoever did not have his or her pocketknife had to pay Foster a quarter.[4] Foster often used his own pocketknife to scrape away decay on dogwoods and laurels and then explain to his children that the decay had occurred because that part of the tree was not receiving sufficient sunlight. He would go on to reference

Christ's teaching on light and darkness in the third chapter of John's Gospel, explaining that those who did wicked things refused to come into the light, and that Christ was the light that gives life to all who believed in him.[5]

Foster and Janet sent Avery away to school at the prestigious Institut Le Rosey in Rolle, Switzerland, in 1930. The family accompanied Avery on the *Vulcania*, an Italian liner. They proceeded across the Atlantic to the Azores, through the Strait of Gibraltar, then to Naples. Foster had purchased first-class tickets for the family, but when they boarded, he learned that the royal suite was unoccupied. Foster was able to secure those rooms at a good fare, and the family spent a luxurious two weeks headed to Europe. They ate breakfast on their veranda overlooking the ocean each morning and had beautiful dinners in the evenings, where Foster selected all the courses, including the meats, cheeses, wines, and desserts. Also true to form, the family skipped lunch.

One stop they made was in Lisbon. The family was set to go ashore for the day and tour the city in a car that Foster had rented. They were all standing on the top deck as the ship docked, and Foster turned to sixteen-year-old Lillias and bet her a nickel that he could pick out which of the cars they were going to take into Lisbon for the day. Foster loved small bets like these, and he was constantly challenging the children to various bets, never for more than a nickel. Lillias, looking at the scores of cars that were taking tourists out to the city, confidently agreed to her father's challenge. When they went down and Foster selected the correct car, Lillias was amazed at her father's uncanny prescience, but when she took out her nickel, her father admitted the truth. He told her that when she wasn't looking, he had peered through binoculars and searched the plates on the cars, identifying the correct one. He refused to accept her nickel.[6]

As the children grew into their teenage and young adult years, Foster would engage them in intellectual discussions, challenging them to think critically and creatively about their views on various issues. Lillias recalled very long and vigorous discussions she had with her father while in college on politics, economics, war, and Communism. Foster was fond of rigorous debate with his children, and it was one of the family's regular pastimes. Lillias would playfully berate her father for being "an old fogy," and Foster thought it was good for her to learn liberal ideas in college. Friends of the family observed how close Foster was to his children, that he wanted them to learn resourcefulness, good morals, practical skills, and how to cultivate those skills over a lifetime.[7] He played Ping-Pong, backgammon, bridge, and tennis with them. He taught the boys how to play chess (Foster didn't teach Lillias because he was opposed to girls playing chess) and took them to boxing matches and baseball games. He saw to it that Lillias had an elegant coming-out party and encouraged her interest in music. Lillias described her father as more attentive to her and her siblings than were the fathers of anyone else she knew as she grew up.[8]

But Foster could be hard on his children at times, too. Foster was not particularly concerned with Lillias's education and was not enthusiastic about her going to college—because she was a girl. Also, he spoiled her while he was strict with his sons. "I could get away with everything," Lillias said.[9] Foster wanted both of his boys to adhere to Dulles tradition and attend Princeton; John went to Princeton, but Avery went to Harvard. Foster also wanted his sons to follow in his footsteps—by becoming lawyers and going into business. Both sons started out trying to honor their father's wishes, but ultimately they both bucked his plans, and Foster deeply struggled emotionally with the paths they each pursued.

John graduated from Princeton in 1935 and went on to Harvard Business School, then began a banking career at the Bank of New York with Foster's encouragement. He hated it. He went to Foster's close friend and Sullivan and Cromwell colleague Arthur Dean for advice. Dean introduced him to the chief metallurgist for the American Metal Company, and John decided to move across the country to the University of Arizona to study metallurgy. He took a position with Hannah Mining Company in Mexico and Brazil, where he became fascinated with Latin American history. In 1962, he began an academic career as a historian at the University of Texas, where he taught for forty-six years right up to his death at age ninety-five. In his nineties, he rode a scooter to class, and after the university banned smoking on campus, he rented his own office on the twenty-seventh floor of an Austin skyscraper so he could continue to puff away on his pipe. Like his father, he was devoted to the yellow legal pad, and all of his twelve books began their lives in handwritten form on the pages of those pads.[10]

Father and son went through a strained period in their relationship. Once John moved away, the two were not particularly close, and for a while, John felt alienated from his father. Journalist and syndicated columnist Marquis Childs described an awkward scene that illustrates the tension. Foster traveled to Mexico City on a state visit in 1958. Bob Hill, the US ambassador, encouraged John, who was vice president of Hannah at the time, to be on the tarmac to greet his father when he arrived. John was reluctant, but he agreed to be there. When Foster got off the plane and greeted Hill and the others who were present, he neglected to greet John. John was furious. "You see," John angrily said to Hill, "you see, you've done me a great disservice. I shouldn't have come here!"[11] Things between the two eventually normalized. The two were together later that day at the American embassy, and when Foster's visit ended, John wrote to his father expressing regret that he was unable to see him off when he boarded his flight back to Washington.[12] They carried on a regular and friendly correspondence until Foster's death months later. But episodes such as this one reveal deep complexities and frequent contradictions in Foster's relationship with his eldest son.

An even more poignant demonstration of such complexity can be seen in Foster's relationship with Avery. Among all the children, Foster seemed to be closest to Avery because the two had shared affinities—sailing and philosophy. Avery was at Le Rosey from 1930 to 1932 and then attended the Choate School in Connecticut until 1936. From 1936 to 1940, Avery was a student at Harvard. Upon graduating, he spent a year at Harvard Law School and in 1941 joined the navy. From his days at Choate and then in his first two years at Harvard, Avery considered himself an agnostic. "It did not enter my mind to consider that the world owed its existence to a wise Creator, that a beneficent Providence watched over and directed it, or that the soul, as the loving work of God's hands, possessed an eternal destiny," Avery wrote. He described his freshman year at Harvard as "a wild and chaotic year, marked by an excess of drinking and corresponding deficiency of sleep." His dorm room was "a center of nocturnal revelry." He had something of a wake-up call after his two best friends were expelled after "a midnight adventure in which the Boston police saw fit to intervene." Avery was involved in this transgression, although he did not specify what it involved. He missed being expelled only because of the support of one administrator.[13]

During his sophomore year at Harvard, Avery began moving away from strict materialism after reading Aristotle and Plato. But the most significant influence in his life during that year was his interaction with a professor named Paul Doolin. Doolin was Avery's tutor, but he left Harvard at the end of the year to take a position at Georgetown. Nevertheless, it was Doolin who played the most significant role in moving Avery in the direction of the Catholic faith. Doolin was a Catholic convert, and Avery described him as a theologian of the medieval sort—"the implacable enemy of materialism, utilitarianism, humanitarianism, pacifism and sentimentality in every form" (23). By the end of Avery's sophomore year, Doolin had not convinced Avery to become a Catholic, but he did open a vista to Catholic theology to Avery that he did not know existed.

In February of his junior year, 1939, Avery spent a dreary winter afternoon in Widener Library reading an assigned section of Augustine's *City of God* for a course in medieval theology. Eventually, he went outside to get some fresh air. He took a walk down the Charles River, feeling the rain in his face. He came upon a tree and noticed that buds were developing on its branches. "While my eye rested on them, the thought came to me suddenly, with all the strength and novelty of a revelation, that these little buds in their innocence and meekness followed a rule, a law of which I as yet knew nothing." As he contemplated the tree, Avery came to believe in God as a person, and not as some vague force called "Nature." When he returned to his room that night, he prayed by his bedside for the first time in many years, in the manner which Janet his mother taught him when he was little. He prayed the Lord's Prayer. "I had to make many new starts before the whole prayer unfolded itself in my mind," Avery later recalled (36–38).

For some months, Avery searched for a religious home. All he knew was Presbyterianism. He had not one Catholic friend, family member, or acquaintance, other than Doolin, who had since left Harvard. He began reading the New Testament carefully and was struck, in a similar way that Christ's original hearers were struck, by the fact that Christ spoke with authority about "things no man had seen." God's Messiah was not merely a moralist, Avery saw. He was persuaded that Christ was the Son of God by fulfilled prophecies in the Old Testament, by the testimony of the apostles who were once weak in their faith, and by Christ's resurrection. And after reading deeply in the Scriptures, he was convinced that the Father was "exactly as [Christ] had described Him—a Father Who would not give a stone in place of bread, or anything but the Holy Ghost to those who asked for It" (51–60).

Avery began attending services at every Protestant church accessible to him but was sorely disappointed in the way the preachers portrayed Christ in their sermons. They distanced themselves from theology and focused their attention on ethics. They treated the Bible as literature and saw Christ in common terms—as a good teacher, as a master of human psychology, or as an effective leader; they ignored his miracles. Protestant preaching was obsessed with self-help, cultural and political commentary, and general sophistry. The risen Christ of the Scriptures was not the same person as what to Avery was a stranger posing as Christ, being preached from Protestant pulpits around Harvard. Perplexed and discouraged, Avery gave the Catholic Church a chance. Even though at first he was repelled by the ceremony and what seemed to him vacuous ritual, he attended Mass every Sunday during his senior year. "I came to understand the action of the Mass, apart from which its trappings are meaningless and even, to some, distasteful." He took up serious engagement with ancient and medieval figures like Augustine, Aquinas, Bonaventure, and Scotus; he also read contemporary thinkers like D'Arcy, Martindale, and Watkin. Of the contemporary figures he read, none were more persuasive than Jacques Maritain and Fulton Sheen. "The more I examined, the more I was impressed with the consistency and sublimity of Catholic doctrine" (84). He decided to see a priest and, after several meetings, was received into the Catholic Church in 1940.

Avery was concerned about how his family would react to his conversion to Catholicism. In every recounting of his family's responses, Avery described them as supportive and encouraging. In his *Testimonial to Grace*, he wrote, "Among my family and friends I found very little hostility to the Catholic religion. Most of them were interested . . . to learn the motives which had prompted me to enter the Church" (90). In an interview for the John Foster Dulles Oral History Project, Avery likened his father's response to his conversion as analogous to his reaction to his decision not to go to Princeton. "I believe my father was surprised when I announced that I wanted to become a Catholic." Avery admitted that Foster's attitude toward Catholicism was largely negative, but his father "didn't try to exercise any kind of pressure on me not to become a Catholic. He went along with it. . . . He never opposed it at all."[14] He went on to say that father and son continued to dialogue about religion from the time of his conversion in 1940 to the end of Foster's life nineteen years later.

What Avery likely did not know at the time was that Foster was thunderstruck by Avery's conversion to Catholicism. Avery assumed that Foster's negative impression of that faith tradition came from what he saw as a basic impracticality, but it likely went much deeper than that. Foster grew up in a religious atmosphere that was decidedly liberal Presbyterian and anti-Catholic. Foster's own father thought the Catholic Church was a false church because he believed it stifled the free consciences of people through what he saw as its authoritarianism. For Allen Macy Dulles, the Catholic Church was anti-Christian because it was tyrannical. He bore this theme out repeatedly in his three-hundred-page book *The True Church*, published in 1907. Foster's views on the Catholic Church were formed in the anti-Catholic moral and intellectual environment that Allen Macy created. What's more, Foster's own perspective on the faith was, and had always been, purely moralistic. He likely would have been comfortable in many of the Protestant churches Avery visited. The Protestant preaching that was a source of disillusionment to Avery was the lifeblood of Foster's faith system.

Days after Avery's announcement about his conversion in 1940, Foster called on his closest friend at the time, Arthur Dean. "I want you to cancel all your appointments. The greatest crisis of my life has come up," Foster said to Dean. Foster drafted a letter to Avery that read, in part, "Never darken my door again. Never speak to me again. Never communicate with me again. You are no longer my son."[15] He showed it to Dean and asked for his advice.

Dean could see that Foster was in shock. Foster thought he had utterly failed as a father. Catholicism was repugnant to Dulles family tradition, Foster believed; he also probably thought that Catholicism, which he was brought up to perceive as repressive, was un-American. They talked all that afternoon and well into the evening. Dean and his wife convinced both Foster and Janet not to disown Avery, that doing so "would be a great mistake and a bitter pill."[16] As a result of his conversation with Dean, Foster wrote Avery a reassuring letter and did not send the harsh one. Their subsequent correspondence for the next eighteen years until Foster's death accurately reflects what Avery said about their fruitful discussions on faith. During the 1950s, Avery regularly sent Foster lines from Ignatius of Loyola, Thomas Aquinas, and other Catholic figures to encourage his father during challenging days at the State Department.[17] To further complicate matters, Avery contracted a bad case of polio while serving in the Mediterranean in the fall of 1945 and nearly died. Fearing either Avery's death or his complete paralysis, Foster and Janet received updates on Avery's condition from Vice Admiral William Glassford, commander of US Naval Forces, Northwest African Waters, and from Secretary of State James F. Byrnes.[18] To Foster's intense relief, Avery made a full recovery, and by the time he became a priest in 1956, his father was no longer in crisis over his son's faith.

None of Foster's children turned out quite as he desired. He wanted his sons to follow Dulles family traditions: Princeton, law, and business. He wanted Lillias to focus her attention on being a wife and mother, like Janet. During the course of their childhoods, Foster raised them in settings of his own making and under his strict control. He had to adjust to the fact that his children, once they came of age, were determined to take their own paths—John to engineering and teaching, Lillias to education and the ministry, and Avery to the Catholic priesthood and theology. It took Foster some time to accept the children on their own terms, and there were tensions between them during his period of adjustment. But he came around. Their relationships were multifaceted and complex, but it is inaccurate to describe them as estranged. Foster was not a neglectful father, as some biographers have alleged.[19]

Duck Island

Just as Foster and his siblings had been reared in a close family whose early years centered on Lake Ontario, Foster raised his own children in a similar context. The importance of the natural world and of immersion into that world through sailing is hard to overstate for Foster, including in the context of raising his children. During the 1930s, Foster sailed the *Menemsha* a total of more than twenty-five thousand nautical miles, covering territory from Lake Superior to Cold Spring Harbor on Long Island.[20] He regularly took his entire family on cruises, sometimes quite long ones. The logs they kept on those trips describe a close family that enjoyed themselves and one another. On one cruise from Rochester Harbor to Georgian Bay in 1933, fifteen-year-old Avery kept the log, noting half-playfully the crewmembers as "John Foster Dulles, skipper; Janet A. Dulles, cook; Lillias P. Dulles, bottle-washer; John W. F. Dulles, crew; Charles Avery Dulles, crew; Robert Hart, 1st Mate and able seaman."[21] Bob Hart was one of Foster's closest companions on the lake from 1931 until Foster's death. Hart saw Foster as a father figure, and he was fiercely loyal. He took care of *Menemsha* during the winters for Foster, and when Foster purchased Duck Island in 1941, Hart managed Foster's fishing business. He was also caretaker of the island when Foster was not there. After Foster's death, Janet gave Duck Island to Hart, and he owned it until his death in 1977. Today, it is managed by Parks Canada and remains accessible only by boat.

Once World War II broke out in 1939, Foster was anxious to sell *Menemsha* because he was concerned that having a yawl would not be practical during another world crisis, this one perhaps much more profound than the one from 1914 to 1918.[22] Foster did, in fact, sell the *Menemsha* in 1941. That same year, Hart discovered that another opportunity to buy Duck Island had presented itself. In May 1938, "King" Claude Cole died of a heart attack and left the island to his wife, Sarah Ann. By early 1941, Mrs. Cole was anxious to sell. Foster purchased Main Duck and Yorkshire Islands from Sarah Ann Cole, along with fishing rights, for $12,000 in July 1941.[23] Shortly after the purchase was finalized, Lillias and her new husband, Robert, enjoyed their honeymoon on the island.[24]

From 1941 until his death, Duck Island was Foster's sanctuary. Dick Benson, a pilot who flew Foster to and from Duck when Foster was secretary of state, spoke of how much Foster loved the island. They flew from Watertown airport about twenty minutes to the island in a Grumman G-44 Widgeon. Foster enjoyed being in the copilot's seat on the flights to the island, and on the way out, he would strain his eyes to catch the first glimpse of the island ahead. "He'd sit up there in front with me, and . . . was so anxious to see it. And you could almost see him relax."[25] As soon as he purchased the island, Foster engaged Hart at a salary of $100 per month to manage a fishing operation from the island.[26] Once the United States joined the Allies as an active belligerent, the army purchased fish from Foster's Duck Island fishery to supply the troops training at Pine Camp on the Black River near Watertown (now Fort Drum).[27]

Almost immediately after buying the island, Foster began planning to build a cabin for himself and Janet. Foster designed it 625 feet square with a main room (where he and Janet slept), a fireplace, and three small rooms behind the fireplace—a kitchen, a dressing room, and a bathroom. In early May 1943, Hart contracted local First Peoples to build the cabin with some materials that were purchased and shipped over, and some materials from the island.[28] Foster hand-selected all the stones for the fireplace and laid them out in the way he wanted them to be assembled. The cabin was built on a bluff about twenty feet above the water. Hart and Foster set up a surplus block and tackle rig from the *Menemsha* to draw water straight out of the lake with a bucket.[29] By early July, the cabin was complete. "The Cabin, I am glad to report, is finished as far as the building of it is concerned and I think looks marvelous and as you wanted it to," an elated Hart wrote to tell Foster.[30]

Duck Island is indeed beautiful. It is just over seven hundred acres of broad meadows, hardwood forests, and pebble beaches. For the Dulleses, the only way to get there was by boat or by plane, and once there, Foster and Janet were totally isolated. The only exceptions to this isolation were the Canadian lighthouse on the western tip of the island, with two light-keepers, and Hart, who as caretaker had a small cabin on the southeast corner. The lighthouse had a radio, which Foster could use in cases of necessity. But Foster loved being cut off from the world, and he and Janet took every opportunity they could to spend as much time as possible on the island.

"What do we do at Duck Island?" Foster said in an interview with a Picton, Ontario, newspaper. "We keep ourselves living very comfortably and that takes considerable time and effort."[31] Their days were spent in leisure, but their leisure was typical for the Dulles family—leisure governed by a regimented schedule and a practiced routine, but one that yielded palpably pleasant results. Foster and Janet rose at six in the morning to light the fire and go for a cold swim in the lake at eight. Then they prepared their breakfast of oranges, bananas, berries, oatmeal, and cream. They also ate corned beef hash with eggs, or ham and bacon with toast and marmalade on the side. Midmornings they spent cutting wood, making beds, crafting candles, and dusting and sweeping. Janet sometimes worked crossword puzzles, and Foster took notes on local birds he observed in the early morning.[32] On a 1944 trip out to Duck, Foster scrupulously recorded various kinds of thrushes, sparrows, ducks, kinglets, warblers, and woodpeckers, along with bluebirds, robins, eagles, meadowlarks, and several other kinds of birds he daily observed.[33]

In the afternoons, Foster and Janet tapped maples and boiled the syrup, depending on the season. They also shot targets with a .22 and hunted ducks during legal season. Midafternoons found the Dulleses reading leisurely in the sun, canoeing, and swimming. On rainy days, Foster wrote speeches while Janet typed them. As always, it was their custom never to have lunch but to eat a large breakfast and feast on a sumptuous dinner.

The Dulleses prepared their dinners over an open fire. They enjoyed cocktails—Janet's favorite was a martini and Foster drank rye whiskey (Old Overholt). They had hickory nuts gathered from the island, plus raw carrots and celery. They made hot pancakes served with caviar and sour cream or mushrooms on a hibachi. Janet prepared soup, which would be followed by a main course of beef or lake trout. Sometimes they prepared chicken with rice. They roasted all their meats over an open fire. They unfailingly concluded dinner with desserts of pie or pudding, like apple betty, bread or rice pudding, or custard. They had cookies or homemade cake. Sometimes they would have gingerbread. Along with their sweets, they ate cheeses for dessert, like Canadian cheddar. They always drank cognac with their cheeses, cakes, cookies, and pies. All this they prepared and savored with no electricity and no running water. As nights drew near, the Dulleses finished their days with walks or brief canoe trips along the shores and in the sheltered coves of the island. Bedtime was at nine, and the last hour of their days found them sitting around the fire reading—Foster with his mystery novels and Janet with her travel books.[34]

For Foster, the outdoors reflected a natural order that was innately moral as well as practical. From 1940 to 1946, when he served as chairman for the Commission on a Just and Durable Peace for the Federal Council of Churches, and later as adviser to the US delegation to the San Francisco Conference that produced the United Nations Charter, Foster hammered on the thesis that the moral law corresponded exactly with physical law. To him, since God was actively at work in the world, moral truths played out in nature and in human relationships in analogous ways. For years, Foster made his case that moral weapons were more powerful, and thus more necessary, than material weapons, and that righteousness could always be counted on to prevail over wickedness. Foster's detractors, from the 1940s until the end of his life, questioned his sincerity and charged Foster with simply trying to use the churches for personal political gain. But Foster was a true believer. Some of the strongest evidence of his sincerity is found in his devotion to nature. For Foster, it was in nature that God's hand was most evidently observed, and it was in human relations—specifically through the churches—that God's redemptive purposes for the world's nations were fulfilled. In nature as in human relations, when humans submitted to, and cooperated with, God's work, peace and life were the result.

The relationship between moral law and physical law can be seen in one of Foster's favorite maxims out on the lake: "everything is fine until you relax." Hart described Foster's meaning—Foster believed that "as long as you're on your toes and watching everything, you get along fine, but the minute you relax then things happen—the minute you think everything's all right."[35] Storms and high seas, unseen hazards underwater, unexpected mechanical failures on board ship, and a host of other vagaries faced when sailing were representations of national and world crises to Foster. He applied the same principle in nature as he applied in international crises. Some years later, as World War II ended and merged into the Cold War, Foster would drive this principle home again and again.

The Dulles Commission and the Peril of Relaxation

In late 1940, the FCC created the Commission for the Study of the Bases for a Just and Durable Peace. This commission was birthed out of the dynamics of controversy within the FCC that intensified as Hitler's armies went from strength to strength during the course of the year. Reinhold Niebuhr sounded an alarm for American churches in a 1939 series of articles he wrote for the *Christian Century* entitled "Leaves from the Notebook of a War-bound American."[36] He argued that Britain and France were the only nations standing between freedom and tyranny, and that American help was indispensable. In January 1940, he penned the draft of a statement entitled "The American Churches and the International Situation," in which he sympathized with the idea that war was unchristian and that all nations were responsible in some way for the nascent world crisis. Still, Niebuhr said, "this admission of common guilt as regards the *origins* of the present wars must not blind us to the incalculable issue at stake in the *outcome* of these wars." Niebuhr also conceded that freedom and justice were not guaranteed if the Allies and China prevailed over Germany and Japan. But if the Axis powers were to prevail, the death of "justice, freedom of thought and worship, and international cooperation" would certainly occur.[37] Because the crisis was fundamentally moral, the United States should ready itself for intervention.

Niebuhr's call for intervention exposed a fault line within the FCC between interventionists and noninterventionists. The fault line was thin at the beginning of 1940, but it continued to enlarge after France was conquered and the Nazis started to bomb population centers in Britain. Foster reluctantly consented to sign the Niebuhr statement on January 16, 1940, but by March he had come to regret his decision. Foster's problem was less with the statement itself and more with the way the media was cherry-picking from the statement to portray the Allies as righteous and the Axis powers as evil. He did not want to side with any group that, as he saw it, could be portrayed as equating self-serving national interests with justice and morality. America and the Allies were just as culpable as the Germans and the Japanese in that regard, and he insisted that the war should not be cast in moral terms.[38]

In April, Foster's ambivalence to the interventionist position hardened further. In a letter to Thomas Debevoise, a friend and attorney based in Manhattan and an interventionist, Foster argued that total war itself, rather than any particular nation, was the real threat to civilization. He estimated that American losses could total up to two million lives if it committed to sending troops to Europe. He also downplayed the threat posed by Nazi Germany. He doubted that Italy would join the war on the side of Germany, and he also thought Russia was harmless. In fact, if Germany were to win, the German government might moderate over time—even though Foster was quick to say that he deplored such a potential state of affairs. Finally, propping up Britain and France with American power would only serve to ensure their status quo as the dominant world powers. Dynamic change would undo all efforts to preserve that status.[39]

One of the more stinging criticisms Foster received for his hesitation about intervention came from a Sullivan and Cromwell colleague, Rogers Lamont. He was the son of Foster's colleague from the Versailles days, Thomas Lamont. Rogers resigned his position as partner at Sullivan and Cromwell, went to Canada, and joined the British army. He received a commission as captain of artillery and was killed in France on May 27, 1940. He was the first American to be killed in action in World War II.

About three weeks before his death, Lamont wrote Foster a lengthy and frank letter in which he took his former boss to task for being not much more than a dreamy idealist. He read a speech that Foster delivered in Detroit the previous October, in which he rehearsed all his familiar themes about the defects of the sovereignty system; the selfish ambitions of the Allies after Versailles; the reasons why Germany, Italy, and Japan turned to violence; and the need for a new world order marked by cooperation, federalism, and national self-sacrifice.[40] An apt, one-word summary of Lamont's reply might be—hogwash. In the middle of his fifteen-page handwritten letter from the field, Lamont stated, "we ought to forget about magic world orders to solve our difficulties—and face realities. Don't aim at the moon and fall into another cesspool such as we're in now." He went on to say, "we might as well ask a cow to digest pork as to ask the human race . . . to take on a new world order." And why should America think about crafting new world orders after the war when it refuses to pay the price now, Lamont asked. Foster, Lamont said, might tell the youth of America that a victorious Germany might mellow in the future, but do not tell them that Americans could create a new world order without getting in the fight—that would be telling them they could get something for nothing.[41] These were strong words from a man who was willing to demonstrate his convictions with his actions. There is no record of Foster ever answering Lamont's criticisms, directly or indirectly, even after he was killed in action.

In late spring of 1940, France fell to the Germans. The FCC crafted another interventionist statement under the leadership of Walter Van Kirk, secretary of the FCC's Department of International Justice and Goodwill, and William Adams Brown of Union Theological Seminary. Foster refused to sign it. But he also refused to align himself with noninterventionist groups like America First.[42] He wanted to stay above the fray and serve as a mediator between doves, like Roswell Barnes, and hawks, such as Van Dusen. Since the FCC was in danger of a permanent rupture between the interventionists and noninterventionists at the upcoming biennial meeting, Van Kirk and Barnes (associate general secretary of the FCC) called a meeting at Van Kirk's home on October 4 to work out a strategy that might bring the competing groups together. Twelve persons were in attendance, including Foster, Harry Emerson Fosdick, Henry Sloane Coffin, Samuel M. Cavert, and Harold Hatch, among others. Everyone in attendance agreed that Foster should draft a new statement that would, as Foster described it, "emphasize and seek to preserve the essential unity of the churches in the face of temporal issues which are divisive."[43]

By October 18, Foster had a draft ready for consideration entitled "The American Churches and the International Situation"—the same title as Niebuhr's statement from the previous January. Foster urged that the churches show that the Christian faith was dynamic, not static. Basing his new statement on the assertion that during wartime, "human and demonic forces operate most violently to divide mankind and . . . impair that spirit of universal brotherhood," Foster made several recommendations. Those included strengthening the ecumenical movement, evangelism, relief work in war-torn areas, freedom from hate, spreading freedom around the world, and boldness in proclaiming the gospel. The American churches, Foster wrote, "form part of Christ's Church" and should see themselves as "that Tree of Life whereof the leaves serve the healing of the nations."[44] At the FCC biennial meeting in December, the six hundred delegates present voted to accept Foster's statement. The success of the statement led directly to the forming of the Commission for the Study of a Just and Durable Peace, and Foster was the unanimous choice to lead it.

The genius of Foster's December 1940 statement was that it took attention off the present controversy of whether the United States should actively intervene in the war on behalf of the Allies or stay out. Foster instead shifted attention to the future postwar condition, one in which individual human dignity took the place of national interest as the basic standard of value in world relations. He boldly stated, "Churches can and should create the underlying conditions indispensable to the attainment of a better international order."[45] Foster crafted a statement that brought basic unity to the FCC, and this unity was sustained for the duration of the war largely because of his efforts on the commission.

Foster became chair of the newly created commission in February 1941. From the start, the commission was unquestionably "his show," as Van Dusen described it.[46] He also was determined that this commission—the name was shortened to the Commission for a Just and Durable Peace (or informally, the Dulles Commission)—would play an indispensable role in educating people in the churches about the importance of working to create an international organization that would promote collaboration and keep peace. And as Barnes said, Foster knew that if he accepted the chairmanship, he was going to be a hands-on leader. "He would not accept that role and then allow somebody else to set policy and direction and then rubber stamp it," Barnes said.[47] At home, on the lake, and at Sullivan and Cromwell, this was exactly the posture that Foster always adopted—command.

Space does not allow a full consideration of Foster's activities with the FCC from 1940 to 1946. Other fine treatments exist that lay out those details.[48] Here we will consider a few of the major themes that Foster articulated in his writing and speaking as chair of the Commission for a Just and Durable Peace. Foster saw himself in a position to right the wrongs of the Versailles peace. The League of Nations had failed to keep the peace. The Versailles Treaty had cast the status quo in stone, in an attempt to isolate the dynamic nations. The sovereignty system, which more than any other factor set the stage for war, was secured. And the American public never grasped the singular nature of their opportunity to lead the world to a just and durable peace. But the war in Europe presented Americans, and particularly American Christians, with another chance to establish a world order marked by justice, cooperation, self-sacrifice, and human flourishing everywhere, even among former enemies. Foster was determined to put the commission in a position to cast a moral vision for the postwar world.

This mandate required the commission to make its case in the form of clear statements and then provide forums for the churches to come together and sharpen the commission's vision. It also required a considerable effort of mass dissemination of the commission's statements through a variety of channels. Further, the commission needed to expand its vision beyond the churches of the United States. The commission's efforts needed to be international and ecumenical in scope. And the government would have to be convinced that a just and durable peace was not possible without the direct support and action from the churches.

Foster and his commission produced scores of statements, essays, study guides, and public addresses from 1940 to 1945. Selected documents include "A Just and Durable Peace" and "Long Range Peace Objectives" in 1941; "Peace without Platitudes," "A Righteous Faith for a Just and Durable Peace," and "Statement of Guiding Principles" in 1942; "The Six Pillars of Peace" and "Christian Messages to the Peoples of the World" in 1943; "The Churches and Dumbarton Oaks" in 1944; and "Statement on Control of the Atomic Bomb" in 1945. The commission also hosted national and international conferences in an effort to mobilize church leaders to carry out its vision for postwar peace. The first conference was held at Ohio Wesleyan University in Delaware, Ohio, March 3–5, 1942. The next was the International Roundtable of Christian Leaders, held at the Princeton Inn (now Forbes College) in Princeton, New Jersey, July 8–11, 1943. Lastly, the National Study Conference took place in Cleveland, Ohio, January 16–19, 1945. These activities played a central role in the development of the United Nations Charter in 1945. They were also critical in the shaping of American public opinion, which directed the United States to break from its mistake in refusing to join the League in 1919–1920, and instead, to take its rightful place of leadership in the newly created United Nations.

The prominent theme animating the Dulles Commission's vision was the primacy of moral law. In the 1942 document "Statement of Guiding Principles," the primacy of moral law became the first and foundational principle. "We believe that moral law, no less than physical law, undergirds our world."[49] Foster wrote an article entitled "Peace without Platitudes," which appeared in the January 1942 issue of *Fortune,* and observed that the Axis powers had overwhelming power in material weapons but were morally and spiritually bankrupt. To him, while the Axis had an important apparent advantage, the Allies "will offset this by a moral and intellectual initiative."[50] Later in 1942, Foster developed his theory of moral law to include faith and mission. In a collection of essays produced by the commission in 1942, Foster wrote a fiery piece calling on America to recover a faith that had been squandered after Versailles. In that essay, he asserted that Americans had allowed their once strong faith in the form of manifest destiny to weaken into sloth and self-satisfaction. But now, "we seek that strength which is to be found in the propulsion of a deep faith and sense of high mission in the world."[51] The Axis powers had a dynamic faith—it was "shot through with evil," and "evil men readily came into leadership," resulting in a faith without a basis in the moral law. But Americans could revive a righteous faith inasmuch as they followed Christ in championing religious and economic freedom, relief for the suffering, international cooperation, and a moral example of "creative purpose." Foster cited Christ's words from the Sermon on the Mount in Matthew 5—"Let your light so shine before men that they may see your good works." The

Second World War had opened up "a chance to become a positive force for human betterment."[52]

Foster had come a long way since arguing in 1940 that the war should not be understood or cast in moral terms, and to do so would mean falling into the trap of national selfishness. By 1942, Foster definitely saw the war in starkly moral terms, but he avoided the lure of conflating national interest with morality. In 1943, the commission went so far as to assert that the war had a supernatural element to it, that it was far more than merely a war between nation-states. Rather, "it is a clash of ideologies. Germany is controlled by . . . demonic forces."[53] From the basis of moral law came the commitment to human freedom and dignity and individual responsibility, and the need for collective action in the direction of righteousness. Furthermore, Foster first added the concept of a divinely inspired mission for Americans as part of his articulation of moral law during World War II.

Foster wanted Americans to get behind the cause of establishing a world organization dedicated to righteousness, and the war provided an opportunity to do so. Thus, starting a world organization was another prominent theme emerging from the Dulles Commission. Foster's keynote address opening the National Study Conference at Ohio Wesleyan in 1942 asked the question, what is government? Foster returned to earlier ideas about the development of group authority, the need for law, and the genius of American federalism. He also reminded his hearers that the modern world was a world of interdependence, not independence. Foster placed three choices before the audience—nationalism, isolationism, or internationalism. Human political evolution had only advanced to the stage of the nation-state, Foster said. The world must actively take the next step in evolution. That step, Foster stated, was to "expand areas of common political authority so that these will more nearly coincide with the economic interconnections and interdependence upon which decent living in fact depends."[54] In other words, human beings needed to evolve into internationalism.

The commission responded with a statement to the Dumbarton Oaks Conference, which met in the late summer of 1944. At Dumbarton Oaks, delegates from the United States, Great Britain, the Soviet Union, and China came together to further develop the idea of a world organization to succeed the defunct League of Nations. The concept was first proposed in the Moscow Declaration of 1943. Foster and the commission had been arguing for such an organization since 1941, and in November 1944, the commission issued a cautious endorsement of the Dumbarton Oaks proposals. The commission's concern was that the "Big Four" were still acting on the assumption of a military alliance rather than a permanent world governmental structure. Still, it recognized a good start when it saw one, but "success will depend not merely upon political measures but upon more general acceptance throughout the world of common moral judgments about national conduct." To the commission, the value of the human individual meant that all international conduct should be oriented toward human dignity over national interest.[55]

The most important statement issued by the Dulles Commission was the "Statement of Political Propositions," commonly known as the Six Pillars of Peace. First, the military alliance known as the United Nations needed to become a formal organization for world collaboration, and it should include all nations, not merely the Allies. Second, national governments must consider other nations' interests when they pursue their own economic interests, and they must recognize that the benefits of the world's resources are for all. Third, treaties that resulted from the peace must be flexible. Fourth, colonies should be set on the path to independence, and the international organization envisioned in the first pillar must realistically guide those processes. Fifth, armaments of all nations, victors and conquered alike, should be regulated. Sixth, the peace must champion religious and intellectual freedom. The commission's goal was to educate the public via the churches on these propositions and to encourage the American public to push its government to make them official policy. The commission also wanted to see other nations adopt these propositions so that world collaboration could be made a reality. Foster said of the Six Pillars, "the many who believe the things we believe and who desire, as citizens, to do something about it have here a field for action."[56]

Foster's commission was successful in accomplishing many of its goals. Foster, Barnes, and Henry St. George Tucker met with President Roosevelt to discuss the Six Pillars, once in March 1943 and again in February 1944. FDR was enthusiastic about the commission's vision, encouraging Foster that the Six Pillars was almost worthy of being preached from the pulpit. He added that the commission ought to do all it could to get the document into the hands of every church in the nation.[57] Foster was way ahead of the president, telling him that sixty thousand churches had already been sent the document, and that more churches would be reached.

While Foster for years had been stridently hitting the themes of the primacy of moral law, the need for international collaboration, and the benefits of economic interdependence, his was among many voices advocating for such notions. Franklin Roosevelt's Neutrality Address of September 3, 1939, echoed these ideas, and Secretary of State Cordell Hull had been working to advance them while a senator and in the early months of the war leading up to American intervention. Undersecretary of State Sumner Welles chaired the Advisory Committee on Problems of Foreign Relations, established in September 1939 to "survey the basic principles which should underlie a desirable world order" after the war was over.[58] Foster's particular contribution was advancing these ideas effectively *to the churches* under the auspices of the FCC and articulating them as part of the essential mission of the United States to aid humanity.

One other conspicuous theme, particularly in Foster's writings and speeches, was his admonition to Christians to stay vigilant and resist the temptation to relax. This theme appeared most obviously in the closing months of the war and in 1946. Foster's tone toward the end of the war became more alarmed at what he perceived to be a creeping spiritual lethargy in the churches. He often cast American history in terms of a declension narrative and preached the need to recover a dynamic faith. In his keynote address to the National Study Conference at Cleveland on January 16, 1945, Foster celebrated the fact that the Dulles Commission had mobilized Christians all over the world toward the goal of establishing a world organization. "The churches represented at this Conference did decisively contribute to the ground swell of public opinion which moved our political leaders to action." But, Foster stressed, this was not the time for Christians to rest on their laurels. "That does not entitle us to relax, with the pleasurable feeling that our task is done." American Christians had a responsibility commensurate with their influence to see the goal through to its completion.[59] This responsibility was not only to themselves but to all humanity, including generations yet unborn.

On April 5, 1945, Foster resigned as chairman of the Commission for a Just and Durable Peace.[60] He had been invited by Secretary of State James Byrnes to serve as general adviser to the American delegation at the San

Francisco Conference, which would be establishing the UN Charter. Foster received this invitation due to the efforts of his friend Senator Arthur Vandenberg of Michigan, who had been lobbying at least since February to get Foster to come to San Francisco in some capacity.[61] Vandenberg believed that before, during, and after the conference, Foster's contribution was of inestimable value. After the conference ended, Vandenberg gushed to Foster, "It is *literally* true that you were my chief reliance and my chief inspiration throughout the San Francisco adventure. . . . It is my deliberate and considered opinion that you made a greater contribution to the San Francisco Charter than *any* other one man who was present at the Golden Gate."[62] Foster was indeed thrilled with the charter, exulting in the first steps toward what he believed were real prospects for world peace and collaboration.[63] But he remained cautious, realistic about the tendency of humans to rest on their laurels. "The present danger is that the millions who compelled the achievements in San Francisco will now relax, feeling that the battle has been won and the Organization can carry on alone at this point."[64]

World War II came to an end on the deck of the battleship *Missouri* in Tokyo Bay on September 2, 1945. Yet the war had barely ended before Foster began to express serious concern about a new ideological threat—the Soviet Union. But Foster was seriously torn between his hopes for international cooperation and the need for meeting this threat. On the one hand, Foster saw that the world at the end of the war needed a basis of trust more than at any other time in human history because of the development and use of the atomic bomb. In early to mid-1946, Foster supported international control of atomic weapons, as expressed that July in the Baruch Plan, one that Bernard Baruch laid out before the UN Atomic Energy Commission, which built on the earlier Acheson-Lilienthal report and became the official American proposal.[65] In an essay he wrote for *Christian News-Letter* earlier that January, Dulles argued that if the United States insisted on monopolizing atomic weapons, the world would no longer trust it. "We have set up the [UN] General Assembly to be the 'town meeting of the world.' Let us invite, and heed, its judgment of what we should do [with atomic weapons]," he wrote.[66] But on the other hand, Foster was concerned that the Soviets were not altogether trustworthy. In a two-part series he wrote for *Life* in June 1946, Foster laid out a detailed analysis of Soviet foreign policy. A striking feature of these writings is that, while the world stopped fighting World

War II in 1945, Foster kept right on going. He continued the fight over ideology after the war—he simply pivoted to a new foe. He described the Soviets as animated by a dynamic, yet evil, faith, just as he described the Nazis in 1942. He argued that moral weapons would prevail over material arms, just as he did in the context of World War II. And he acknowledged that everyone was ready to have peace. The last thing anyone wanted in 1946 was another war. But that desire, while understandable, was fraught with peril. "We feel we have earned the right to a period of relaxation. . . . These are attitudes which contribute to war."[67] Relaxation led to satisfaction; satisfaction led to complacency; complacency led to fear of change; fear of change led to efforts to fix the status quo; efforts to fix the status quo guaranteed a violent outbreak. And a violent outbreak with nuclear weapons was an unthinkable prospect. At the same time, Foster became more and more convinced that the Soviets were not to be trusted.

Thus, in the middle of 1946, Foster began entering a phase in which he apparently turned away from internationalism and toward nationalism. There is much truth to this analysis. But Foster was never an idealist. He was a pragmatic realist, and as such, he reacted to crises as they arose, as if he were sailing on Lake Ontario or tapping maples on Duck Island and a storm suddenly emerged out of a clear blue sky. He did not anticipate Avery converting to Catholicism, nor did he foresee that his cherished hopes for universal brotherhood among nations would be thwarted by the Soviet Union, America's ally against the Axis powers. His positions on issues, in his private and public life, evolved around the contours of the crises he faced. As the Communists presented more of a threat to international cooperation and the American way of life, Foster became more concerned about meeting that threat and less optimistic that international unity could be achieved as long as the Soviets pursued an expansionist foreign policy and held the veto power in the UN Security Council. Still, one feature in his thought remained constant from 1940 to the end of his life—his commitment to the idea that moral laws were reflected in nature as much as in diplomacy and politics. And just as in calm seas, an observer of international relations ought never let her guard down. As Foster liked to say, everything is fine until you relax.

6

"Give a Man a Revolver"
(1946–1952)

I could not help but think as I heard the encomiums pour out
from both sides here, that much more of it and [John Foster
Dulles] will be a dark horse.

—Senator Alexander Wiley[1]

On a spring morning in 1942, Foster boarded the Lexington Avenue
express train at the Chrysler Building headed south to his office at
48 Wall Street in lower Manhattan. As he stepped off the platform and
into a car in the rear of the train, he sensed a man following him unusu-
ally closely. While he was stepping into the vestibule of the car, a "heavy,
thick-set, and tough appearing man" cut in front of Foster, so that he was
squeezed in between the two men. Just inside the car, the large man in
front abruptly turned, apparently to make his way off the train and onto the
platform. In his statement to the police, Foster said that the man "did not
try to pass on either side of me, but pushed into me in quite a violent manner."[2] Both the big fellow and the man behind Foster hurriedly left the train
and turned north. Other passengers, Foster noted, observed the loud and
aggressive manner (even by New York City standards!) in which the large
man pushed his way off the train. Foster dismissed the awkward incident
from his mind—until he arrived at his office. He found that the contents
of his left hip pocket—a set of papers and a sum of cash—were missing.
Foster had been robbed on the IRT Lexington Avenue southbound line.

The partners in crime had made off with $102, "a commutation ticket to Cold Spring Harbor, an American Airlines scrip card, and one or two miscellaneous slips of paper and notes." The loss of the cash was regrettable, more so than most of the other things. But one item the thieves got away with was more valuable to Foster than the other scraps of paper: his concealed pistol license, No. C20862.[3] Foster applied for the license because he owned two residences, one on Cold Spring Harbor and one in the city. "I have large amounts of money, jewelry, and valuable papers in each. Frequently, I drive alone at night to and from these places with money and valuable papers on my person," he wrote on his license application. Foster listed Thomas E. Dewey as a character reference, his friend and the future governor of New York and the 1944 and 1948 Republican nominee for president. His weapon of choice was a Smith and Wesson .38 caliber revolver.[4] Foster was obviously taking his personal security seriously, for he was aware of all that he had to lose. His being a victim of pickpocketing on a subway train only seemed to confirm the fact of an insecure world, and of his perceived need for vigilance against others who would steal from him or otherwise try to do him harm. After all, falling prey to plunder at the hands of an evildoer could happen with such suddenness that the victim might not even realize what was happening until it was too late, such as in Foster's unfortunate case in the New York subway.

Security in the Face of the Soviet Threat

A few years later, in 1949, Foster gave an interview to the editors of *US News and World Report* on American-Soviet relations. By that time, the two former allies had become hostile rivals in Europe and the Pacific. By the end of that year, the Soviet Union would explode its first atomic bomb and the Chinese Communists under Mao Tse-tung would take control of mainland China, chasing the pro-Western Nationalist Chinese government under Chiang Kai-shek to the island of Formosa (Taiwan). Foster had come to believe since the end of World War II that the Soviet Union was actively directing a general strategy of global domination. Furthermore, it possessed the initiative as a dynamic power, in the same way that Japan, Italy, and Germany did as "dynamic powers" during the 1930s. He argued that while the people of Russia were peaceful, their leaders were wicked and were not interested in better relations with the United States "because of the fact that fear is one of their stocks in trade." Thus, the countries of the free world, including the United States, needed to arm themselves against the threat of aggression. Foster thought it was lamentable, but necessary, that four years after the most destructive war the world had ever seen, America and Western Europe needed to rearm. If nothing else, Foster believed, it would make those countries feel more secure. And the feeling of security was just as important as actually being secure. He said, "If you give a man a revolver he feels safer in a dangerous world than if he is totally unarmed. . . . The psychological fact is that until they have some military force there is going to be fright [of the Red Army], and some military force will appreciably allay that fright."[5] Perhaps there was something present in Foster's own psychology inspiring this statement, put there by a couple of hoodlums on the New York City subway in 1942.

In any case, by the late forties and early fifties, Foster had become deeply concerned about security against the Soviets for the United States, for Western Europe, and for the countries in the Pacific—Australia, New Zealand, the Philippines, and Japan. During the 1930s, Foster had been suspicious about the quest for security. He believed that at Versailles, the victorious Allies had tried to cement their security into a permanent status quo, keeping Germany weak and keeping Japan in its place. This obsession of the "haves" to maintain their power at the expense of the "have-nots" resulted in war. Ironically, Foster's postwar concern about security served as the impetus for arguably his greatest diplomatic achievement—the Treaty of San Francisco, ratified by the United States Senate in 1952, that formally ended World War II in the Pacific. This treaty went far toward establishing that just and durable peace Foster had championed so strenuously and vociferously during the war, and it created the basis for stability and security in the Pacific for the rest of the twentieth century.

Not long after hostilities between the Allies and the Axis powers had ceased, the Cold War began in earnest. World War II had been a victory, in John Lewis Gaddis's words, "over fascism only—not over authoritarianism."[6] To put it more specifically, the war was a victory over one kind of ideology and a setup for another ideological confrontation that would continue for five decades. Barely a year after V-E and V-J Days, on March 5, 1946, Winston Churchill spoke in President Harry Truman's home state to cast the Soviet Union in dark terms, saying that Moscow was the emanating center of an emerging tyranny that threatened the peoples of Eastern Europe and of all "Christian civilization." To Westminster College in Fulton, Missouri, Churchill memorably said, "From Stettin in the Baltic to Trieste in the Adriatic an iron curtain has descended across the Continent. Behind that line lie all the capitals of the ancient states of Central and Eastern Europe. Warsaw, Berlin, Prague, Vienna, Budapest, Belgrade, Bucharest and Sofia; all these famous cities and the populations around them lie in what I must call the Soviet sphere, and all are subject, in one form or another, not only to Soviet influence but to a very high and in some cases increasing measure of control from Moscow."[7]

Just weeks earlier, the American *chargé d'affaires* in Moscow, George Kennan, sent the State Department his famous eight-thousand-word "Long Telegram" outlining his interpretation of the Soviet posture toward the postwar world, the long-range Soviet policies toward engaging that world, and how United States foreign policy should be conducted in light of the Soviet outlook. Kennan asserted that, for the Soviet Union, "in the long run there can be no permanent peaceful coexistence" with capitalistic countries. The Soviets, Kennan continued, planned to deepen the differences and heighten the tension between Communism and capitalism with the goal of inspiring revolutionary movements in capitalist countries, in addition to colonies and former colonies within the capitalist spheres of influence. Further, America should expect the Soviets to pursue a dramatic increase in their armed forces, "great displays to impress outsiders," and the maintaining of profound secrecy of their activities both foreign and domestic. The United States must realize, Kennan insisted, that the Soviet pursuit of world domination was less an act of expansion for the sake of expansion than an act of expansion for the sake of its own survival. Kennan wrote, "we have here a political force committed fanatically to the belief that with US there can be no permanent *modus vivendi,* that it is desirable and necessary that the internal harmony of our society be disrupted, our traditional way of life be destroyed, the international authority of our state be broken, if Soviet power is to be secure."[8] Kennan's "Long Telegram" became the basis for the Truman Doctrine, which Harry Truman articulated in an address to Congress in March 1947. The Truman Doctrine, first applied in Greece and Turkey, committed the United States "to support free peoples who are resisting attempted subjugation by armed minorities or by outside pressures."[9] It would dominate American foreign policy for the next twenty-five years.

Between 1948 and 1952, the free/Communist world binary that Churchill and Kennan warned against increasingly seemed vindicated by events that unfolded in Europe and Asia. In February 1948, Stalin aided Czechoslovakian Communists in staging a coup in that country and overthrowing the only pro-Western government in Eastern Europe. Also in 1948, the Soviets attempted to expel the British, French, and Americans from West Berlin and to consolidate their hold on East Germany by means of a blockade. The Allies responded with a massive airlift of supplies to the city consisting of nearly 200,000 flights between June 1948 and May 1949. On August 29, 1949, the Soviets exploded an atomic bomb, ending American nuclear hegemony. And on October 1, 1949, the Chinese Communists under Mao Tse-tung seized control of the Chinese mainland—what Americans would characterize for years as "the loss of China."[10]

Then, on June 25, 1950, North Korean forces crossed the thirty-eighth parallel and invaded South Korea. The events leading up to this are important to recount. As World War II was winding down in the summer of 1945, Soviet forces occupied the northern portion of the Korean peninsula; American forces occupied the southern portion in preparation for the planned invasion of Japan, scheduled for September 1945 (the dropping of atomic bombs on Hiroshima and Nagasaki made the planned invasion unnecessary). The thirty-eighth parallel was established as a temporary boundary between the Communist North and the pro-Western South by agreement between the United States and the Soviet Union at the Potsdam Conference in 1945, pending the formation of a unified Korea after Japan's defeat. Soviet and American forces had withdrawn from Korea by 1949, but North Korea remained a Soviet-supported Communist state, whereas the US-supported Republic of Korea (South Korea) was created as a result of UN-supervised elections. The leaders of both North Korea and South Korea had voiced their desires to forcefully unify the peninsula. Kim Il-sung, leader of North Korea, received Stalin's blessing for the invasion early in 1950. Gaddis wrote that Stalin wanted to open up a second front against the Allies in Asia, which "would maintain the momentum generated by Mao's victory the previous year."[11]

To complicate these matters, Americans were growing more suspicious of Soviet espionage in their midst. Soviet espionage had been a concern among Americans well before 1950, and the conviction of State Department official Alger Hiss for perjury that year, after he had denied being a Soviet spy under oath, served to heighten existing fears. Hiss had been best known for his work on Far Eastern affairs as well as his contributions toward the creation of the UN Charter. He worked in the State Department from 1936 to 1946 and left to head the Carnegie Endowment for International Peace. At the time of his departure, he enjoyed the respect and gratitude of acting secretary of state Dean Acheson. Acheson said of him in December 1946, "he has a vast number of devoted friends and admirers in the Department and they all shall regret his departure, wish him well and shall follow his career with very great interest in the future."[12] Hiss was forced to resign from the Carnegie Endowment in 1949, and in 1950, Wisconsin senator Joseph McCarthy began leading a crusade against suspected Communist infiltrators planted in influential institutions like the State Department. How could China's fall to Communism and the Soviet development of the atomic bomb have occurred so quickly, so unexpectedly, McCarthy asked? His only answer was that the Soviets were getting valuable information from spies in key positions in the US government. One of the ways in which Truman sought to counter McCarthy's charges was to demonstrate that his administration was committed to maintaining a united front of Democrats and Republicans to contain the Soviets, which meant utilizing top Republican John Foster Dulles at the United Nations and negotiating with the Soviets as the Allies worked to bring World War II to a diplomatic conclusion in both Europe and Asia.

Since resigning from his post with the Federal Council of Churches in 1945, Foster's career went in varied, dramatic, and sometimes unexpected directions. He served as adviser to three secretaries of state—James Byrnes, George Marshall, and Dean Acheson—at the Council of Foreign Ministers (CFM) meetings in London (1945), Moscow (1947), London (1947), and Paris (1949). The CFM comprised representatives from the United States, Britain, France, and the Soviet Union. They came together to negotiate outstanding territorial, political, and economic issues mostly in central, eastern, and southern Europe. Foster served as United States representative to the first, second, third, and fifth sessions of the General Assembly of the United Nations from 1946 to 1949 and again in 1950. He was chief foreign policy adviser to Thomas E. Dewey during his unsuccessful bid for the presidency in 1948. Dewey returned to service as governor of New York following his loss, and in the summer of 1949 he tapped Foster to fill out the vacant Senate seat of Robert Wagner, who stepped aside due to health reasons. Foster resigned as managing partner of Sullivan and Cromwell, took up his senatorial duties in July, and ran in the special election that November but was defeated by former New York governor Herbert Lehman. After his defeat, Foster turned to writing his second book, entitled *War or Peace*, which was published in the spring of 1950. From April 1950 to March 1952, Foster advised both the secretary of state and the president and served as the personal representative of the president in the negotiations that finalized the peace treaty with Japan, a treaty signed by forty-nine nations in San Francisco. During the 1952 presidential campaign, Foster drafted the Republican Party platform and served as Dwight Eisenhower's chief adviser on foreign policy. Upon his election to the presidency, Eisenhower nominated Foster to be the fifty-second secretary of state, a fulfillment of a lifelong ambition.

By the time he began work on the Japanese peace treaty, Foster had come to see the Soviet Union as the personification of atheistic materialism, diametrically opposed to the moral law and human freedom as rooted in universal dignity. He perceived the world in binary terms, dividing it into two categories in opposition to one another—the free world led by the United States and the Communist world directed from Moscow. He also only allowed for two potential outcomes for any and all levels of conflict between these two sides—victory or defeat. As the Cold War began from 1945 to 1948, he continued to conceive of the moral law as universal, just as he had since writing "The Road to Peace" in 1935. But as the decade of the 1950s opened, Foster increasingly tended toward the view that the United States was the paradigmatic expression of the moral law in the world and the Soviet Union was its nemesis.

Mark Toulouse, in his landmark text *The Transformation of John Foster Dulles*, argued that Foster went through a dramatic "transformation" between 1937 and 1950 from "prophet of realism" to "priest of nationalism." Toulouse argued that Foster's transformation took place in the way he defined and articulated the concept of the moral law from his participation in the 1937 Oxford Conference to his authoring of *War or Peace*.[13] Whereas in 1937, Foster conceived of the moral law in universal, transcendent terms, by 1950 he saw it in immanent terms. The earlier Foster saw force and the threat of force as useless in maintaining peace, but the later Foster believed that deterrent force was necessary to counter the evil the Soviets represented. Foster's commitment to the moral law as the foundation for human activity as evidenced in nature did not wane during this period of change. Nor did Foster's fundamental belief in the power and indispensability of human liberty change. But by 1952, Foster saw the United States as the innocent nation, and American interests and actions in the world as inherently righteous. This perception represented a marked distinction from that of 1937, when he was careful in *War, Peace, and Change* to argue that all nations were guilty of outrages and none were in a position to claim the righteous high ground, including the United States.

Toulouse's thesis is smart, persuasive, and difficult to challenge. Since Foster's understanding of moral law was not rooted in a developed, carefully considered theological system but instead was the product of observations from experience in the natural world and based in pragmatic philosophy, it is understandable that his views would be susceptible to dramatic change. And herein lies a potential key to understanding why Foster's views shifted. Again and again, Foster argued that change was inevitable. He had seen the forces of change affect the world in dramatic ways from his service with the Reparations Commission at Versailles in 1919 to his nomination as secretary of state after Eisenhower's victory in the 1952 presidential election. And Foster's posture toward world events tracked right along the course of those changes. For example, when Hitler invaded Poland in 1939, Foster was a noninterventionist, asserting that Germany was a dynamic power rebelling against the harsh strictures arbitrarily imposed on it by Britain and France. By the time the United States joined the war in December 1941, Foster was a committed belligerent. At the 1943 International Roundtable of Christian Leaders in Princeton, the Dulles Commission characterized the war as a clash of ideologies. It defined the Nazis as evil and controlled by demonic forces.[14] By the end of the war, and as a result of his experiences on the CFM, Foster began to see that the ideological war that had just concluded was morphing into a new ideological war with a new enemy, one that possessed nuclear weapons. Foster's conception of moral law changed right along with the circumstances—circumstances that were unprecedented in their narrow margin for error or misunderstanding.

We in the twenty-first century tend to conceive of the Second World War as one historical category with a definite beginning on September 1, 1939, and a definite end on September 2, 1945. Popular images of ticker-tape parades, surrender ceremonies on battleship decks, and sailors kissing nurses on the streets of New York reinforce that conception. We then shift to a separate conception of the Cold War as historical category distinct from World War II, beginning with the Truman Doctrine and ending in 1991 with the collapse of the Soviet Union. But unlike us, Foster did not isolate World War II from the Cold War because he was not considering the two events from a position of hindsight. He was living within the realities of those wars, and he was reacting to circumstances as they unfolded before his eyes. Change was occurring, and Foster responded to those changes. Foster saw World War II as a war between ideologies. But as World War II merged into the Cold War, Foster never stopped fighting the ideological war he began fighting in 1941. He simply pivoted to a new enemy. The old enemy, the Nazis, had been conducting a program of world domination from the political and ideological center of Berlin. The new enemy, Foster believed, was pursuing the same program of world domination from its political and ideological center, Moscow. Hitler had been the personification of Nazi evil during World War II. Stalin, for Foster, became the personification of Communist evil in the early years of the Cold War. Once the Nazis were vanquished, Foster set the Soviets into the place formerly occupied in his mind by the Nazis. The frightening difference between these two menaces, for Foster, was the calculus of atomic power. This awesome contrast between the nature of the Nazi threat and the nature of the Communist threat in Foster's thinking meant that the diplomatic and military stakes were higher than any human being had ever before comprehended. If the world was going to escape the tyranny of Communist ideology and its Soviet promoters, the United States was the only nation powerful enough to provide the moral and physical resources and leadership for it to do so. It was also the only nation with what Foster continually called a "sense of destiny," a divine mandate to do so. Foster considered the Japanese peace treaty, signed in 1951 and ratified by the United States in 1952, as the first test of American moral and physical leadership of the free world.

Foster's views on Soviet foreign policy and the nature of the Soviet threat evolved over time. In 1945 and 1946, Foster urged Americans not to relax, not to become complacent in the face of the very real, dangerous, and novel challenge the Soviets presented. In the same way that there were two sides during the war, one righteous and the other evil, Foster saw new lines being drawn by Soviet intransigence, especially in Europe. But the universalism that still characterized his early views on the moral law and human dignity would not allow him to strike an entirely pessimistic tone. In the first months after the end of the war in 1945, Foster believed that atomic weapons should and could be placed under the control of the United Nations, that the Soviets could be cooperated with, that the United States should be tolerant of different philosophies, and that America could change the Soviet Union by the force of its example of justice and freedom. By 1946, his optimism about continued US-Soviet cooperation had melted away. And by 1950, Foster was convinced that the Soviets were the greatest enemy the United States had ever faced. The free world needed the leadership of an America characterized by the moral law against a foe that would stop at nothing to achieve its global, godless ambitions.

A few examples from Foster's activities demonstrate this evolution. Just over a month after the B-29s over Hiroshima and Nagasaki released their payloads, the executive committee of the FCC issued a statement urging the United States government to propose that the UN consider control of the production and use of nuclear weapons as "their first order of business."[15] The statement was produced with Foster's knowledge and assent. Also, in an article he wrote in January 1946, Foster argued that the UN should determine what the United States should do with its atomic weapons. If we were to insist on keeping atomic energy to ourselves, Foster wrote, how could the world trust us?[16] And during a conference with Truman on March 16, 1946, Foster urged upon the president the necessity of "the maintenance of ultimate control of atomic energy in civilians as against military."[17] But by June of that year, Foster was preoccupied with the Soviet threat such that he expressed doubts about the wisdom of internationalizing control of atomic weapons. He wrote in *Life* magazine that Soviet ambition was to create a *"Pax Sovietica,"* and it would be a gamble to entrust American atomic technology to an international body that included as one of its most powerful members one that would "use ruthless methods to conform others to their particular pattern."[18]

Still, even though Foster was already fearful of the Soviets and hesitant about handing American nuclear know-how to the UN by that summer, he still held out hope that the Soviets could be turned to American-style liberal democracy. After all, did not the Christian faith advocate for many of the same ideals as Communism? There were many Christians in Russia, after all, and furthermore, Foster observed, "communism as an economic program for social reconstruction has points of contact with the social message of Christianity as in its avowed concern for the underprivileged and its insistence on racial equality." And even though the difference between democracy and Communism could be boiled down to the difference between theism and atheism, Foster still held out hope that two competing ideologies could coexist in peace. It was necessary for both sides to realize that the presence of conflicting beliefs among human beings was normal, and that a festering spirit of intolerance sets the stage for conflict. The United States, as the world's leading Christian nation, should model tolerance. The governments of the United States and the Soviet Union ought to cooperate together in, as Foster put it in using one of his favorite phrases, the "curative and creative tasks envisaged for the United Nations." Moreover, Foster considered that "it is not unreasonable to believe that if Soviet leaders were confronted with a . . . strongly backed American program of this order, they would respond."[19] Thus, in 1946 Foster thought it was still possible to win the Soviet Union over by modeling the example of a transcendent moral law. It was the duty of a Christian nation to engage in this exemplarist project. "We would each hope," Foster wrote in June 1946, "that our example would be so good that men everywhere would follow it."[20]

By 1949–1950, much had changed in Foster's thinking. As a United States senator, Foster had come to equate Soviet Communism with the fascism that had lately been defeated in World War II. Both programs were atheistic, both were obdurately evil, and both rejected the moral law outright. In an address to his old church in Watertown, standing in front of the pew in which he sat as a boy, he articulated this common ground between fascism and Communism in order to bring into sharp relief just how dangerous the Soviets were. He went on to say, "Orthodox Communists believe . . . that there is no such thing as universal and equal justice . . . and they think it quite right to use force and violence to make their way prevail."[21] On the floor of the Senate, Foster had also given up on the idea of America attempting to turn the Soviets from evil to good purposes by the force of their example. Senate tradition dictated that very junior senators should remain deferentially silent among their senior peers, but despite feeling "wrapped in senatorial swaddling clothes rather than in a senatorial toga," Foster rose to the podium on July 12, 1949, to give a lengthy endorsement of the Senate's ratification of the North Atlantic Treaty.[22] Later, on September 21—two days before President Truman announced that the Soviets had exploded their own atomic bomb—he addressed his Senate colleagues to characterize the Soviets as being bent on "world domination" through means of "political penetration, fifth column activities, and revolution." But the collective security provided by the North Atlantic Treaty, combined with the atomic weapons held by the United States, would go far in correcting the imbalance of power between the as-yet weak West and the four-million-man Red Army.[23] And in his 1950 book *War or Peace*, Foster characterized the Soviets as being obsessed with world rule, an obsession they would attempt to carry out by whatever means necessary. "They believe it right to use fraud, terrorism, and violence, and any other means that will promote their ends. They treat as enemies all who oppose their will."[24]

Thus, by 1950, Foster had abandoned all hope that the Soviet Union would change course from its tyrannical designs on its own people and the peoples of the world. The force of American moral example would not be adequate. Since World War II, Foster had become accustomed to drawing lines between the righteous and the evil. The difference for Foster by 1950 was that Communism, unlike fascism, could not be seen as a temporary anomaly to be dispatched in due time. Soviet Communism was a titanic menace to the whole world, and its methods were crafty and subtle, unlike those of the Nazis, who preferred direct aggression. In World War II, Foster believed that each of the major Allied powers, the Soviets included, understood the need for international collaboration and desired peace. By the end of the 1940s, he was no longer convinced of that. The Soviets, Foster believed, had placed themselves outside of the moral law by rejecting its existence and utilizing terror, fear, and fraud to advance their interests.

Forging a Treaty with Japan

The beginning of the Cold War and developments in Europe and Asia through 1949 made concluding a peace treaty with Japan an urgent matter. The military phase of World War II was over, and American policy makers sensed the need to end the war diplomatically and ensure security in the Pacific after the fall of mainland China to the Communists in 1949. American forces began their occupation of Japan in 1945, overseen by the supreme commander for the Allied powers (SCAP), General Douglas MacArthur. As early as 1947, various parties had cast disparate visions for a peace treaty. MacArthur wanted generous terms for Japan in order to avoid alienating the Japanese people by prolonging the occupation. The War and Navy Departments wanted to rearm Japan against the Soviet Union. And two groups in the State Department offered ideas for the treaty. The Borton Group, under Columbia University historian Hugh Borton, special assistant to the director of the Office of Far Eastern Affairs, wanted to impose stringent reparations on the Japanese. The Policy Planning Staff, led by George Kennan, wanted to indefinitely extend the occupation to strengthen Japan's economic power and guard against Communist aggression in the Pacific.[25] By November 1948, the National Security Council (NSC) had decided to finalize a strategy for a peace treaty that drew most of its inspiration from Kennan's desire to strengthen Japan's economic potential and MacArthur's desire to end the occupation. Historian Frederick Dunn marked this decision by the NSC in 1948 as "*the* turning point in America's postwar policy toward Japan."[26]

Reflecting on his 1947 vision for peace with Japan, MacArthur wrote that his desire for a generous treaty was rooted in the belief that after about five years, occupations became counterproductive. MacArthur believed that the defeated nations become "restive" and the victorious nations take on the features "of entrenched power."[27] The NSC concurred with this view and envisioned a treaty setting the conditions for the creation of a self-sufficient Japan that was friendly to the United States. The NSC also saw a peace treaty as serving the primary purpose of establishing national security for the United States in the Pacific. MacArthur, as SCAP, understood the American strategic western frontier to be, not the West Coast, but "the littoral islands extending from the Aleutians through the Philippine Archipelago."[28] In any Asian war, MacArthur said, the United States would strike from, and protect, this frontier. Because Japan was located in the center of this line, it held singular strategic importance to American interests and should be a key consideration in the making of the treaty. The treaty Foster forged between 1950 and 1951 was the culmination of both MacArthur's and the NSC's original vision. Dunn made the important point that Foster should be seen as the principal figure bringing "a previous blueprint" into reality rather than "as 'the architect of the Japanese peace treaty,' as has often been done."[29]

Foster received his appointment as foreign policy adviser to the secretary of state on April 6, 1950. Truman appointed Foster in an effort to receive bipartisan support for his policy of containment of Communism in the Pacific. The appointment came at just the right time for Foster because he was between jobs. He had resigned from Sullivan and Cromwell to accept Dewey's appointment to the Senate in July of the previous year, but then he lost his campaign against Lehman in the special election four months later. He wrote *War or Peace* during the winter of 1949–1950 because he had not much else to do. Arthur Vandenberg came to Foster's rescue, recommending "the very able John Foster Dulles" to Acheson, noting that bringing Foster to the State Department would "restore some semblance of bipartisan unity at the water's edge."[30] Foster had already distinguished himself in negotiations on European issues, and Truman needed a Republican to assist with matters in Asia and the Pacific. And Foster was committed to bipartisanship, in principle. He wrote in *War or Peace* that the acrimony of the 1948 presidential election worried foreign governments, and it was essential for the United States to demonstrate a united front in foreign policy. "Everyone concedes that there must be a large measure of national unity to meet grave national peril from without," Foster wrote a few months prior to his appointment.[31] He wrote to Acheson to stress the necessity for unity to achieve victory over the Soviets. Characterizing the postwar situation as one of "grave peril" and one "more insidious than any our nation has yet faced," Foster said, "I hope and believe that traditional American good sense will reassert itself and that we shall find the . . . good spirit . . . needed to win the cold war and win the peace."[32] In a telegram responding to Foster, Acheson said, "I agree completely."[33]

Foster enjoyed the complete support of both President Truman and Secretary Acheson while he led the treaty negotiations, and in the words of historian Bernard C. Cohen, "his power often exceeded his responsibility."[34] During the negotiations, Foster spoke with the authority of the president overseas and the authority of the State Department at home. And having served as a United States senator, even for just a few months, Foster enjoyed the unique legitimacy of having been a member of one of the most exclusive "clubs" in the world. The network Foster cultivated in the Senate, with its constitutional power of treaty ratification, was of enormous value once the treaty with Japan went before that body for consideration in early 1952. Further, because Foster was so closely tied in with the Federal Council of Churches, he was in a position to muster popular support for the treaty by making many of his appeals from church pulpits around the country. In short, Truman and Acheson saw Foster as the most competent, well-positioned person in the United States for the task of leading the negotiations for the Japanese peace treaty and getting the American people behind it.

Memories of Versailles haunted Foster for decades. The failure of that treaty to ensure a lasting peace, and the failure of his own Reparations Commission to balance justice with mercy, had pounded in Foster's head like a dull headache ever since 1919. His references to those failures over thirty years were legion, and here was his chance to redeem what had been lost at Versailles. Foster wanted a simple and brief treaty with Japan, in contrast to the loquacious and florid 1919 settlement. He wanted Japanese sovereignty to be completely restored and Japan to be treated as an equal among equals. He sought no restrictions on the Japanese economy, military, political philosophy, or society. He had learned that a retributive peace that stripped the vanquished of their dignity and autonomy would birth another nightmare of militarism and expansionism, one that might subsume the world into another conflagration. Foster believed that a magnanimous peace seeking restoration and reconciliation in the spirit of Christianity was required to restore Japan and rebuild the countries that it ravaged. Most importantly, it would make Japan a powerful ally and a bulwark against Communism.

Security against Communism was Foster's primary goal. Bernard Cohen, in his study of Foster's work on the treaty from February 2, 1951, to February 18, 1952 (just prior to submission to the Senate for ratification), categorized the major themes that Foster referenced in his speeches. By far, "policy and security considerations" dominated Foster's rhetoric. Forty-seven percent of the 4,728 total lines of Foster's speeches about the treaty, both at home and abroad, were devoted to security. The next most prominent theme was "economic and financial considerations," which comprised only 11 percent of Foster's words.[35] Within the category of security, Cohen listed four subcategories of topics in order of prominence in Foster's speeches—"security in non-US areas," "threat from Soviet and Communist world," "collective security and alliances," and "Japanese sovereignty: effects on free world security."[36] Moral and military defense against Communism dominated Foster's perspective.

Foster made four trips to the Far East between the summer of 1950 and the end of 1951: in June 1950, January-February 1951, April 1951, and December 1951. On his first visit to Japan, Foster made a short trip to South Korea to consult with President Syngman Rhee, primarily to reassure him that the United States would not allow Japan to reoccupy Korea.[37] He was also given a tour of the South Korean defensive lines along the thirty-eighth parallel. One photo taken by a South Korean photographer on June 18, 1950, shows Foster peering across the boundary into North Korea through binoculars, surrounded by Republic of Korea army officers. North Korean artillery pulverized the spot where Foster stood prior to an infantry and armor assault of ninety thousand troops—eight divisions and an armored brigade—just seven days later.

Foster was in Tokyo when the North Koreans invaded South Korea. He wrote a top-secret memorandum in which he observed that the Japanese people were "shocked . . . into realization of the need of acceptance of United States defensive strength in Japan."[38] The Communist attack on South Korea thus amplified the nature of the threat that Foster believed emanated directly from Moscow. It underscored for him the fact that the "North Korean Reds . . . did not do this purely on their own but as a part of the world strategy of international communism," Foster said in an interview with CBS a few days after the invasion.[39] Most pertinently, Foster thought the North Koreans invaded in order to throw the peace negotiations into chaos and perhaps upset them altogether. If the Soviets could control the whole Korean peninsula, then the Communists could isolate Japan entirely with the help of the Chinese. "Japan would be between the upper and lower jaws of the Russian Bear," Foster said. It would be ripe fruit for the plucking.

Thus, at the start of the Korean War the moral imperative of securing a peace treaty in the interest of security was overwhelming to Foster. On October 23, 1950, Everett Case, president of Colgate University, convened a meeting of a study group of the Council on Foreign Relations to consider the problems inherent in a peace treaty. Case invited Foster to lead the meeting and also extended invitations to twenty-eight other people, including John Allison of the State Department; Arthur Dean of Sullivan and Cromwell; Herbert B. Elliston of the *Washington Post*; Joseph Grew, former American ambassador to Japan; and Henry P. Van Dusen of Union Theological Seminary. Foster gave a lengthy summary of his vision for the treaty, beginning with a clear statement of his two guiding principles. First, the late war needed to be formally concluded. Entailed in that goal, Japan had to be protected from Communist overthrow. Foster sought to shake the group out of its pre–World War II assumptions, namely, that Japan presented a threat to its neighbors in Asia and the Pacific. Yes, the treaty needed to prevent a recurrence of Japanese aggression, but Foster envisioned a treaty that would address the *post*-World War II situation. Thus, Foster's primary goal was "the prevention of the overpowering of the free world by the Soviet world."[40] The means by which this goal would be accomplished, Foster explained, was by providing for the end of the occupation and the complete evacuation of all American forces from the four Japanese home islands: Hokkaido, Honshu, Shikoku, and Kyushu. And assuming Japan would become a member of the United Nations, it would be responsible for contributing armed forces for international peacekeeping. Since the Japanese constitution (1947) prohibited the existence of its own military, Japan could invite the United States to maintain forces on its soil. This would achieve the purpose of preventing a "power vacuum" in Japan and would assuage any concerns, especially from Australia and New Zealand, of renewed Japanese aggression. Finally, the presence of American forces would be a powerful deterrent against any Communist invasion of Japan. "No attack could be made upon Japan without the certainty of becoming involved with the United States in a major war."[41] The Communists simply would not dare attack Japan with American troops in their path.

Of course, Foster's talking points to the Council on Foreign Relations in the fall of 1950 were purely academic. The Americans would have to convince the Japanese of the need for maintaining US forces in Japan after the occupation. Moreover, the Japanese would also have to be persuaded that the peace treaty itself would be necessary to Japanese security. Australia, New Zealand, the Philippines, Britain, and the forty-five other nations involved in the treaty discussions—including the Soviet Union—had their own conditions for the treaty. How would Foster address these disparate parties?

In Japan, Foster conferred with diplomats, members of the press, business figures, missionaries, leaders of each political party, labor unions, individual members of the National Diet, and delegates to the Far Eastern Commission (FEC)—the Soviet Union, the United Kingdom, the United States, China, France, the Netherlands, Canada, Australia, New Zealand, India, and the Philippines.[42] In one meeting with the Japanese press, Foster described his plan of convincing the Japanese government to invite US forces to provide a deterrent. He justified this by telling his hearers that countries like Britain in Western Europe already had cooperative security arrangements with the United States. "They want to have US troops and airplanes in Europe. . . . We have air forces in England today. . . . And I would think that the problem for Japan should be looked at the same way."[43] By February 1951, Japanese prime minister Shigeru Yoshida came around to Foster's position. He was persuaded that close and continued cooperation with the United States was necessary for Japan's future as a sovereign nation. In an address to the Diet, Yoshida said that it was impossible for Japan to stand alone against the Soviet and Chinese Communists and that he supported Foster's proposal for collective security. He said, "In conversations, Dulles' mission made known US willingness to provide us, if we want, armed assistance against outside attack. We conducted conversations on the premise that cooperative arrangement with US is the best practical solution under existing international situation and that this would be heartily welcomed by the great majority of people."[44] Katsuo Okazaki, Japan's chief cabinet secretary during peace negotiations, said that Yoshida, prior to the North Korean invasion of South Korea, had favored neutrality with security guaranteed by the UN. Seeing this was not a feasible option, Yoshida ultimately accepted Foster's proposal for American troops to return ninety days after the termination of the formal occupation. They were to serve as a deterrent force.[45]

Australia and New Zealand were concerned, first and foremost, with preventing Japan from ever again becoming a menace to their security. In an address to the Australian Institute of International Affairs in Sydney, Foster agreed that international security was the primary issue concerning the peace treaty. The real threat to security, though, was not Japan but Soviet designs on "the off-shore island chain which starts with the Aleutian Islands and runs on down through Japan, the Ryukyus, the Philippines, Australia, and New Zealand." In a striking anticipation of the famous domino theory of the 1950s and 1960s, Foster argued that every one of these islands formed an interdependent whole. "If any one major link in that chain were lost, it would make it almost impossible as a military matter . . . to hold the other links in the chain." If Japan fell to the Communists, the Soviets and the Chinese would use a Japanese conscript army to threaten Australia and New Zealand. If it required six years of effort for the Allies to defeat Japan by itself, Foster argued, imagine how difficult it would be to subdue a Japan occupied and controlled by millions of Soviet and Chinese soldiers. While Australia and New Zealand wanted Japan disarmed, Foster contended that forcing German disarmament was one of the great mistakes of Versailles. Versailles proved that forced disarmament only "produces the very evil that you want to correct." Security was the prime consideration in this treaty, Foster said, and the United States was committed to working out a cooperative arrangement for defense of Australia and New Zealand as part of the Japanese peace treaty.[46]

Whereas security was on the minds of the Australians and New Zealanders, reparations were the principal demand of the Philippines. Japan despoiled the Philippines in its five-year occupation. At a luncheon hosted by the Institute of Pacific Relations in Manila, Foster expressed sympathy with this demand. "That is natural and inevitable, and certainly every consideration of justice and equity calls aloud for the maximum possible reparations for the terrible wrongs that have been committed here." But, Foster said, Versailles taught bitter lessons about reparations. The French had a just claim to massive reparations against Germany, which had invaded and occupied northern France during World War I, but Germany was too devastated itself to pay. Foster told his Filipino audience that they reminded him of the French in 1919—"the feeling of the French in those days was very much akin to the feeling which I find here today, and for the same reason." But the fact was, as Foster explained, if the treaty required Japan to pay reparations, that nation would fall to the Communists. Foster thought Communism represented an unprecedented menace, one that had to be contained and ultimately rolled back. What was more for Foster, the Soviets wanted nothing more than to absorb the industrial power of Germany and Japan. With that power, Foster said, "that combination of Russia, Communist China, plus Japan and Germany, would then be in a position to dominate the rest of the world and carry out the program of world conquest which was outlined by Stalin some 25 years ago." Foster called on the Philippines—largely on the basis of fear—to work alongside the United States to find just solutions for themselves and the Japanese that would effectively correct the wrongs of the past war and prevent a third world war from occurring. And lest Filipinos get the idea "that we love Japan more than we love the Philippines," Foster pleaded with his audience to remember that America considered the Philippines among its closest friends. The Philippines, after all, had been a US colony, liberated by the Americans and given its independence in 1946.[47]

The Soviets made numerous charges of hypocrisy and faithlessness against the United States. Foster provided James Reston of the *New York Times* written responses to each of the Soviets' nine specific charges. The first charge was that the United States had cut the Soviet Union out of all the treaty negotiations. Foster replied that he had consulted regularly with Yokov Malik, the deputy minister of foreign affairs, from October 1950 to January 1951 and that the Soviets had been supplied with treaty drafts with the invitation to provide comments. The Soviets did provide written comments, and the Americans replied between May and July 1951. "The Soviet Union," Foster remarked, "cannot deny 'participation' in the treaty-making process except by reversing the usual sense of words." The Soviets also objected to the process by which the treaty negotiations took place. Instead of being produced through the collaboration of the CFM, it was pursued through a series of bilateral talks between the United States and Japan. False, Foster said. "There was never any agreement to negotiate the Japanese peace treaty through the Council of Foreign Ministers." The Soviets had tried to get the treaty negotiated through the council, but the United States was unwilling to allow them to stymie the negotiations by persistently applying their veto power, as they were doing in the treaty negotiations concerning Austria and Germany. And among the other charges, the Soviets complained that the United States cut the Chinese Communists out of participation. But since Mao's China was nothing more than a puppet of Soviet Russia, Foster replied, that nation did not represent legitimate Chinese ideas. Furthermore, the United Nations regarded Communist China as an aggressor, and if Chinese interests were going to be represented, then "a Chinese Government which is peacefully disposed" ought to be the one participating in negotiation.[48] Foster simply waved off each of the Soviet protestations as illegitimate and absurd.

On September 8, 1951, forty-nine countries signed the Treaty of San Francisco with Japan. In addition to the peace treaty, security treaties were concluded between the United States, Australia, and New Zealand (the ANZUS alliance); the United States and Japan; and the United States and the Philippines. President Truman submitted these treaties to the Senate on January 10, 1952, for ratification. The four treaties were designed to be interdependent, in that the ultimate goal for each one was security for the nations in the Pacific, regarded strategically as the western American frontier. The four treaties together provided interlocking defense arrangements that established a network of collective security against Communist aggression, whether that aggression took direct form, such as invasion, or indirect form, such as infiltration. The peace treaty restored complete sovereignty to Japan; it defined its sovereign territory and allowed for United States forces to be hosted at the invitation of Japan after the end of the occupation. It also released Japanese prisoners of war, freed Japan from all restrictions on trade and commerce, and opened up formal relations between Japan and the Republic of Korea. On the issue of reparations, the treaty called for an arrangement whereby the Allied countries hurt by the war would send raw materials to Japan for processing into manufactured goods. In this way, just reparations could be attempted in a manner that Japan had the ability to discharge. Finally, with regard to Japan's relations with China, Japan agreed to renounce all claims and interests in China and was given leave to conclude a separate treaty of peace with that nation. Of course, by "China," the treaty meant "China as one of the Allied victors in the war,"[49] that is, Nationalist China. Foster acknowledged that the treaty was not perfect, but he hailed it as an unprecedented example of unity to fulfill the goal of a just and enduring peace.

The Senate Committee on Foreign Relations held hearings on the treaties between January 21 and 25, 1952. In his statement to the committee, Foster grounded his negotiating efforts on six premises: (1) Japan needed the community of free nations, (2) the community of free nations needed

Japan, (3) freedom was essential to Japan, (4) Japan was trustworthy and ready to be welcomed into the community of free nations, (5) Americans must have faith in freedom, and (6) the United States must clearly articulate its concern for the Pacific region. "The community of free nations needs to deny to the Soviet Union the chance to use Japan for evil and it needs for itself Japan's great capability for good," Foster said. Furthermore, Foster testified, if Japan and the free community were to live together and benefit from one another, Japan had to be free. It certainly had to be free from Soviet domination, but it also had to be free from American occupation. And Foster insisted that "Monroe Doctrine language" ought to be used with reference to the nations of the Pacific. The peace treaty with Japan and the Pacific security treaties, as part and parcel with one another, served "to liquidate the old war" and "to strengthen the fabric of peace in the Pacific as against the hazard of a new war."[50]

At the San Francisco Conference, in which all the peace delegates from the countries party to the treaty gathered, Foster was delighted with how the Soviets responded to the proceedings. When asked whether he thought the Soviets experienced a "diplomatic defeat" at the conference, Foster said that "it was a much broader defeat" than merely diplomatic. For Foster, the Soviets experienced "a great moral defeat."[51] While they tried to obstruct the signing of the treaty, they utterly failed. The unity among the delegations, Foster insisted, was what ultimately stymied Communist efforts to undermine the conference. And this unity was certainly obvious to others besides Foster. Delegates from the Latin American countries that had declared war on Japan wrote to Foster and praised him for promoting such unity. Rafael de la Colina of Mexico thanked Foster for the chance "to have cooperated with you . . . in this historic undertaking." Guillermo Sevilla Sacasa of Nicaragua expressed his appreciation that the conference exemplified his life's vision of promoting "the unity of our American States." J. E. Valenzuela of Honduras hailed the significance of "the unity of the American States." And Felix Nieto del Rio of Chile committed his nation to "the continuance and strengthening of that unity as a contribution to a peaceful world."[52] The unity that Foster achieved was indeed remarkable, and it resulted in one of the greatest achievements of durable peace and security in American history. The Senate ratified the treaty on March 20, 1952, and President Truman signed it into law on April 15, 1952.

An article Foster wrote for the *Christian Century*, entitled "A Diplomat and His Faith," was published the day before Senate ratification took place. In it, he reflected on the treaty's achievement and on how he saw the Christian dimensions of the treaty. He had learned important lessons from the failure of Versailles to establish a real and lasting peace. "As one who had had close contact with the making, and then the unmaking, of the Treaty of Versailles, I realized how undependable was a peace treaty that was discriminatory, that had to be forcibly imposed and that gave expression to the evil passions which war leaves in its aftermath." He wrote that he drew his inspiration from the "Statement of Guiding Principles" adopted by the Commission for a Just and Durable Peace in 1942. Specifically, the statement's stress on the universality of the moral law inspired him most as he negotiated the treaty, as well as the "special responsibility that devolved upon the United States to bring international relations into conformity with that moral law." Japan had been a bitter foe during the war, but the war was over. The time for forgiveness and reconciliation was at hand, and Christian nations were duty bound to extend the hand of friendship to a former foe once the fighting had ceased. "So we drafted a treaty which invoked the spirit of forgiveness to overcome the spirit of vengefulness; the spirit of magnanimity to overcome the spirit of hatred; the spirit of humanity and fair play to overcome the spirit of competitive greed; the spirit of fellowship to overcome the spirit of arrogance and discrimination; and the spirit of trust to overcome the spirit of fear." This treaty was the culmination of everything Foster had been working on with regard to war, peace, internationalism, and the role of the churches for thirty years.[53]

But Foster did not mention a powerful foil to this narrative that appeared just one day after his testimony before the Foreign Relations Committee. The Presbyterian clergyman A. J. Muste testified against the treaty on behalf of a national pacifist organization called the Fellowship of Reconciliation. Muste called the treaty a "fraud." Since the United States would be stationing forces in Japan for the indefinite future, how could it be said that Japan was no longer an occupied country? Furthermore, the presence of American forces violated the Japanese constitution, since that constitution banned armed forces. Muste contended that the American presence in Japan would only deepen the resentment of Pacific peoples, as they would experience yet another form of Western imperialism in effect, which would only drive them closer to the Soviets. Muste called for the United States, coincidentally enough, to resist relying on material weapons for security and look to the "spiritual forces" of nonviolence as taught by Gandhi. If we do not "mind our own business," Muste urged, "we shall run the risk . . . of committing suicide in order to prevent Russia from killing us."[54] Curiously, much of what Muste said in his testimony resembled the "prophetic realism" that Foster articulated in his earlier days, and served as a blunt contrast with the later Foster.

Foster displayed a remarkable consistency in applying the moral law to the Japanese peace treaty in addresses he gave to audiences in the United States and abroad during the period from 1950 to 1952. Indeed, Foster's references to the moral law occurred regularly in all his speeches and writings going back to 1935. A palpable change took place, however, when Foster eventually applied the moral law to the "community of free nations" and considered the Communist nations, having denied the existence of that law, as outside its reach. The universality of unity and peace that Foster championed prior to 1946 was largely gone by 1952. Universal ideals were important to Foster, but after 1950, he universalized defense and security rather than peace. He did this to arrive at a future goal of universal peace and human freedom that could only be attained once Communism no longer posed a threat to those ideals.

7

"A Faith Linked with the Pursuit of Justice"
(1953–1959)

[John Foster Dulles] saw the necessity for a faith linked with
the pursuit of justice—a faith even more dynamic than the
evil faiths represented by the totalitarian systems of his day.

—Avery Dulles, SJ[1]

On December 16, 1950, President Truman issued Presidential Proclamation 2914, entitled "Proclaiming the Existence of a National Emergency." North Korea had invaded South Korea the previous June. UN troops
under American command counterattacked, and by late November they
had advanced almost to the Yalu River, the frontier dividing North Korea
from China. Victory was at hand until 300,000 Chinese troops attacked
all along the UN front on November 26. By the middle of December, UN
forces had been driven back into South Korea, dashing American hopes
for a conclusive victory over the Communists by Christmas. "I summon
all citizens to make a united effort for the security and well-being of our
beloved country and to place its needs foremost in thought and action
that the full moral and material strength of the Nation may be readied
for the dangers which threaten us," Truman's proclamation stated.[2] In this
context, Truman issued Presidential Proclamation 3004 two years later,
on January 27, 1953, entitled "Control of Persons Leaving or Entering the
United States." Building on Proclamation 2914, Truman laid down rules
for American citizens and noncitizens traveling in and out of the United
States. Specifically, citizens coming and going from the United States "shall

be subject to the regulations prescribed by the Secretary of State" and "the Secretary of State is hereby authorized to revoke, modify, or amend such regulations as he may find the interests of the United States to require."[3] Four days after Proclamation 3004 was issued, John Foster Dulles took office as the fifty-second United States secretary of state. In the context of the ongoing Red Scare led by Senator Joseph McCarthy, Proclamation 3004 was potent stuff.

As secretary of state, Foster took steps to deny passports to American citizens who were Communists on the basis of these two proclamations. He also did so in accordance with two acts of Congress, the Passport Act of 1926 and the Immigration and Nationality Act of 1952. Numerous citizens were affected, including African American historian and civil rights activist W. E. B. Du Bois. Du Bois was denied a passport by the State Department due to his Communist sympathies. He addressed a letter directly to Foster on February 22, 1957, requesting passports for his wife, Shirley, and himself to travel to Ghana to celebrate its independence from Britain upon the invitation of the new prime minister, Kwame Nkrumah. Du Bois wrote, "three times since 1952, I have been refused the right to travel with no specific charges, but with the apparent assumption that because I differ with dominant American opinion, in some respects I have therefore no right to travel, speak or think. These rights I have always regarded as the fundamental rights of a 'free democracy' which you continually call the United States."[4]

In 1958, the Supreme Court handed down a decision consistent with Du Bois's argument. Like Du Bois, an artist named Rockwell Kent, an alleged member of the Los Angeles County Communist Party, had been repeatedly denied passports for travel to Europe during the early 1950s. Associate Justice William O. Douglas wrote the majority opinion, arguing that citizens could not be denied freedom of travel on the basis of their convictions. To him, "the right to travel is a part of the 'liberty' of which a citizen cannot be deprived without due process of law under the Fifth Amendment."[5] Specifically, the Court decided that the secretary of state did not have the authority to refuse to issue passports to Communists. The case was *Kent v. Dulles*. The vote was close—five to four. It was decided on June 16, 1958. Eleven months later, John Foster Dulles was dead.

This case illustrates Foster's exquisite consistency regarding his anti-Communist beliefs. Not only was he committed to the containment, and ultimately the defeat, of Communism abroad, he was also the enemy of Communism at home. Throughout the 1950s, Foster argued that Communism was a faith system, albeit atheistic, just as Christianity and the other major religions of the world were faith systems. But Communism was at war against theistic faith and freedom, which Foster believed were rooted in the moral law and sacred human dignity. Because Communism was antithetical to freedom, the moral law, and human dignity, it was an affront to God. Foster was committed to an all-out defense of these values as integral to the American spiritual heritage, and he believed that Communism could not prevail over them in the final analysis. His actions as secretary of state, actions that bore on both foreign and domestic policy, bear witness to the sincerity of Foster's commitment and his determination to carry it through regardless of impediments or difficulties. In fact, Foster believed that it was America's responsibility to lead the free world in defense of the moral law wherever Communism threatened it. But Foster's life ended before he could complete his tenure as secretary of state during the second term of the Eisenhower administration. He died of abdominal cancer on May 24, 1959, at age seventy-one.

The trajectory of Foster's life demonstrates that he was a man of complexity. While he suffered no unusual tragedies during the course of his life, and though he enjoyed the privileges of wealth, a powerful support network, and the singular opportunities that attended those privileges, Foster has remained a person notoriously difficult for historians to pinpoint. The keenest historian of Foster's diplomacy, Richard H. Immerman, described Foster as "an extremely elusive subject."[6] This book is a religious biography: it has offered consideration of Foster's fundamental beliefs as they evolved (or even "transformed") and as they remained constant throughout his lifetime. One of Foster's most cherished and unchanging commitments was to the concept of freedom based on human dignity. He was first exposed to the concept of human freedom in a political context through his grandfather Foster, and in a religious context through his father, Allen Macy. Foster applied this concept to the reparations problem after World War I, contending for freedom of the seas, free movement of trade and people, and lenient and realistic reparation payments for Germany. He also championed freedom of thought during the Presbyterian controversy between 1923 and 1925, specifically in the cases involving Fosdick and Van Dusen. He carried this commitment through his work with the FCC during World War II, the creation of the UN Charter, and in leading negotiations for the finalizing of the Japanese peace treaty. Foster's virulent anti-Communism was rooted in a lifelong commitment to freedom, and he sought to defend freedom against what he saw as its greatest threat. Furthermore, he saw the United States as the only nation with the necessary material and moral strength to confront Communism; a strength sourced in a Christian heritage defined by what his father described as "evangelic," or free, as opposed to "Catholic," or hierarchical and tyrannical. Toulouse was correct in assessing Foster as a changed man between 1937 and 1950. But Foster was actually more consistent than Toulouse gave him credit for during this period, despite the changes Toulouse correctly identified and tracked in his biography. Foster's concept and application of the moral law underwent a transformation, to be sure. But Foster's belief in the concepts of the moral law, freedom, and the American way of life was deeply rooted. For him, if they were worth having, they were worth defending. And the cost of defending those good things reflected their value.

Foster became secretary of state on January 21, 1953, after an easy Senate confirmation. Cancer compelled him to lay down his duties on April 22, 1959. His activities during those six years and three months were the most consequential of his entire life. A book-length study is required to offer a mature account of Foster's years as secretary of state, and indeed many excellent diplomatic histories treat various features of his career under Eisenhower's presidency.[7] It is beyond the scope of this book to explore those features. In what remains, I will confine myself to a contextual examination of Foster as a religious man, and as someone whose beliefs defined him even though those beliefs are best characterized, in a way that Foster himself might endorse, as dynamic.

Dwight Eisenhower first met Foster in 1949 while he was president of Columbia University. They met again in May 1952, and Eisenhower found that they initially hit it off on the need for the United States to resist isolationism and to establish networks of collective security around the world. By the beginning of June, Eisenhower was impressed enough with Foster to say to him, "Well, you're the kind of man that I'd like to see as Secretary of State."[8] Eisenhower admired Foster for his sincerity and his expertise. Richard Nixon, who served as vice president under Eisenhower, believed that Eisenhower relied fully on Foster with regard to foreign policy. As early as August 1952, just weeks after the Republican National Convention had concluded, Eisenhower leaned heavily on Foster for his counsel on foreign policy. From that time, Nixon assumed that Eisenhower, if elected, would nominate Foster as secretary of state, and he did. "There was no question but that Eisenhower, in his own mind, relied on Dulles more than anybody else at that point. I just assumed he would be the man," Nixon recalled in 1965.[9] It took time for the two men to develop a basis of complete trust and affinity. But on looking back on their professional and personal relationship, Eisenhower remembered how devastated he was when Foster died. He described his deep satisfaction in working with Foster, and that his trust in Foster was complete. Furthermore, Eisenhower recognized early on in the relationship how much Foster wanted to head the State Department. When the chief justice of the Supreme Court, Fred Vinson, died in September 1953—only eight months into his first term—Eisenhower offered to nominate Foster to the bench to serve as chief justice, promoting him out of the State Department. Foster, according to Eisenhower, did not hesitate to turn down his offer. "My entire interest is in the job I have," Foster told Eisenhower. "As long as I am satisfying you there, I don't want any other governmental job."[10]

Foster's religious faith informed a wide range of his foreign policy positions during his secretaryship, but three are important for our purposes here: the "liberation" of Communist-held regions, "massive retaliation," and "brinkmanship." None of these policies, for Foster, were isolated from each other. They were explicitly part of the grand strategy embraced by the Eisenhower administration known as "New Look" by 1955. New Look was a strategy for meeting the Communist threat wherever and however it appeared in the world. Foster applied these policies to the salient crises of the Eisenhower years in the Middle East, Indochina, Formosa, Europe, and Latin America. They were controversial and helped set Foster up for criticism—much of it quite fair—for being an American imperialist, a nuclear warmonger, and a paper tiger. These positions stemmed primarily from religious, not political, convictions.

Liberation

As Foster prepared for the presidential election in 1952, he crafted a critique of the Truman administration policy of containment and advocated for a new policy of liberation. Under the Truman Doctrine and the Marshall Plan (inspired by Kennan's "Long Telegram"), the United States provided billions of dollars in economic aid and technical support to non-Soviet-dominated European countries in an effort to prevent Communist takeover. The United States was, in effect, taking responsibility for the rebuilding of Europe, and it was a brilliant strategic move against Stalin. Though Stalin was offered aid through the Marshall Plan, he refused it and also forbade all countries in Eastern Europe under his control from accepting any aid. Gaddis wrote, "Stalin fell into the trap the Marshall Plan laid for him, which was to get *him* to build the wall that would divide Europe."[11]

Despite the brilliant success of the containment strategy in Europe, it was a failure in Asia. Communism was not contained within the borders of the Soviet Union in the East. China fell to the Communists in 1949, and North Korea was not deterred from attacking South Korea in 1950. The UN attempt to liberate the Korean peninsula from Communism in late 1950 failed when the Chinese intervened and reconquered the North. By 1952, Foster believed the inherent problem with containment was that it sought to maintain the status quo in the face of dynamic change—an idea he had been promulgating for almost twenty years. Furthermore, containment was immoral, because it signaled to Soviet-dominated countries that America was ambivalent about their future and that they would never be free.

In a May 19, 1952, piece in *Life* entitled "A New Foreign Policy: A Policy of Boldness," Foster pointed out the irony that those most committed to human freedom were also most committed to political stasis. Moral forces were more powerful than material forces; the dynamic prevailed over the static; and "there is a moral or natural law not made by man which determines right and wrong," Foster asserted. Foster predicated his entire piece on this statement: "We should let these truths work in and through us. We should be *dynamic*, we should use *ideas* as weapons; and these ideas should conform to *moral* principles." If Americans followed this counsel, then containment and stalemate would give way to liberation. But Foster was careful to stress that this liberation would be peaceful. It would take place through the dissemination of ideas and moral example. "We can be confident," Foster wrote, "that within two, five or 10 years substantial parts of the present captive world can peacefully regain national independence."[12]

At his Senate confirmation hearing in January 1953, Foster restated these ideas. When asked what his vision was for American foreign policy, Foster maintained that containment was merely defensive and no victory was ever gained through defensive strategies alone. "It is only by keeping alive the hope of liberation . . . that we will end this terrible peril which dominates the world." Still, Foster quickly added, liberation did not entail violent means. Liberation would be effected through ideas and moral example. Foster called upon Abraham Lincoln's belief that the principles of the Declaration of Independence were not for Americans only but for all of humanity.[13] Toward the end of his tenure as secretary of state, Foster seemed to content himself with a containment policy in all but name. But his pronouncements about freedom and moral law continued to flow.

Massive Retaliation

As early as 1951, in the midst of crafting the Japanese peace treaty, Foster was developing the foreign policy strategy that came to define his career as secretary of state—what was popularly known as "massive retaliation." The principle behind this ominous-sounding phrase was simple—deterrence against aggression. In Foster's address to the American-Japan Society in Tokyo in February of 1951, he drew an analogy between securing personal goods in a home and security on a national level. Communities created police forces to deter crime. While police officers were not stationed at every individual home, criminals would think twice before invading someone's home because, as Foster put it, "the likelihood of failure is a deterrent to aggression." Nations were duty bound to protect their liberties, Foster said. The way to protect liberty from the Communists was to construct a network of collective security so powerful that no aggressor would dare challenge it. "An armed aggressor would be subjected to a striking power," Foster explained, "the immensity of which defies imagination."[14] The collective security arrangements entered into by the United States, the Philippines, Japan, Australia, and New Zealand were the culmination of this vision as Foster presented it in 1951.

Foster continued to develop the idea in his *Life* piece from May 1952, "A New Foreign Policy: A Policy of Boldness," in which he called for peaceful liberation of Communist-dominated countries. Foster argued that the

United States was, materially, the most powerful nation in the world. But one thing it lacked—faith in human liberty. Such faith Americans ought to recover, Foster believed. The free world held the moral high ground, because freedom sprung from the moral law and was thus invincible. "The free should not be numbed by . . . this vast graveyard of human liberties" in Russia, Eastern Europe, and Asia, Foster contended. "It is the despots who should feel haunted. They, not we, should fear the future."[15] And even in the face of the threat of vast Soviet and Chinese armies, numbering well into the millions, the free world need not be daunted. Rather, it should establish the will to "retaliate instantly against open aggression by Red armies, so that, if it occurred anywhere, we could and would strike back where it hurts, by means of our own choosing," Foster said.[16] The free world already possessed the material means to face and defeat Communist aggression. What it lacked was the spiritual determination to defend human liberty, which was founded on a dynamic faith in the moral law.

These early statements served as prototypes of Foster's deterrent strategy of massive retaliation based on collective security. But by the beginning of 1954, Foster occupied the most important post in the American Foreign Service, and arguably the most powerful post of its kind in the world. He was no longer a mere ambassador, nor was he just a thought leader. He played a principal role in making American foreign policy and carrying it through to completion when possible. So when Foster put his ideas forth from his lofty position of United States secretary of state, the effects were exponentially more consequential than when he was working for the FCC, or even when he was negotiating the Japanese peace treaty.

On January 12, 1954, before the Council on Foreign Relations, Foster outlined a summary of the Eisenhower administration's overall approach to foreign policy. The problem with foreign policy under Truman was that the United States only reacted to the actions taken by the Soviet Union. There was no long-term goal in the minds of Truman-era policy makers. But the Communists, said Foster, had long-term goals. They were patiently taking small steps, barely noticeable, to aggravate divisions between the Allied nations and weaken those nations by inflicting pressure at multiple points in the world, forcing them to spread out their resources. The answer to Soviet long-range policy that promoted the expansion of tyranny was to promote the defense, and the ultimate expansion, of liberty. That answer came in the form of collective security. Collective security differed from local defense forces, which were too weak to withstand the might of Soviet or Chinese armies. When the free nations combined their strength, the result was "a maximum deterrent at a bearable cost." Local defenses, Foster said, were important, but they were no match for Communist aggression. They "must be reinforced by the further deterrent of massive retaliatory power," Foster argued. Such power would have the ability to strike offensively at times and places of its own choosing, and this was the critical factor. Foster informed his audience that the president and the National Security Council had already made policy decisions putting this deterrent strategy in place. "Now the Department of Defense and the Joint Chiefs of Staff can shape our military establishment to fit what is our policy, instead of having to try and be ready to meet the enemy's many choices," Foster said. Thus, even if setbacks were to occur, their effects would be mitigated. And most importantly, "massive retaliation" was meant to correct the mistake of "containment," in that it meant establishing an offensive posture to advance liberty rather than a defensive one that merely sought to maintain the status quo. Foster stressed that freedom built a spiritually, intellectually, and materially rich heritage. Thus, Foster said, "we intend that our conduct and example shall continue . . . to show all men how good can be the fruits of freedom."[17]

As it turned out, the main problem with massive retaliation was its application. The primary deterrent in America's arsenal was, of course, atomic weapons. And on November 1, 1952, the United States exploded its first thermonuclear device, a fusion bomb code-named Ivy Mike, with a 10-megaton yield, many hundreds of times more powerful than the Hiroshima bomb. The Soviets detonated their own hydrogen bomb the following year, on August 12, 1953. Under what circumstances could such devastating weapons be used, when it was obvious that widespread use of fission and fusion devices in warfare would render the planet uninhabitable? The impracticality of nuclear weapons in limited wars such as Korea and Vietnam became clear, and in the absence of those weapons, the efficacy of deterrence was mitigated. Yet, for the very reason of their fearsomeness, nuclear weapons were useful in preventing total war. Gaddis wrote that Eisenhower "insisted on planning *only* for total war. His purpose was to make sure that no war at all would take place."[18]

Brinkmanship

James Shepley, the chief of the Time-Life Washington Bureau, penned an article in January 1956 entitled "How Dulles Averted War." Shepley set out to show how Foster's strategy of deterrence—"massive retaliation"—was working. "In the conduct of his office," Shepley wrote, "Dulles not only radically revised the 'containment' policy of the Truman administration but also altered drastically the basic concept of the job of Secretary of State."[19] In short, Shepley wrote that Foster prevented a third world war in Korea (1953), in Indochina at Dien Bien Phu (1954), and in the Formosan Straits, specifically at two tiny Nationalist outposts on the islands of Quemoy and Matsu (1954–1955). In each of these three instances, Shepley maintained, the Russians and the Chinese knew that they had more to lose than to gain if they attempted to force the return of Communist POWs to North Korea or China in 1953, tried to invade and conquer all of Southeast Asia in 1954, or reached for Formosa in 1954–1955. "Deterrence, as practiced by Dulles, has not only prevented the 'big' hydrogen war but the littler wars as well," Shepley claimed.[20]

Shepley interviewed Foster to get his thoughts on the success of massive retaliation. Foster said the risk of war was unavoidable. There would always be risk of war in the pursuit of peace, Foster said. Then he made one of the most controversial statements of his career. "Some say that we were brought to the verge of war. Of course we were brought to the verge of war. The ability to get to the verge without getting into war is the necessary art. If you cannot master it, you inevitably get into war. If you try to run away from it, if you are scared to go to the brink, you are lost. . . . We walked to the brink and we looked it in the face."[21]

The day after the Shepley piece ran on January 16, Foster called a press conference to clarify his meaning. The statement created enduring controversy, and his January 17 press conference did not allay widespread perception that Foster was, in a word, crazy. Some of the criticisms were withering. Herblock, a syndicated cartoonist for the *Washington Post*, sketched a depiction of a chubby Foster dressed in a Superman costume, shoving a panicky and unwilling Uncle Sam over a cliff, telling him, "Don't be afraid, I can always pull you back." Adlai Stevenson, the 1952 and 1956 Democratic nominee for president, attacked Foster for "boasting of his brinkmanship—

the art of bringing us to the edge of the nuclear abyss."[22] Nevertheless, Foster tried to explain himself by reverting to a familiar theme: "I believe . . . that there are basic moral values and vital interests, for which we stand, and that the surest way to avoid war is to let it be known in advance that we are prepared to defend these principles, if need be by life itself."[23] Foster was, if nothing else, consistent.

No one who knew Foster in his FCC days, between 1937 and 1945, could fail to notice a change in the man who crafted and championed the Six Pillars of Peace and was now advocating for "massive retaliation" and "brinkmanship." When Foster became secretary of state, he disassociated himself with all official involvement in the ecumenical movement, just as he did with Sullivan and Cromwell. But he kept his friends, and sometime in 1954—the records are unclear as to exactly when—Foster hosted a dinner and conversation with his former FCC friends and colleagues at his home in Georgetown. It had all the makings of a reunion. Attending was Fred Nolde, who collaborated with Foster on the 1942 Cleveland Conference and the 1943 International Roundtable in Princeton. Also attending was Roswell Barnes, one of Foster's closest friends, who would ultimately preside over Foster's funeral. Retired Harvard philosopher William Hocking was present, along with Samuel M. Cavert, who was instrumental in forming the National Council of Churches out of the old Federal Council. John Mackay, president of Princeton Theological Seminary, was also in attendance, along with Walter Van Kirk, who helped arrange the meeting.

The men had dinner and then retired to Foster's study for a conversation that lasted several hours. Foster missed his old friends, and the feeling was mutual. Several of them, however, felt more than the distance of time and circumstances separating them. Cavert certainly did. After Foster's death, Cavert said that he had changed so much that by the 1950s he hardly recognized him from the man he knew in the 1930s and 1940s.[24] Mackay went further, confronting Foster head-on about his rhetoric of massive retaliation. "It seems to me, Mr. Dulles," said Mackay, "that there are cases in which the threat of massive retaliation will prove to be quite futile and will not achieve the objective for which it was designed." Mackay believed that the Chinese, for example, were prepared to sustain tremendous losses in order to achieve their ambitions and would not be deterred even by atomic weapons. His primary concern was that massive retaliation went against

Christian principles, particularly those advanced at the 1937 Oxford Conference, at which Mackay led the session in which Foster presented his paper,
"The Problem of Peace in a Dynamic World." Mackay believed that negotiation and face-to-face interaction were the surest way to achieve stability
in the world, and that Foster had also once believed that. "I cannot but feel
that in this, Mr. Dulles was not really true to his deepest self and to insights
which he had formerly expressed, but that he became . . . responsible for a
kind of foreign policy which has not been creative or constructive . . . and
which must be rethought."[25]

Mackay was not willing to grant Foster any consideration regarding the
different roles he occupied at the State Department and with the FCC. But
interestingly enough, both Cavert and Nolde conceded later that Foster,
unlike themselves, did not have the luxury to merely theorize concerning
diplomacy in the nuclear age. Cavert, even after expressing disappointment
and perplexity over Foster, admitted that his role was far different than the
one he filled as chairman of the Commission for a Just and Durable Peace.
Nolde took a different view of Foster's shift altogether. Whatever criticisms
he may have had at the meeting, he kept them to himself. Reflecting on that
meeting years later in 1965, Nolde blamed the Communists for stubborn-
ness and sympathized with Foster in having to deal with them. He also sympathized with Foster because he thought Foster was misunderstood with
regard to massive retaliation and brinkmanship. Nobody, observed Nolde,
accused John F. Kennedy of brinkmanship during the 1962 Cuban missile
crisis. "I think that in seeking to explain what was an obvious difference
in public posture between Dulles in the 'forties and Dulles while Secretary
of State, this factor has to be taken into account—I mean the factor of la-
bels, descriptives, misunderstanding, and also the factor . . . of the man in
power who has the responsibility and can't take as many chances."[26] While
Foster's former FCC colleagues recognized that changes had occurred in
his thinking, they differed on whether or not Foster was justified in making
the changes. Cavert and Mackay held views similar to Toulouse's analysis,
that Foster had "transformed" from a "prophet of realism" to a "priest of
nationalism." Nolde was more nuanced in his understanding of Foster's
position. Still, Nolde, Mackay, and Cavert all agreed on one aspect of that
dinner with Foster: he was a gracious host, heard everyone voice all their
concerns, was open to adjusting some of his own views, and did not attempt

to convince anyone in the group to come to his side of issues. In other words, he was open to their concerns and invited their candor. None of his guests expressed surprise that Foster was open to criticism. This was the Foster they had always known.

Foster consistently carried his commitment to the moral law through the early Cold War, even though his application of that commitment had changed. It differed because the circumstances differed, and because his role was not that of theorist but of policy maker. His decisions prior to 1945 affected few outside his circle of influence, but those he made after 1953 had consequences that could determine whether human life continued or not. He did universalize security, but not for security's sake. He saw collective security as indispensable to peace. "Peace is not just the drab business of seeking security. Peace is a positive and creative state which can and should enrich the life of every individual, of every nation and of the whole society of nations," Foster said to the American-Japan Society in 1951, as he was out-maneuvering the Soviets on the Japanese peace treaty. But peace would have to be won, just as wars were won. It would take titanic effort and profound sacrifice. It would involve material and moral weapons. And the United States was, in fact, the only nation with the resources and credibility to lead the free world in the pursuit of peace, as Foster understood it. While Foster was working to confront the new challenges of the postwar world, some of his former FCC colleagues like Mackay and Cavert were still operating under prewar presuppositions. The inexorable logic of Mackay's point of view, for example, would have led to what A. J. Muste proposed as he testi-fied against the Japanese peace treaty in 1952—total American withdrawal premised on absolute nonviolence. During the 1950s, Foster feared that the Soviets would move to isolate the United States and ultimately destroy it. His fears were based on careful study of Soviet Communism under Stalin, Soviet and Chinese actions in Europe and Asia, and other sources such as Kennan's "Long Telegram" that were widely accepted as credible at the time. For Foster, withdrawal and disarmament in the face of such a threat were tantamount to national suicide. It was simply out of the question.

Foster warned against nationalism that deified the state in his 1937 book *War, Peace, and Change.* During the 1950s he frequently asserted Amer-ican indispensability, because it was uniquely founded on transcendent ideas. But Foster did not believe that American ideals were for the benefit of Americans alone. When he extolled the founders and their ideals, he hastened to add that the founders wanted those ideals shared, not self-ishly hoarded. He said the founders "created here a society of material, intellectual, and spiritual richness the like of which the world had never known. It was not selfishly designed, but for ourselves and others."[27] That is why Foster rebuked those who sought to return to an isolationist for-eign policy after World War II, represented in particular by conservative Republican senator Robert Taft of Ohio. Foster was susceptible to error, to moral compromise, and to national arrogance. He was willing to give Iran and Guatemala over to authoritarian regimes, for example. He believed that authoritarian regimes in the American orbit were much to be preferred over totalitarian Communist regimes that the Soviets could use as a base to attack or destabilize the United States or its allies. As secretary of state, Foster no longer functioned as a churchman. He functioned as the chief diplomat of the United States, and as such, he believed his first duty was to defend American interests, allies, and ideals when he perceived they were threatened by Communist aggression. Not all his actions resulted in free-dom and human dignity for everyone in the world, but he strove to protect and advance those ideals with the resources and knowledge he had. His detractors saw Foster as rigid, but he took comfort in the fact that he did not make decisions based on whether or not they would be popular.

What remained constant in Foster's beliefs? His love of Lake Ontario, his attraction to the natural world, and the connection he saw between the dynamics of natural forces and those of human relationships. A year before his death, in the early summer of 1958, Foster went to his friend Bob Hart to see if he might organize a sailing trip. Hart spoke to Bob Purcell, an old friend of Foster's who owned a thirty-five-foot sailboat on Lake Ontario. Purcell was president of a Wall Street investment trust organization named Investors Diversified Services. Hart and Purcell had known each other from active sailing on the lake as early as the 1920s. The three of them, joined by Art Eldredge, another of Foster's old sailing buddies, took a nine-day cruise on Lake Ontario surrounding the Labor Day weekend. The Chinese had begun to shell Quemoy and Matsu, as they had done in 1954. But Foster received permission from Eisenhower to continue with his trip, so they proceeded on. Foster was completely cut off from communication with Washington for most of those nine days, and Purcell described him as totally relaxed. They sailed in rough weather, which Foster relished; they ate like kings; they swam in the freezing water; and they carried out five-and ten-cent bets on trivial details like the weather, activities, and cruising routines that Foster had enjoyed all his life. Purcell said, "this cruise had just the aspect of four old friends from Jefferson County going out for a little cruise, and nothing significant about it at all."[28] It was Foster's last cruise on Lake Ontario before he died.

One of the reasons Foster was relaxed was that he knew his brother, Allen, was at the helm of the Central Intelligence Agency and that his sister, Eleanor, was the head of the Berlin desk for the State Department. The siblings were close, both personally and professionally. Neither Allen nor Eleanor was particularly religious. Allen, though married to his wife, Clover, had a playboy's reputation. He was an extrovert, at home in social situations, and preferred attending parties to home life. Eleanor earned a PhD in economics from Harvard in 1926, and through her memoirs and her biography of Foster, she is an important source for Dulles history.[29]

Siblings who are personally close often experience strain in their relationship when they interact with one another professionally. And particularly when one sibling is superior in rank to another in an organization, things can get awkward. According to Dulles family biographer Leonard Mosley, Foster's relationship with Allen during the 1950s was amiable, professional, and complementary. They respected one another, and Allen was deferential to Foster in public and private settings. But Foster's relationship with Eleanor was more complicated. Early in his tenure as secretary of state, Foster tried to move Eleanor out of her State Department position in Berlin and transfer her to the newly created Foreign Operations Administration, which was under the leadership of Harold Stassen. Without consulting Eleanor, he set up a meeting between her and Stassen and insisted that she go. "I don't think you can stay in the State Department," Foster told her. "You go and see Stassen. He'd like to give you a job." Eleanor went ahead with the meeting; Stassen offered her a job working on European aid and trade relations. But when he told her that she would not be allowed to attend staff meetings, she refused his offer. Eleanor later described Foster's reaction to the news as "annoyed," and he gave her a month to prove herself in Berlin. Exactly thirty days later, Foster called her and abruptly said, "Eleanor, it's all right. I guess it's all right. Goodbye." As she reflected on Foster's attempt to move her out of the State Department, Eleanor came to the realization that while there was personal and sincere love between them, there was not professional respect.[30]

In his personal life, Foster enjoyed competition on Lake Ontario, but he was not one to enter his own name as a contestant in sailing races. He did establish a race on the lake for Dragon class yachts in 1955 for the Crescent Yacht Club in Chaumont, New York, of which Foster was a member. He established the race partly because he saw international unity between Canada and the United States represented by the lake: another analogy he was fond of drawing between nature and human relationships.[31] In the first year of the race, Bob Purcell finished in second place. The winner of the trophy was a man named Bruce Huston.

Foster established the race around the trophy. He donated the trophy, manufactured by Steuben Glass, to be awarded annually to the winner. The trophy was just over thirteen inches tall and included the inscription "John Foster Dulles Secretary of State Trophy." Engraved on the trophy was the seal of the US secretary of state, a Dragon class yacht, and four points of the compass with the flag of the Crescent Yacht Club. It sat on a lighted stand, which gave the glass trophy a striking feature. Sadly, in November 1957, the trophy was accidentally tipped over during a banquet at the Genesee Yacht Club and shattered. The commodore of the Genesee Yacht Club, A. P. Manning, notified Hart about the accident, since he served as a trustee of the Dulles Trophy. As one might expect, Manning urged Hart not to tell Foster about the accident.[32] Apparently, Foster never found out, although the trophy was replaced. And in 1957, he did not have long to live.

Foster was admitted to Walter Reed Hospital on February 10, 1959, for a hernia operation. Just over two years earlier, Foster had been diagnosed with abdominal cancer and underwent what was thought to be a successful operation. He was hospitalized for a week in December 1958 with an inflamed colon. After attending a NATO meeting in Paris later that month, and taking another trip to Europe on February 2–9, Foster went into the hospital for the hernia procedure. The surgeons found that Foster's abdominal cancer had returned, and he began radiation therapy. He received eighteen radiation treatments and was released to spend some time at Hobe Sounds, Florida, to get some rest.[33]

Foster told Eisenhower that he was willing to resign and even drafted a resignation letter on March 30, just before leaving for Florida. Eisenhower refused it. But when Eisenhower consulted with Foster and his doctors just after his return to Walter Reed on April 13, the president was told that the cancer was terminal. Also, a tumor had developed on Foster's vertebrae in his neck. Eisenhower accepted Foster's resignation on April 15.[34] Undersecretary of State Christian Herter, a protégé of Foster's, replaced him as secretary. On April 23, Eisenhower appointed Foster as special consultant to the president with cabinet rank. Foster wrote to Eisenhower accepting the appointment. He said in his letter, "I am grateful to you for wanting me to serve in this capacity. I accept in the hope that I shall thus be able to assist you and the Secretary of State in the solution of problems which will continue to confront our nation in its quest of a just and honorable peace."[35] In his final weeks, Foster received visits from Winston Churchill, British prime minister Harold Macmillan, and Jean Monnet, one of the founders of the European Union, among many others. Eleanor brought a branch from a dogwood tree and set it up in Foster's room to brighten it. In the last weeks of his life, Foster enjoyed the hymns that he had sung around his mother's piano. His favorite was "Work, for the Night Is Coming." Just a few rooms down from Foster at Walter Reed was General George C. Marshall. He would die five months after Foster. Foster died on the morning of May 24, at 7:49 a.m. After the nurse stopped counting Foster's pulse, Janet looked down at Foster's face and said quietly, "My life, too, has ended."[36] West German chancellor Konrad Adenauer said of Foster, "He was my warm and true friend. He was not only a great statesman but a good and great human being."[37]

The state funeral was the largest since Franklin Roosevelt's in April 1945. Thousands of people passed by Foster's coffin to pay their respects May 26 and 27 as Foster's body lay in state in Bethlehem Chapel of Washington National Cathedral; an honor guard was posted around the coffin. At two o'clock on May 27, the funeral service featured a boys' choir singing "O God, Our Help in Ages Past" and "Through the Night of Doubt and Sorrow." Roswell Barnes officiated, along with Paul Wolfe of Brick Presbyterian Church and Edward L. R. Elson of National Presbyterian Church in Washington, DC. Several passages of Scripture were read, as well as a passage from John Bunyan's *Pilgrim's Progress*.

And as he went down deeper, he said
Grave, where is thy Victory?
So he passed over, and all the Trumpets sounded
For him on the other side.[38]

The funeral procession made its way from the cathedral to Arlington National Cemetery, on top of the hill adjacent to the memorial to the battleship *Maine*, destroyed in Havana harbor in 1898. Crowds of mourners lined the streets down the route of the funeral procession from National Cathedral all the way to Arlington. Andrei Gromyko, the Soviet foreign minister, flew to Washington to attend the funeral. Dwight Eisenhower wept as he followed the caisson up the slope where the grave was prepared. Honorary pallbearers included Dulles family friends Pemberton Berman, Arthur Dean, Bob Hart, C. D. Jackson, John D. Rockefeller III, Dean Rusk, and Henry P. Van Dusen, among several others. Konrad Adenauer marched in the procession, and several other heads of state came to the funeral. Jean Monnet of France, Dag Hammarskjöld of the United Nations, and Paul-Henri Spaak of NATO were present. Foreign ministers from sixteen nations were also in attendance, including Foster's protégé Christian Herter, who succeeded him as secretary of state. Dulles biographer Townsend Hoopes observed that Americans hardly knew how the nation would proceed in the Cold War without Foster. Foster "seemed in death to be recognized by admirers and critics alike as a man who had occupied so large a part of the diplomatic horizon for so long a time that his departure suddenly stirred anxiety because the void he left seemed of such immense proportions."[39]

At Arlington Cemetery, Foster was buried near General Leonard Wood, who commanded the Rough Riders during the Spanish American War, first as colonel, then as brigade commander. When Janet died in 1969, she was buried alongside Foster. Chief Justice Earl Warren, whom Eisenhower nominated to that office instead of Foster, also died in 1969. His grave is a few steps away from the Dulles plot.

Eisenhower heard of Foster's death while spending time at his farm in Gettysburg, Pennsylvania. Immediately, he wrote a tribute to Foster in longhand, and the *New York Times* published it on the front page of the newspaper on May 24. Eisenhower described Foster as "one of the truly great men of our time" and "a foe only to tyranny." He emphasized Foster's belief in human brotherhood, freedom, and dignity as well as just and durable peace. "In the pursuit of [peace], he ignored every personal cost and sacrifice, however great."[40] Foster's obituary in the *New York Times* reported that "when Mr. Dulles had to withdraw from the international scene one word was heard over and over among the diplomats of Europe and Asia: 'Indispensable.'"[41]

EPILOGUE

Civil Religion, Progressive Christianity, and John Foster Dulles

I'm not bloodthirsty, but I hope the Soviets never stop thinking I am.

—John Foster Dulles[1]

S ince Foster's state funeral, his star has fallen. Even before he died, Foster was becoming caricatured in the American imagination. Although *Time* named him its "Man of the Year" in 1954, Carol Burnett performed a parody song about Foster just three years later in August 1957 on *The Ed Sullivan Show* and *The Tonight Show* entitled "I Made a Fool of Myself over John Foster Dulles." Reflecting on those performances for the Paley Center for Media in 2015, Burnett glibly remarked, "At that time our Secretary of State was John Foster Dulles, who was *aptly named*" to much laughter.[2] British prime minister Harold Macmillan mused in 1957 that Foster's "speech was slow, but it easily kept pace with his thoughts."[3] In 1986, Mark Russell of the *New York Times* described Foster as the "man for whom the Homburg hat must have been invented."[4] Richard Immerman observed that Foster was unpopular in the State Department. Foster was reserved, shy, and more comfortable spending quiet evenings at home with Janet and his dog than being in the center of the Washington social scene. Furthermore, his public persona was vastly different from his private one. "In public, he displayed none of the humor, warmth, or sensitivity that he did in private," to people like his secretary, Phyllis Bernau Macomber, according to Immerman.[5]

In the public imagination, Foster's image continues to be defined by

188

gloom, farcicality, pigheadedness, and religious fanaticism. In a way, Foster contributed to this image. For example, Foster repeated the mantras of moral law, the righteousness of the American founders, the need for dynamic faith, and the evils of Soviet Communism again and again. To read his speeches and statements gets tedious because he repeated himself so often! His ideas had the tendency to sound like platitudes over the course of his tenure as secretary of state. One Herblock cartoon depicted Foster as a sleepy proprietor of a grocery market, presiding over a display of "Frozen Attitudes," "Frozen Platitudes," and "Foster's Frosted Fruitless Policies." An exasperated shopper asked the indifferent Foster, "Don't you ever have anything fresh?" Nevertheless, such depictions as these are simplistic and unfair.

John Foster Dulles was one of the most consequential figures to hold the office of secretary of state in the twentieth century. He was a complicated figure because his life and career represented a complex interplay between change and constancy, or as Foster might have said it, dynamism and the status quo. As has been noted, Foster was not interested in theological ideas, nor did he have a deeply considered system of dogmatic convictions rooted in Scripture or the Protestant intellectual tradition. What he did have was a firm basis in moral law. And even though his understanding and application of moral law underwent a change when he was secretary of state, that inward change can be attributed to the outward change of circumstances and the role that he occupied in relation to those changes. But he was not double minded; he was not tossed by the wind and waves of circumstances. His commitment to human dignity and freedom, as rooted in the Christian faith and the moral law, remained. He saw them as worthy of a stout defense. That fact does not make every motive of Foster's pure, or every action righteous, or every word spoken unambiguous. But that fact does make him human.

It was easy for many of Foster's peers to judge his actions from 1953 to 1959 on the basis of an anachronistically constructed paradigm of 1937 to 1945. Likewise, it is easy for us to condemn Foster by means of an anachronistic twenty-first-century paradigm. Foster was a religious man in a position of great power in the United States government, and his religion was primarily ethical. He was trained in philosophy and the law, and he approached his secretaryship as a lawyer committed to his client, the United

States. And he was bringing old family traditions into his approach to the issues of his day: a religious tradition represented by the Dulles family and a diplomatic tradition represented by the Foster family. He could be rigid, abrupt, and insensitive one moment and yet open-minded, warm, and compassionate the next. He was complicated, just as every human being is.

Foster the Religious Human Being

Any credible assessment of John Foster Dulles as a major figure of American diplomatic history from 1919 to 1959 must reckon with him first and foremost as a human being. And any reckoning with Foster's humanity must seriously consider his religious life, in order to make sense of its many complexities. In the more than sixty years since his death, only one historian, Mark Toulouse, has produced a book-length treatment of Foster's religion. Toulouse's work, while important, focuses narrowly on Foster's "transformation" from internationalist to nationalist from 1937 to 1952, and only lightly treats his early life and overlooks his career as secretary of state altogether. This biography examines Foster's religious development beginning in the context of his family line and concluding with his death in 1959. Foster's religious life as it animated his career as lawyer, churchman, and diplomat can be summed up as a blend of exceptionalist civil religion and progressive Christianity. That potent mixture produced John Foster Dulles. In our own day, elite white male Anglo-Saxon Protestant predominance has been largely eclipsed by more diverse cultural and religious expressions in American diplomacy, politics, and society. Making sense of Foster's life and significance to American history requires us to understand him in his world, a world vastly different from our own. And Foster was, from birth to death, deeply affected by some of the particular expressions of Protestantism that predominated on the American scene prior to what Charles Murray called the "coming apart" of white America, a phenomenon that included a decisive shift toward secularism and away from Protestant assumptions and practices.[6]

On May 7, 1954, Ho Chi Minh's Viet Minh forces overran the French citadel at Dien Bien Phu in northern Vietnam as the French made their last stand in a long and costly war to maintain control over their colonial possessions in Indochina. Ho's victory meant that he would have serious credibility representing Vietnamese Communists at the Geneva Conference scheduled for late that spring. With impeccable timing, his forces defeated the French shortly after the conference had gotten under way. All but one of the involved powers—the United States—agreed that, given the combination of Ho's popularity among the Vietnamese people and his raw staying power, resisting him would be all but futile. Ho would be negotiating with anti-Communist Vietnamese representatives as well as those from Cambodia, Laos, Britain, France, China, the Soviet Union, and the United States.

Foster led the American delegation at Geneva. His primary attention was on establishing a lasting peace on the Korean peninsula after the armistice ending the Korean War the previous year. He maintained that he would have nothing to do with any compromise with the Communists on the future of Vietnam. Foster was unabashedly contemptuous of the Chinese Communists and was convinced that Ho Chi Minh was a Chinese puppet. And he was confident that America could succeed in building up an anti-Communist bulwark in Indochina where the French had failed.

At a London press conference held prior to the official gathering, on April 13, 1954, Foster had the following exchange with a reporter:

Q: What would you regard as a reasonable satisfactory settlement of the Indochina situation?

Foster: The removal by the Chinese Communists of their apparent desire to extend the political system of Communism to Southeast Asia.

Q: That means the complete withdrawal of Communists from Indochina?

Foster: That is what I would regard as a satisfactory solution.

Q: Is there any compromise that might be offered if that is not entirely satisfactory to the Communists?

Foster: I had not thought of any.[7]

Foster's intransigence continued into the conference. When a reporter asked him two weeks later in Geneva if he planned on having any private conversations with Chou Enlai, the Chinese foreign minister, Foster's dry response was, "Not unless our automobiles collide."[8] Ultimately, the three-month-long conference produced an agreement among all parties that Vietnam would be divided along the seventeenth parallel, that Ho would lead North Vietnam from Hanoi, that Western powers would shape a non-Communist government based in Saigon in South Vietnam, and that a general election would be held in 1956 to decide which government would permanently unite Vietnam. And American entanglement in Southeast Asia began in earnest.

Foster's inflexible posture toward the Chinese Communists in particular represented the general attitude most Americans held toward Communism during the immediate post–World War II period. During the 1950s, Americans were willing to expend enormous resources in a simmering and uncertain conflict with what they saw as Soviet-led expansionism right after fighting the most devastating war in human history. Americans saw the Cold War in starkly religious terms, as a struggle between good and evil, light and darkness, and true religion and what Harry Truman called "a false philosophy which purports to offer freedom, security, and greater opportunity to mankind."[9]

The Cold War spawned an awakening of civil religion in America after 1945. While not a conversionistic awakening like the First Great Awakening in the eighteenth century or the Second Great Awakening of the nineteenth, it was a theistic revival identifying the United States as the paragon of righteousness and freedom. It was a revival led most significantly by President Eisenhower, with preachers coming alongside the president to reinforce civil religion. This new postwar civil religion cast America as the champion of God-fearing people everywhere against what Americans generally saw as an aggressive atheistic system centered in Moscow's Kremlin and bent on subjugating the world. Nineteen fifties religious theism was Ameri-centric but pluralistic, embracing what sociologist Will Herberg called the "Protestant—Catholic—Jew" religious landscape that prevailed in the United States in 1954.[10]

Religious leaders, both Protestant and Catholic, conservative and liberal, railed against "godless Communism" and extolled America's God. Billy Graham, Carl McIntire, Norman Vincent Peale, Edward L. R. Elson, and George M. Docherty were Protestants; Bishop Fulton Sheen, Francis Cardinal Spellman, James Francis McIntyre, and John Courtney Murray were Catholic. Billy Graham was vaulted onto the national scene after his 1949 Los Angeles crusade, and became the confidant to presidents for the next sixty years. Civil religion historian Raymond Haberski wrote that Graham helped Cold War presidents see the struggle in terms of "a moral crisis rather than a moral paradox."[11] Fulton Sheen brought his fiery rhetoric to a radio and television audience of up to thirty million people. In his 1948 book entitled *Communism and the Conscience of the West*, Sheen wrote, "*Communism is not to be feared just because it is anti-God, but because we are Godless*, not because it is strong, but because we are weak, for if we were under God, then who could conquer us?"[12]

Politics was also "awash in a sea" (as Yale historian Jon Butler might say)[13] of civil religion during the 1950s. In 1951 and again in 1953, Senator Ralph E. Flanders of Vermont sought to renew interest in the Christian Amendment, which was popular during the late nineteenth and early twentieth century. The proposed amendment asserted that America was a Christian nation and explicitly named Jesus Christ as the God of the United States. Congress called for a National Day of Prayer to be proclaimed each year by the president, starting in 1952. Dwight Eisenhower became the first president to be baptized in office (he was baptized by his pastor, Edward Elson of National Presbyterian Church) and successfully advocated for the phrase "under God" to be added to the Pledge of Allegiance, which occurred in 1954.[14] Eisenhower filled a pastoral as well as a political role during his presidency. The Republican National Committee hailed him as both the political and spiritual leader of the nation. Eisenhower was able to fuse religious and political rhetoric, and in doing so, he mobilized the country to prepare for something of a holy war against Soviet Communism.

Progressive Christianity, while it predominated between the Civil War and World War I in America, remained a significant cultural and intellectual force at the beginning of the Cold War. It was forged by figures like Washington Gladden, pastor of the First Congregational Church of Columbus, Ohio; Walter Rauschenbusch, author of *A Theology for the Social Gospel* (1917); Frances Willard, president of the Women's Christian Temperance Union; Shailer Mathews of the University of Chicago; William Newton Clarke of Colgate Theological Seminary; William Adams Brown of Union Seminary; and Harry Emerson Fosdick of Riverside Church in Manhattan, among many others. Theologically liberal, progressive Christians chafed against confessions of faith, emphasis on doctrine, and religious authority based in Scripture, tradition, or the institutional church. Progressive

Christianity was modernist, and as an intellectual system influenced by evolutionary theory, it prevailed over fundamentalism by the 1920s. Foster was at the center of both the civil religious awakening of the 1940s and '50s and the progressive Protestant movement of the interwar period, both shaping and being shaped by these religious dynamics.

Foster, Civil Religion, and Progressive Christianity

How did Foster form, and how was he formed by, civil religion and progressive Christianity? First, consider civil religion. In his brilliant history of religion in American foreign policy, Andrew Preston observed that religion served as an example of continuity amid vast changes in American diplomatic history. Since the eighteenth century, Americans have seen themselves as a divinely chosen people to *be* something and to *do* something. They were to *be* as a city upon a hill, a beacon of freedom and progress. And they were to *do* righteousness in the world by spreading their founding ideals where they did not exist and championing them where they were threatened by tyrannical forces. In Preston's formulation, Americans saw themselves at times as brandishing a "shield of faith" to the world through "Christian pacifism, anti-interventionism, anti-imperialism, and internationalism." At other times, Americans took up the "sword of the Spirit" in righteous warfare, thereby "serving [God] and fulfilling his will," in Preston's words.[15] Thus, Americans have habitually embraced the idea of their own exceptionalism, and consistently have done so in religious terms. Sometimes religious exceptionalism was exemplarist (Preston's "shield of faith"), and other times it was imperialist (Preston's "sword of the Spirit"). Exemplarism and imperialism at times were complementary, and at other times mutually exclusive. Promoters of both brands of religious exceptionalism historically have envisioned an American indispensability in the world.[16]

Foster's approach to foreign policy changed during his career. During the 1930s through the mid-1940s, he was an internationalist. From 1946 to 1950, he became wary of Soviet ambitions and feared a new world war. By 1950, he had given up on any form of partnership with the Soviet Union and saw Communism as outside the international world order and the moral law that served as its basis. He also believed that the United States was the only power that could thwart Soviet ambitions to dominate and enslave the world. In that sense, Foster was a nationalist, although he never gave up on internationalism as an ideal. Foster's change was tempered by the constancy of religious faith. It was his religious faith that animated his brandishing a "shield of faith" during his internationalist years, and that same religious faith moved him to wield a "sword of the Spirit" in efforts to deter Communist aggression while serving as secretary of state.

Foster frequently asserted that America was unlike any nation the world had ever known, because it was founded as a Christian nation. Since Christianity was the essence of American identity, America had a responsibility to share its blessings with the rest of the world, especially in light of the threat the Soviets posed to human freedom. In his 1952 *Life* editorial, "A Policy of Boldness," Foster wrote that if the United States turned its back on the world while its people faced the threat of absorption into Soviet Communism, there would be nothing to stem the Communist threat. "Such [isolationist] policies would really give 100 percent cooperation to the Soviet Communist effort to encircle and isolate us, as a preliminary to a final assault. Once Asia, Europe, Africa, and probably South America were consolidated against us, our plight would be desperate."[17] In Foster's mind, Western European powers could unite against the Soviet threat, as could free governments in Asia, Latin America, and Africa. But without American leadership, resolve, and spiritual and material power, Communism could not be contained or rolled back.

After all, America's uniqueness was not only found in the circumstances of its founding. American material prosperity outpaced that of every other nation in the world, including the Soviet Union. That was one of the reasons why Foster continually reminded Americans of their need to reinvigorate their spiritual and moral power. Foster believed that because of unprecedented material prosperity, Americans would place their hope to check and defeat Communism in material forces only. Still, America was the most powerful nation in the world. "Looked at in any impartial way, we are the world's greatest and strongest power. The only commodity in which we seem deficient is faith. In all material things we have a productivity far exceeding that of Russia: our steel production is about three and one half times that of the Soviet Union, and in aluminum, petroleum, and electric power our superiority is even greater. Our people have a standard of education, an inventive talent, and a technical skill unmatched by any of the peoples under Soviet rule."[18] Despite these material strengths, Foster worried that Americans might lose faith in their moral and spiritual principles and be divided along partisan lines. As he closed his piece, he urged his readers to remember, "Only a united America can unify the free world."[19] Unity would come through the ideals that formed America's unique spiritual heritage. American unity would preserve and extend freedom in the world and ultimately prevail over the Communist threat.

American indispensability was, and continues to be, central to exceptionalist civil religion. Civil religion is closely related to progressive Christianity. The bridge linking the two was a Manichean belief in a cosmic war between light and darkness taking place in space and time. Since the colonial period, Americans have cast their identity in terms of the righteous pitted against the evil. Reality has been, for much of the American experience, a zero-sum game between the forces of light and the forces of darkness. For colonial and national Americans, historical villains since the seventeenth century have variously included Native Americans, French, British, Spanish, Mexicans, Germans, Russians, Japanese—not to mention various groups cast at sundry times in terms of the Inferior Other, such as African Americans, or Asian, Irish, Jewish, Latino, and Catholic immigrants. As historian Richard M. Gamble described, Americans "have seen themselves as a progressive, redemptive force, waging war in the ranks of Christ's army, or have imagined themselves even as Christ Himself, liberating those in bondage and healing the afflicted."[20] Thus, in exceptionalist civil religion, America has always represented the forces of light, righteousness, and truth; its enemies are the manifestations of darkness, evil, and falsehood, and must be neutralized.

Early and mid-twentieth-century progressive Christianity reflected this Manichean concept. Gamble rightly identified several assumptions held by progressive Christians of this period, the most prominent of which was a belief in inevitable progress. Informed by evolutionary theory, progressive Christians saw history moving toward an ethical and spiritual *telos*, which was the kingdom of God. Time was advancing, the past was inferior to the present, and the future was where hope lay. Related to the assumption of inevitable progress was the idea of developmentalism, a theory that proposed change as the constant of history. For progressive Christians, developmentalism meant that the faith was constantly adapting to new scientific advancements and the Bible should be interpreted as the product of chang-ing human experience rather than static revelation given in ageless form to humankind for all time. Fundamentalists, or conservatives, embraced the concept of "the faith that was once for all delivered to the saints" (Jude 3). But progressives, or modernists, believed it was the churches' collective responsibility to adapt to change and to direct change toward the ultimate goal of the realization of the kingdom of God.[21]

The major theological upshot of inevitable progress was that progres-sives rejected the Augustinian dichotomy between the city of man and the city of God, a dichotomy that had been largely assumed since Augustine completed his magnum opus in the fifth century, *De Civitate Dei.* For Au-gustine, the city of man was temporal, transitory, hubristically pitted against God, and doomed to final destruction. The city of God was anchored in the hope of the eternal kingdom of God to be fully realized at the end of the age with the descent of the new Jerusalem and the new heavens and the new earth after Christ's second advent (Rev. 21:1–2). For Augustine, true follow-ers of Christ looked with hope to their citizenship in heaven, regarded their time on earth as a sojourn, and lived according to the teachings of Christ, the King of kings and Lord of lords.

Fifteen centuries later, progressive Christians denied the Augustinian distinction between the two cities and, furthermore, denied that there was any conflict between the two. Progressives stressed the immanence of God—that is, God's activity and presence in this world—over his transcen-dence, or his rule over and above the world. In so doing, they stressed that salvation came to the world in space and time, and the kingdom of God would be brought about by the activity of human beings as they made the world according to God's will, as in Christ's plea in the Lord's Prayer: "Thy will be done on earth as it is in heaven."[22]

While Foster was no theologian, theologians and religious thinkers who were close to him personally and professionally influenced him. The closest theologian to Foster was, of course, his father, Allen Macy Dulles. In his 1907 book *The True Church,* Allen Macy articulated a classic pro-gressive theology of the church. He wrote that the triumph of the church was inevitable, that it was "unconquerable by evil forces," and "that all the power of darkness shall be unable to resist its triumphant march to vic-tory."[23] What did the triumph of the church consist in? Simply put, that human beings experienced salvation by attaining the pure moral character of God. Salvation consisted of a this-worldly sense. It was an ethical salvation, not a salvation from condemnation because of sin. Allen Macy wrote that salvation was "to make man perfect in the likeness of God" and "the perfection of the Christian character."[24] God worked immanently to save, that is, in the world through the church, and particularly through faithful Christians who endured hardship and persecution since the first century. No matter the obstacles, "the True Church" would always advance and "shall at last be gathered together" at Christ's second advent. "The Church comes; fair as the morn, clear as the sun, terrible as an army with banners. The ransomed of the Lord come to Zion with songs and everlasting joy, to be welcomed by the Captain of their salvation, to take blissful possession of the new heaven and the new earth wherein dwelleth righteousness."[25] Foster identified closely with his father's understanding of the church, and particularly its responsibility to ensure peace and brotherhood in a world threatened with destruction.

Lionel Curtis was another important influence on Foster, especially during the 1930s and 1940s while Foster was thinking about ecumenism, the evils of national sovereignty, and the need for a federalized world order. Curtis, one of the early proponents of world government in the early 1900s, wrote a world history entitled *Civitas Dei*, in which he advanced the thesis that Christ's life and teachings were the moral basis for human prosperity, and that the only way to end human misery was to build a world government predicated on Christ's ministry and his teaching on the kingdom of God.[26] Pure human brotherhood would find its culmination in the kingdom of God, and this kingdom would not be realized solely through the supernatural, miraculous work of God. The kingdom would be attained by human effort, and specifically, the effort of faithful Christians. Indeed, the bringing about of the kingdom was humanity's most important responsibility. "To create His Kingdom on earth," Curtis wrote, "is the first and foremost duty of man." God left it up to human reason to build the kingdom, and the kingdom would necessarily entail, according to Curtis, "the organisation of all human society in one commonwealth," a "world commonwealth."[27] After Curtis sent Foster a copy of the first edition in 1937, Foster wrote him to say, "I find it exceedingly stimulating and what you say has appreciably influenced my thinking."[28]

A Pragmatist on Israel and Race

And yet, Foster was not a progressive ideologue. One example of how Foster's pragmatism overrode ideology was in his approach to the state of Israel, which had come into existence in 1948. Foster bucked progressivism in one principal aspect—he was not consistently anti-Zionist, as many progressives were. True, he had anti-Zionist sympathies prior to becoming secretary of state. He was a member of the anti-Zionist Holy Land Emergency Liaison Program, which was connected with the American Council for Judaism, but as political theologian Samuel Goldman observed in his *God's Country: Christian Zionism in America*, he had resigned from this group by 1952 because "it was too critical of Israel."[29]

While his contemporary American Jews and Israelis did not always view Foster as pro-Zionist,[30] he was arguably not anti-Zionist while he was secretary of state. At the very least, Foster pursued a policy toward the Arab-Israeli conflicts during his tenure at State in terms of "friendly impartiality,"[31] as he said to the Senate Foreign Relations Committee in February 1956. Even more explicitly, though, the Republican presidential platform of 1952, which Foster endorsed, called for "peace between Israel and the Arab states" but also "a national home for the Jewish people."[32]

In a 1956 statement to the Senate Foreign Relations Committee, Foster proposed the sending of nonmilitary aid specifically to Israel and also said, "the United States does not exclude the possibility of arms sales to Israel at a time when it will preserve the peace."[33] By July 1956, the State Department announced an aid package of $3.5 million for "scientific and humanitarian projects in that country."[34] All this was to shore up Israeli security in the face of growing alienation with Egypt and the onset of the Suez crisis in the fall of 1956 in an effort to undermine Soviet designs on the Middle East. As ever, Foster's commitment to Israel, which became more explicit after the 1956 Suez crisis, was practical rather than doctrinal.

Foster's break with progressive Christians on the issue of Israel is perhaps most evident in his dealings with prominent members of the anti-Zionist CIA front group, the American Friends of the Middle East (AFME). The AFME was active in Congress as it sought to undermine Israel even after it was recognized by President Truman (whose Zionist bona fides might themselves be questioned, given his support of the Bernadotte Plan, which called for the partition of Israel after its May 1948 declaration of independence). And several figures close to Foster were either actively involved in the AFME or were closely associated with it, such as Kim Roosevelt, a grandson of Theodore Roosevelt with close ties to Allen from their time in the Office of Strategic Services during World War II and, later, the CIA. Perhaps most pertinent to Foster was the fact that Edward L. R. Elson, pastor of the National Presbyterian Church in Washington, DC, of which Foster and his wife Janet were affiliate members, became a member of the board of the AFME in 1954.

Elson wrote frequently to Foster, sending him copies of sermons, inviting him to special services (always making sure to reserve the pew occupied by his famous grandfather and uncle, who had also been secretaries of state), and asking him to serve on various church councils and committees. Elson was a shameless flatterer, praising Foster for things like "how superlatively I believe you are handling the responsibilities of your high office."[35] He also regularly exerted pressure on Foster to tack toward the AFME and its agenda, especially from 1955 to 1957. Foster was not swayed by Elson's overtures but always politely resisted his pastor with regard to the AFME. For example, in 1957, Cornelius Engert and Elson, both members of the AFME board, invited Foster to a special dinner, from which Foster begged off specifically because his staff advised him, "the organization is a partisan Arab group."[36] In early 1958, Elson brazenly insisted that Foster make a special stop in Cairo, which would have interrupted a trip to attend a Baghdad Pact meeting in Tehran. Elson thought it would be important for Foster to cultivate "a better working relationship between the Egyptian Government and the United States." Furthermore, Elson wrote, "some of our real and trusted friends would be greatly encouraged by your personal appearance in Cairo."[37] Foster rebuffed Elson, telling him that visiting Cairo would encourage Nasser to perceive such a visit as weakness. In fact, each time Elson brought up issues pertaining to the Middle East in his correspondence with Foster, the secretary either rejected his proposals or simply ignored him. It appears from the evidence then, that far from exerting anti-Zionist influence on Foster as an AFME board member and the pastor of one of the most prominent mainline Protestant churches in the nation, Elson had no tangible influence on him.[38]

Race represented another set of issues in which Foster cannot be seen as a progressive ideologue. Progressive Christianity was a major religious and intellectual influence in the life and work of Martin Luther King Jr. during the civil rights movement. King read Rauschenbusch's *Christianity and the Social Crisis* while studying at Crozer Theological Seminary and was deeply moved by the book. While he rejected Rauschenbusch's embrace of inevitable progress, he identified strongly with his teaching that Christianity was a religion for the whole person, physical, social, and spiritual. In his 1958 essay "My Pilgrimage to Nonviolence," King wrote, "It has been my conviction ever since reading Rauschenbusch that any religion which professes to be concerned about the souls of men and is not concerned about the social and economic conditions that scar the soul, is a spiritually moribund religion only waiting for the day to be buried."[39]

Foster would have agreed with King's statement, to a point. C. D. Jackson, publisher of *Fortune* magazine and an active supporter of the United Negro College Fund (UNCF), invited Foster to speak at a luncheon hosted by the UNCF in New York on March 20, 1955. The event was the first of its kind, because all thirty-one presidents of the historically black colleges supported by the UNCF at the time were in attendance. In addition to being a supporter of the UNCF, Jackson was an important anti-Communist figure, having served as an adviser to President Eisenhower on psychological warfare during World War II. He later served in the Eisenhower administration as "special assistant to the President, with special responsibilities in the 'cold war' planning of this Administration," in the words of Sherman Adams, Eisenhower's chief of staff.[40] Jackson had a special interest in inviting Foster to speak to the UNCF because Jim Crow segregation was a public relations liability for the United States in the Cold War. Foster heartily agreed, and he said as much in his remarks at the luncheon. But he also admitted that the United States simply had not lived up to the promises of its founding ideals with regard to how it treated its African American citizens. "We must recognize with contrition," Foster said, "that we in this country have not always lived up to the ideals of our Declaration of Independence." He went on to praise the educators and financial backers of the UNCF for looking to material needs as well as spiritual needs of African Americans. "Private charity and benevolence are an essential reflection of the brotherhood of man through the Fatherhood of God," Foster said.[41] His remarks anticipated the theme of King's "promissory note" in his "I Have a Dream" speech and also looked back on Rauschenbusch's theme of Christianity for the whole person.[42]

Still, Foster was hardly an outspoken advocate in the African American freedom struggle of the 1950s. He did not, for example, lend a voice alongside that of his old friend and Eisenhower administration colleague Herbert Brownell, who served as attorney general from 1953 to 1957. Both of them had been powerful New York attorneys—Brownell had been with the law firm Lord, Day, and Lord since 1929, and the two had worked together for Thomas Dewey in his campaigns for governor and president during the 1940s. Brownell also worked for Foster in his failed 1949 Senate campaign, and their friendship was a warm one.

But their mutual interests did not seem to include racial justice. Brownell, along with Maxwell Rabb, was one of the most forward-thinking members of the Eisenhower administration on race. He wrote the 1953 amicus brief expressing the administration's position on school desegregation at the request of Supreme Court chief justice Fred Vinson while the Court was considering the *Oliver Brown v. Board of Education of Topeka* case. Brownell asserted that the Fourteenth Amendment rendered segregation unconstitutional and urged the Court to strike it down. Thurgood Marshall, chief legal counsel for the NAACP, "publicly praised" Brownell for his brief, according to historian William I. Hitchcock.[43] Brownell also persuaded Eisenhower to make passage of civil rights legislation a priority in his 1957 State of the Union message. And he guided Eisenhower through the tense standoff with Arkansas governor Orval Faubus during the Little Rock crisis over school integration. But when Brownell introduced the concept that became the 1957 Civil Rights Act, Foster opposed him. When Brownell offered a proposed bill to the Eisenhower cabinet for discussion, he included a provision for federal authority to sue local and state governments in civil court for violating African American citizens' voting rights. Foster argued against it believing that the measure crossed a line, saying that Brownell's proposal "deviated too far from accepted mores."[44] The provision ended up being included in the bill, and Eisenhower signed the bill into law on September 9, 1957. It was the first federal civil rights legislation since Reconstruction, initiated by Herb Brownell. But Foster did not take the opportunity to join Brownell in pushing for commonsense civil rights reform when he had it.

Earl Warren became Eisenhower's pick to succeed Fred Vinson as chief justice of the Supreme Court in 1953, not Foster. Warren skillfully guided the Court to issue a unanimous decision in striking down school segregation in the *Brown v. Board* decision in 1954, and he did so intentionally. He knew that a decision with such moral and legal gravity had to come from a Court speaking with one voice. Could Foster have accomplished this? Would his heart have been in it? It is impossible to know, but given the apparent ambivalence Foster had toward American apartheid in the 1950s, it is likely he would not have been a champion for African Americans had he led the Supreme Court rather than the State Department.

While Foster may not have been a paradigmatic progressive Christian of the first half of the twentieth century, progressive Christianity and civil religion continue to serve as tools in interpreting Foster's significance in American history. Seeing Foster's evolving positions on foreign policy, national sovereignty, war, internationalism, free trade, treaty making, nuclear deterrence, human freedom, the role of churches in the world, and the many issues he addressed in his career through the lenses of civil religion and progressive Christianity helps solve some of the troubling paradoxes present in his career broadly considered. For example, how could Foster have embraced internationalism and world organization, first through the League of Nations and then the United Nations in the 1930s and 1940s, but later have "transformed" (in Toulouse's words) into seeing the United States and the Soviet Union in a Manichean struggle of light against darkness in the 1950s? One possible answer is that progressive Christianity was fluid. Progressive Christianity allowed for a Manichean interpretation of ethical conflict, and it also made room for religious ecumenism and world commonwealth in terms that the Federal Council of Churches and Lionel Curtis endorsed. Foster was thus being true to progressivism in both periods of his career. But he was also acting in accord with exceptionalist civil religion in both periods. He saw the American federal system as being indispensable to keeping peace between rival polities in the 1930s and '40s and desired a world federation modeled on the American system. He never gave up on the moral superiority of American ideals at any point in his career, but his expression and application of those ideals changed with circumstances.

Biographers have often fretted over how difficult Foster is to understand over the broad sweep of his lifetime. Most biographers since the early 1970s have preferred to see Foster in negative terms. And he cannot seem to escape the decades-long curse of being the butt of a joke. But every human being is a complex mixture of varying experiences, paradoxes, flaws, and virtues. Foster certainly was. But whether we praise Foster as a champion of freedom, censure him as a war criminal, or anything in between, we should do so based on clear historical thinking. Foster is from the past. Making sense of the past in the present takes hard work. But the rewards are rich. Richard Weaver wrote that knowledge of the past gives us a perspective that both warns and affirms. It warns us against the futility of trying to perfect humanity and affirms us in the reality of our humanity in the present. Thus, in studying a past life like Foster's, we receive the gift of wisdom when considering our own lives. "Let us pause long enough to remember that in so far as we are creatures of reflection, we have only the past," Weaver wrote. "The present is a line, without width; the future only a screen in our minds on which we project combinations of memory." Weaver continued, "Imagination enables us to know that people of past generations lived and had their being amid circumstances just as solid as those surrounding us. And piety accepts them, their words and their deeds, as part of the total reality, not to be ignored in any summing-up of experience."[45] And as we think on the peoples of the past, let us remember the wisdom of the Latin funerary inscription *Viator, viator! Quod tu es, ego fui; quod nunc sum, et tu eris.* Traveler, traveler! What you are, I was; what I am now, you also will be.[46]

Diplomatic and religious historian William Inboden correctly pointed out that religion is one essential means by which we understand why people of the past acted the way they did. Religion might not be the only explanation, and there may be little or no direct evidence for how religious faith provides the basis for any particular action taken by any particular actor in time. But, as Inboden wrote, "religion helped shape the basic worldview of many American elites. Their actions in turn grew out of this worldview."[47] Foster is dead. He can no longer speak for himself. He had his chance at life and does not have the opportunity to change his mind or express pride or regret in explaining any of his thoughts, words, or deeds. It is left to us in the present to honestly and diligently work to make sense of his life and legacy, and we should do so as we would want others to do the same for us when we are gone. To understand Foster's religion is essential to fulfilling that task. And his religion underscores the centrality of his humanity, as we humans in the present seek to learn from this man of the past.

Notes

Introduction

1. Beth Barton Schweiger, "Seeing Things: Knowledge and Love in History," in *Confessing History: Explorations in Christian Faith and the Historian's Vocation*, ed. John Fea, Jay Green, and Eric Miller (Notre Dame: University of Notre Dame Press, 2010), 77.

2. Leonard Mosley, *Dulles: A Biography of Eleanor, Allen, and John Foster Dulles and Their Family Network* (New York: Dial Press / James Wade, 1978), 88.

3. Statement (not issued): Adolf Hitler, January 21, 1952, JFDP, Box 306.

4. Schweiger, "Seeing Things," 63.

5. "Eleanor L. Dulles of State Dept. Dies at 101," *New York Times*, November 4, 1996, section B, 10.

6. Dwight D. Eisenhower, "The President's Tribute," in *The Spiritual Legacy of John Foster Dulles: Selections from His Articles and Addresses*, ed. Henry P. Van Dusen (Philadelphia: Westminster, 1960), vii.

7. Entry for May 14, 1953, in Robert Ferrell, ed., *The Eisenhower Diaries* (New York: Norton, 1981). Quoted in Richard H. Immerman, introduction to *John Foster Dulles and the Diplomacy of the Cold War*, ed. Richard H. Immerman (Princeton: Princeton University Press, 1990), 3.

8. Kennedy's 1962 remarks are available on YouTube at https://www.youtube.com/watch?v=j4ePWWSyzkU.

9. Stephen Kinzer, *The Brothers: John Foster Dulles, Allen Dulles, and Their Secret World War* (New York: Holt, 2013), 2.

10. "The Ten Best Secretaries of State . . . ," *American Heritage* 33, no. 1 (December 1981), https://www.americanheritage.com/content/ten-best-secretaries

-state%E2%80%A6; Immerman, introduction to *John Foster Dulles and the Diplomacy of the Cold War*, 4.

11. Daniel W. Drezner, "The Post–Cold War Secretaries of State, Ranked," *Washington Post*, July 27, 2016, https://www.washingtonpost.com/postevery thing/wp/2016/07/27/the-post-cold-war-secretaries-of-state-ranked/?utm _term=.a6eb445d5625.

12. Stephen Kinzer, interview by Lawrence Velvel, *Books of Our Time* (Massachusetts School of Law at Andover), December 21, 2014, https://youtu.be /hW2vL76q3yg.

13. Harry S. Truman, Appointment Sheet, March 16, 1946, in *Off the Record: The Private Papers of Harry S. Truman*, ed. Robert H. Ferrell (New York: Harper & Row, 1980), 87.

14. Truman to John Foster Dulles, March 25, 1952, PACC, Box 14.

15. Acheson to John Foster Dulles, March 24, 1952, JFDP, Box 57, Reel 20.

16. Memorandum of Conversation between John Foster Dulles and Harry S. Truman, October 3, 1951, Japan, 1951, JFDP, Box 53, Reel 18.

17. Margaret Dulles Edwards (Mrs. Deane Edwards), oral interview, April 23, 1965, Rye, NY, 23, conducted by Richard Challener, JFDOHC.

18. John Foster Dulles, "I Was a Nominal Christian," *Challenge*, January, February, March 1942, 35.

19. John Foster Dulles, "A Diplomat and His Faith," *Christian Century*, March 19, 1952, 336.

20. Shigeru Yoshida, oral interview, September 30, 1964, Oiso, Japan, conducted by Spencer Davis, JFDOHC.

21. See, for example, Alexis de Tocqueville, *Democracy in America*, ed. Harvey C. Mansfield and Delba Winthrop (Chicago: University of Chicago Press, 2000), 2:428–33.

22. Avery Dulles, SJ, *John Foster Dulles: His Religious and Political Heritage; The Flora Levy Lecture in the Humanities*, ed. Maurice W. duQuesnay and Albert W. Fields (Lafayette: University of Southwest Louisiana, 1994), 8.

23. Thomas E. Dewey, oral interview, January 22, 1965, New York City, 10, conducted by Richard D. Challener, JFDOHC.

24. Lillias Dulles Hinshaw, oral interview, May 29, 1966, Washington, DC, 24, conducted by Philip A. Crowl, JFDOHC.

25. Margaret Dulles Edwards, oral interview, 15, JFDOHC.

26. Henry P. Van Dusen, introduction to Van Dusen, *The Spiritual Legacy of John Foster Dulles*, xiii.

27. Eleanor Lansing Dulles, *Chances of a Lifetime: A Memoir* (Englewood Cliffs, NJ: Prentice Hall, 1980), 3.

28. Townsend Hoopes, *The Devil and John Foster Dulles* (Boston: Little, Brown, 1973), 43.

29. Avery Dulles, oral interview, July 30, 1966, Woodstock College, MD, 16, conducted by Philip A. Crowl, JFDOHC.

30. Herb Cooper, interviewed by the author, Picton, ON, May 25, 2018.

31. Phyllis Bernau Macomber, oral interview, January 8, 1966, Washington, DC, 28, conducted by Philip A. Crowl, JFDOHC.

32. Drew Pearson, "Dulles Defended Reich to Save Client's Money," *Philadelphia Record*, September 28, 1944, JFDP, Box 25, Reel 5.

33. John Foster Dulles to Leech, September 30, 1937, JFDP, Box 16, Reel 3.

34. Mosley, *Dulles*, 91.

35. Mosley, *Dulles*, 92.

36. Memorandum by John Foster Dulles, September 12, 1946, Box 31, folder 12, "Attacks on Dulles," PHS.

37. Ronald W. Pruessen, *John Foster Dulles: The Road to Power* (New York: Macmillan, 1982), 132.

38. Louis Jefferson, *The John Foster Dulles Book of Humor* (New York: St. Martin's, 1986), xi.

Chapter 1

1. Matthew Watson Foster to John Watson Foster, September 8, 1862, in John Watson Foster, *Biographical Sketch of Matthew Watson Foster, 1800–1863* (New York: J. J. Little, 1896), 78–79.

2. Robert D. McFadden, "Cardinal Avery Dulles, Theologian, Is Dead at 90," *New York Times*, December 12, 2008, https://www.nytimes.com/2008/12/13/us/13dulles.html.

3. Fred Garry, interview by the author, Watertown, NY, October 25, 2017.

4. Avery Dulles, "Remarks Observing the Two Hundredth Anniversary of First Presbyterian Church of Watertown" (video of service, recorded June 29, 2003, VHS), First Presbyterian Church, Watertown, NY.

5. John Watson Foster, *Biographical Sketch*, 83.

6. The address was later published under this title in *Catholic Mind* 77, no. 1337 (November 1979): 8–22. It also appeared in Avery Dulles, *A Church to Believe In: Discipleship and the Dynamics of Freedom* (New York: Crossroad, 1982), 53–65.

7. Nicola Haslam, "One-Third of Americans Can't Name All of Their Grand-parents," *New York Post*, December 19, 2018, https://nypost.com/2018/12/19/one-third-of-americans-cant-name-all-of-their-grandparents/.

8. Eleanor Lansing Dulles, oral interview, March 26–April 22, 1965, McLean, VA, and Washington, DC, 9, conducted by Philip A. Crowl, JFDOHC. Margaret Dulles Edwards, oral interview, April 23, 1965, Rye, NY, 57–58, conducted by Richard D. Challener, JFDOHC.

9. John W. Foster, *Diplomatic Memoirs*, 2 vols (New York: Houghton Mifflin, 1909), 2:156.

10. Edith Foster Dulles, *The Story of My Life* (privately published, 1934), passim, JFDP, Box 397. The manuscript lacks page numbers.

11. Mark Toulouse, *The Transformation of John Foster Dulles: From Prophet of Realism to Priest of Nationalism* (Macon, GA: Mercer University Press, 1985), 10.

12. Eleanor Lansing Dulles, *Chances of a Lifetime: A Memoir* (Englewood Cliffs, NJ: Prentice Hall, 1980), 15.

13. Samuel Gaillard Stoney, *The Dulles Family of South Carolina* (Columbia: University of South Carolina Press, 1955), 9–14, JFDP, Box 392.

14. Stoney, *The Dulles Family*, 9–14.

15. "Obituary Record of Graduates of Yale University Deceased during the Academical Year Ending in June 1887" (New Haven: Tuttle, Morehouse, and Taylor, 1887), 378–79, accessed December 30, 2018, http://mssa.library.yale.edu/obituary_record/1859_1924/1886-87.pdf. The degree was probably honorary.

16. John Foster Dulles, speech on Bible Society Broadcast, November 20, 1950, JFDP, Box 302. *Which* Bible society he addressed in this broadcast is unclear.

17. The most recent Princeton graduate in the family is Emilie Dulles, who is a member of the class of 2003.

18. Varnum Lansing Collins, ed., "Princeton University General Biographi-cal Catalogue, 1746–1916, for Joseph Heatly Dulles, class of 1873," JFDP, Box 392.

19. Varnum Lansing Collins, ed., "Princeton University General Biographical Catalogue, 1746–1916, for Allen Macy Dulles, class of 1875," JFDP, Box 392.

20. John Watson Foster, *Biographical Sketch*, 6.

21. John Watson Foster, *Biographical Sketch*, 7.

22. Everett Vaughn, "The History of the Foster Family," Otwell Junior Historical Society, JFDP, Box 392.

23. John Watson Foster, *Biographical Sketch*, 84.

24. Eleanor Lansing Dulles, *Chances of a Lifetime*, 3.

25. John Watson Foster, *Diplomatic Memoirs*, 2:102.

26. Eleanor Lansing Dulles, *Chances of a Lifetime*, 6–7.

27. John Watson Foster, *Diplomatic Memoirs*, 1:8–9.

28. John Watson Foster, *Diplomatic Memoirs*, 1:9.

29. "A Gallant Officer," *Washington Evening Star* (Grand Army Edition, Part II), September 22, 1892, *Chronicling America: Historic American Newspapers*, Library of Congress, http://chroniclingamerica.loc.gov/lccn/sn83045462/1892-09-22/ed-1/seq-9/. See also "John W. Foster," ELDP, Box 2, Folder 7.

30. John Watson Foster, *Diplomatic Memoirs*, 1:9. Hereafter, references to this work will be placed in parentheses in the text.

31. John Foster Dulles, interview in "Look Here!" television program, September 15, 1957, JFDP, Box 358.

32. Eleanor Lansing Dulles, *Chances of a Lifetime*, 10.

33. Edith Foster Dulles, *The Story of My Life*. All subsequent quotations in this discussion (from here to note 36) come from Edith's memoir; the document has no page numbers.

34. Her father wrote extensively about these trips on horseback in his *Diplomatic Memoirs*, 1:35–47.

35. See also the first chapter of Mary Raber, *Ministries of Compassion among Russian Evangelicals: 1905–1929* (Eugene, OR: Pickwick, 2016).

36. Edith Foster Dulles to John Foster Dulles, May 21, 1937, JFDP, Box 16, Reel 3.

37. Edith Foster Dulles, *The Story of My Life*.

38. Foster's uncle once told him, "The more I read books on geology, the more I am convinced that the account of creation given in God's word is the only rational theory, both scientifically and historically." John Welsh Dulles II to John Foster Dulles, October 20, 1939, JFDP, Box 18, Reel 4.

39. Frederick H. Kimball, *Years of Faith: A History of the First Presbyterian Church of Watertown, New York: 1803–1953* (Watertown, NY: Hungerford-Holbrook, 1953), 18–19.

40. Allen Macy Dulles, *The True Church: A Study (Historical and Scriptural)* (New York: Revell, 1907), 5.

41. Allen Macy Dulles, *The True Church*, 12–21.

42. Allen Macy Dulles, *The True Church*, 227.

43. Allen Macy Dulles, *The True Church*, 227–28.

44. John Foster Dulles, "The Peace We Seek," YWCA Centennial Luncheon, New York City, January 11, 1955, JFDP, Box 333.

45. William P. Hills, "The Reverend Dr. Allen Macy Dulles, Pastor 1887–1904," First Presbyterian Church, Watertown, NY.

46. Edith Foster Dulles, *The Story of My Life*.

47. Eleanor Lansing Dulles, *Chances of a Lifetime*, 20.

48. Eleanor Lansing Dulles, *Chances of a Lifetime*, 20.

49. Nataline Dulles Seymour, oral interview, July 5, 1965, Henderson Harbor, NY, 4, conducted by Philip A. Crowl, JFDOHC.

50. Allen Welsh Dulles, oral interview, May 17–June 3, 1965, Washington, DC, 10–11, conducted by Philip A. Crowl, JFDOHC.

Chapter 2

1. Diary of Allen Macy and Edith F. Dulles, February 25, 1893, JFDP, Box 582.

2. "A March Blizzard: Washington Cut Off from Communication with the World," *Washington Evening Star*, vol. 70, March 12, 1888, 1, *Chronicling America: Historic American Newspapers*, Library of Congress, https://chroniclingamerica.loc.gov/lccn/sn83045462/1888-03-12/ed-1/seq-1/.

3. Edith Foster Dulles, *The Story of My Life* (privately published, 1934), passim, JFDP, Box 397.

4. Diary of Allen Macy and Edith F. Dulles, passim.

5. Diary of Allen Macy and Edith F. Dulles, April 1890.

6. Diary of Allen Macy and Edith F. Dulles, February 25, 1895.

7. Diary of Allen Macy and Edith F. Dulles, December 25, 1890, and August 10, 1890.

8. Diary of Allen Macy and Edith F. Dulles, June 12, 1890.

9. Diary of Allen Macy and Edith F. Dulles, February 25, 1893.

10. "Social Matters: Baby McKee's Birthday Party—Personal Notes," *Washington Evening Star*, vol. 80, March 16, 1892, 3, in *Chronicling America: Historic American Newspapers*, Library of Congress, https://chroniclingamerica.loc.gov /lccn/sn83045462/1892-03-16/ed-1/seq-3/.

11. Diary of Allen Macy and Edith F. Dulles, March 15, 1892.

12. Nataline Dulles Seymour, oral interview, July 5, 1965, Henderson Harbor, NY, 16, conducted by Philip A. Crowl, JFDOHC.

13. JFD Entrance Exams, Princeton University, PACC, Box 1.

14. Margaret Dulles Edwards, oral interview, April 23, 1965, Rye, NY, 20, conducted by Richard D. Challener, JFDOHC.

15. John Foster Dulles, "My Preparation in English," September 24, 1904, PACC, Box 1.

16. Nataline Dulles Seymour, oral interview, 11, 14.

17. Eleanor Lansing Dulles, oral interview, March 26–April 22, 1965, McLean, VA, and Washington, DC, 4, conducted by Philip A. Crowl, JFDOHC.

18. Allen Welsh Dulles, oral interview, May 17–June 3, 1965, Washington, DC, 10, conducted by Philip A. Crowl, JFDOHC.

19. Allen Welsh Dulles, oral interview, 10.

20. Eleanor Lansing Dulles, *John Foster Dulles: The Last Year* (New York: Harcourt, Brace & World, 1963), 20–23.

21. See Eleanor Lansing Dulles, oral interview, 12, and Margaret Dulles Edwards, oral interview, 29.

22. Eleanor Lansing Dulles, *John Foster Dulles*, 160. See also Eleanor Lansing Dulles, oral interview, 25.

23. Eleanor Lansing Dulles, *John Foster Dulles*, 150–51.

24. Edith Foster Dulles, *The Story of My Life*, passim.

25. Edith Foster Dulles, *The Story of My Life*, passim.

26. JFD Entrance Exams, Princeton University, PACC, Box 1.

27. JFD Entrance Exams, Princeton University, PACC, Box 1.

28. Eleanor Lansing Dulles, oral interview, 11.

29. John W. Foster to John Foster Dulles, December 27, 1891, JFDP, Box 1, Reel 1.

30. Edith Foster Dulles, *The Story of My Life*, passim.

31. Eleanor Lansing Dulles, oral interview, 6.

32. Eleanor Lansing Dulles, oral interview, 7. See also Eleanor Lansing Dulles, *John Foster Dulles*, 161.

33. "King Cole Owned Main Ducks Island," *Picton (ON) County Weekly News*, January 5, 2005, 5.

34. Eleanor Lansing Dulles, *John Foster Dulles*, 126; "University Enrollments," *Daily Princetonian* 29, no. 107 (October 25, 1904), PACC, Box 1.

35. Richard D. Challener, "John Foster Dulles: The Princeton Connection," *Princeton University Library Chronicle* 50, no. 1 (Autumn 1988): 10. See also Gerard B. Lambert, oral interview, May 14, 1964, Princeton, conducted by Philip A. Crowl, JFDOHC, for an example of one classmate who had no recollection of Foster at all from undergraduate days.

36. *Nassau Herald*, 1908, 91, PACC, Box 1. Everard F. Miller, oral interview, October 8, 1965, Glen Head, Long Island, 21, conducted by Richard D. Challener, JFDOHC.

37. Challener, "John Foster Dulles," 13.

38. Miller, oral interview, 11.

39. Miller, oral interview, 12.

40. Edward J. Shedd, oral interview, February 1966, Santa Barbara, CA, 12, conducted by Gordon A. Craig, JFDOHC.

41. Margaret Dulles Edwards, oral interview, 27; Eleanor Lansing Dulles, *John Foster Dulles*, 126. Everard Miller denied he had done this, but based on corroborating testimony from his sisters, he evidently did.

42. Margaret Dulles Edwards, oral interview, 26; Eleanor Lansing Dulles, oral interview, 19–20; Challener, "John Foster Dulles," 15.

43. JFD Scholastic Grades, JFDP, Box 1.

44. Miller, oral interview, 1.

45. John Foster Dulles, "Resolved, That George Washington Deserves to Stand Higher in the Estimation of His Countrymen Than Abraham Lincoln," JFDP, Box 279.

46. *The Princeton Bric-a-Brac*, 104, PACC, Box 1.

47. Princeton University Catalogue, 1904–1905, PACC, Box 1.

48. JFD Scrapbook from the Second Hague Conference, 1907, JFDP, Box 582.

49. Miller, oral interview, 8.

50. John Foster Dulles, "Remarks Introducing Dr. Huber at Bar Association Luncheon," June 4, 1931, JFDP, Box 289.

51. John Foster Dulles, Travel Notes: Netherlands, circa 1907, entry for Friday, June 14, 1907, JFDP, Box 278.

52. John Foster Dulles, Senior Thesis, Princeton University, "The Theory of Judgement," 1908, 16, JFDP, Box 279.

53. John Foster Dulles, Senior Thesis, 62–63.

54. Miller, oral interview, 18.

55. Miller, oral interview, 10.

56. Eleanor Lansing Dulles, oral interview, 37.

57. John Foster Dulles, Senior Thesis, 16.

58. Edith Foster Dulles, *The Story of My Life*, passim.

59. See John Foster Dulles, Diary and Miscellaneous Notes: Paris, Washington, DC, etc., April 3, 1909–May 19, 1911, JFDP, Box 278.

60. See Nataline Dulles Seymour, oral interview, and Allen Welsh Dulles, oral interview.

61. Eleanor Lansing Dulles, *John Foster Dulles*, 128.

62. Eleanor Lansing Dulles, *John Foster Dulles*, 62.

63. John Foster Dulles, Diary and Miscellaneous Notes, January 18, 1911, JFDP, Box 278.

64. John Foster Dulles, Diary and Miscellaneous Notes, January 18, 1911. See, for example, entries for November 25, 26, December 1, 3, 30, 1910; and for January 10, 18, and February 1, 1911.

65. John Foster Dulles, Diary and Miscellaneous Notes, passim.

66. John Foster Dulles, Diary and Miscellaneous Notes, passim.

67. John Foster Dulles, Diary and Miscellaneous Notes, February 18, 1911.

68. Erik M. Jensen, review of *A Law unto Itself: The Untold Story of the Law Firm Sullivan and Cromwell*, *Business Law Review* 133, no. 1 (1990): 138.

69. Ronald W. Pruessen, *John Foster Dulles: The Road to Power* (New York: Macmillan, 1982), 15–16.

70. John Watson Foster to John Foster Dulles, August 20, 1911, JFDP, Box 1, Reel 1.

71. John Foster Dulles, Diary and Miscellaneous Notes, February 18, 1911.

72. Eleanor Lansing Dulles, oral interview, 52.

73. Townsend Hoopes, *The Devil and John Foster Dulles* (Boston: Little, Brown, 1973), 25.

74. Eleanor Lansing Dulles, oral interview, 47.

75. Eleanor Lansing Dulles, oral interview, 47.

76. Eleanor Lansing Dulles, oral interview, 54.

77. Eleanor Lansing Dulles, *John Foster Dulles*, 205.

Chapter 3

1. John Foster Dulles, Memorandum on Behalf of the Presbytery of New York, Respondent, January 15, 1926, 7, PACC, Box 3.

2. Edith Foster Dulles to John Foster Dulles, 1918, JFDP, Box 2, Reel 1.

3. Edith Foster Dulles to John Foster Dulles.

4. Allen Macy Dulles to John Foster Dulles, April 29, 1924, PACC, Box 2. Uzzah was one of the sons of Abinadab who was struck dead for reaching out to steady the ark of the covenant as David was bringing it on an oxcart from Kiriath-Jearim to Jerusalem at the beginning of his reign (2 Sam. 6:1–8). Allen Macy sometimes used simplified spelling in his personal letters, which might explain the misspelling of the name.

5. Ronald W. Pruessen's biographical work is particularly scrupulous in its detail of Foster's legal and diplomatic career. In this section, I am particularly indebted to Pruessen's work.

6. Van Dyke to John Foster Dulles, March 6, 1922, JFDP, Box 4, Reel 1.

7. Lillias Dulles Hinshaw, oral interview, May 29, 1966, Washington, DC, 4, conducted by Philip A. Crowl, JFDOHC, and Avery Dulles, oral interview, July 30, 1966, Woodstock College, MD, 2–4, conducted by Philip A. Crowl, JFDOHC.

8. Ronald W. Pruessen, *John Foster Dulles: The Road to Power* (New York: Macmillan, 1982), 14.

9. Lansing to John Foster Dulles, January 29, 1913, JFDP, Box 1, Reel 1.

10. John Foster Dulles to Lansing, January 31, 1913, JFDP, Box 1, Reel 1.

11. Ronald W. Pruessen, "Woodrow Wilson to John Foster Dulles: A Legacy," *Princeton University Library Chronicle* 34, no. 2 (Winter 1973): 111, and Martin Erdmann, *Ecumenical Quest for a World Federation: The Churches' Contribution to Marshal Public Support for World Order and Peace, 1919–1945* (Greenville, SC: Verax Vox Media, 2016), 6.

12. *War Memoirs of Robert Lansing, Secretary of State* (New York: Bobbs-Merrill, 1935), 314.

13. John Foster Dulles to Executive Assistant to the Chief of Staff, July 23, 1918, JFDP, Box 2, Reel 1.

14. Pruessen, *John Foster Dulles*, 24. See also relevant orders issued to Foster: War Department to John Foster Dulles, November 9 and December 18, 1918, JFDP, Box 2, Reel 1.

15. See John Foster Dulles, Memorandum on requisitioning of Dutch ships in American harbors, March 21, 1918, JFDP, Box 2, Reel 1.

16. John Foster Dulles, Memorandum on "War Service Record," 2, JFDP, Box 392, and Memorandum for Provisional Economic Aid to Russia, October 1, 1918, JFDP, Box 2, Reel 1.

17. Erdmann, *Ecumenical Quest*, 10. See also *Foreign Relations, 1918*, supplement 1, vol. 1, *The World War*, (Washington, DC, 1933), 337–469.

18. Erdmann, *Ecumenical Quest*, 11.

19. Wilson to Lansing, February 23, 1919, JFDP, Box 2, Reel 1.

20. Jan Smuts was the central figure in the formation of the Union of South Africa, a fascinating and complex figure. See Saul Dubow, *Racial Segregation and the Origins of Apartheid in South Africa, 1919–36* (New York: St. Martin's, 1989), and Saul Dubow, "South Africa's Racist Founding Father Was Also a Human Rights Pioneer," *New York Times*, May 18, 2019, https://www.nytimes.com/2019/05/18/opinion/jan-smuts-south-africa.html.

21. John Foster Dulles, Memorandum of Conference Had at President Wilson's Hotel, Paris, April 1, 1919, at 2 p.m., April 1, 1919, JFDP, Box 2, Reel 1.

22. Philip Mason Burnett, *Reparation at the Paris Peace Conference: From the Standpoint of the American Delegation*, vol. 1 (New York: Columbia University Press, 1940), 775–77. Quoted in Pruessen, "Woodrow Wilson to John Foster Dulles," 113.

23. The figure of $32 billion was whittled down further by the Dawes Plan of 1924 and the Young Plan of 1929 after it was clear the Germans were unable to pay. Richard H. Immerman, *Empire for Liberty: A History of American Imperialism from Benjamin Franklin to Paul Wolfowitz* (Princeton: Princeton University Press, 2010), 171, and Pruessen, *John Foster Dulles*, 36–37.

24. Wilson to John Foster Dulles, June 27, 1919, JFDP, Box 2, Reel 1.

25. John Foster Dulles to Janet Dulles, June 28, 1919, JFDP, Box 2, Reel 1.

26. John Foster Dulles, Memorandum on War Service Record, 3, JFDP, Box 392. For a detailed record of Foster's service on the American Peace Delegation, see Pruessen, *John Foster Dulles*, 29–57.

27. Pruessen catalogued a select number of clients and loans that Foster managed during the 1920s in *John Foster Dulles*, 60–72.

28. Van Dyke to John Foster Dulles, November 4, 1925, JFDP, Box 7, Reel 2.

29. John Foster Dulles to van Dyke, November 6, 1925, JFDP, Box 7, Reel 2.

30. John Foster Dulles to Merrill, April 27, and May 6, 1938, JFDP, Box 17, Reel 3.

31. Mark Toulouse, *The Transformation of John Foster Dulles: From Prophet of Realism to Priest of Nationalism* (Macon, GA: Mercer University Press, 1985), 16–17.

32. John Foster Dulles, Memorandum on the Importance to the United States of the Economic Provisions of the Treaty of Versailles, April 5, 1921, 1, 6, JFDP, Box 4, Reel 1.

33. Pruessen, *John Foster Dulles*, 104.

34. John Foster Dulles, "On the Eve of the Washington Conference," November 1921, 5–13, JFDP, Box 289.

35. John Foster Dulles, "On the Eve of the Washington Conference," 22–23.

36. See Oona A. Hathaway and Scott J. Shapiro, *The Internationalists: How a Radical Plan to Outlaw War Remade the World* (New York: Simon & Schuster, 2017).

37. John Foster Dulles, "Outlawing War," circa 1922, 1, JFDP, Box 279.

38. John Foster Dulles, "Outlawing War," 10.

39. John Foster Dulles, "Outlawing War," 11–18.

40. John Foster Dulles, "America's Part in an Economic Conference," December 17, 1921, 2, JFDP, Box 289.

41. John Foster Dulles, "America's Part," 3.

42. John Foster Dulles, "America's Part," 13.

43. John Foster Dulles, "The Allied Debts," *Foreign Affairs* 1, no. 1 (September 15, 1922): 131, JFDP, Box 279.

44. John Foster Dulles, "The Allied Debts," 132.

45. Report of Committee on War Appointed by the New York Presbytery, October 1924, 3, PACC, Box 2.

46. Report of Committee on War Appointed by the New York Presbytery, 3–7.

47. "Paper by John F. Dulles," in Report of Committee on War Appointed by the New York Presbytery, 18.

48. "Paper by John F. Dulles," 19.

49. "Paper by John F. Dulles," 20.

50. Catt to John Foster Dulles, November 8, 1924, PACC, Box 2.

51. John Foster Dulles to Catt, November 14, 1924, PACC, Box 2.

52. Program, Conference on the Cause and Cure of War, January 18–24, 1925, PACC, Box 2.

53. "Women Can Banish War in Generation, Conference Hears," *World*, January 21, 1925, PACC, Box 2.

54. Program, Conference on the Cause and Cure of War.

55. Pruessen, *John Foster Dulles*, 98.

56. "Women Can Banish War in Generation, Conference Hears."

57. Bevan Sewall, "Pragmatism, Religion, and John Foster Dulles's Embrace of Christian Internationalism in the 1930s," *Diplomatic History* 41, no. 4 (2017): 802.

58. Harry Emerson Fosdick, *The Living of These Days: An Autobiography* (New York: Harper, 1956), 109.

59. Fosdick, *Living of These Days*, 122–33.

60. Harry Emerson Fosdick, "Shall the Fundamentalists Win?" *Christian Century* 39, no. 23 (June 8, 1922): 713.

61. Fosdick, "Shall the Fundamentalists Win?," 713–14.

62. Fosdick, *Living of These Days*, 145.

63. Robert Moats Miller, *Harry Emerson Fosdick: Preacher, Pastor, Prophet* (New York: Oxford University Press, 1985), 116–17.

64. "An Overture to the General Assembly Adopted by the Presbytery of Philadelphia," October 16, 1922, Box 12, Folder 33, "Guide to the Presbyterian Church in the USA Office of Stated Clerk Records," PHS.

65. George Marsden, *Fundamentalism and American Culture*, 2nd ed. (New York: Oxford University Press, 2006), 175.

66. "An Affirmation Designed to Safeguard the Unity and Liberty of the Presbyterian Church in the United States of America," December 26, 1923, Box 12, Folder 34, "Polemical Publications, Articles, Sermons, Clippings, 1922–1924," PHS. By May 5, 1924, there were 1293 cosigners.

67. Edgar Whitaker Work et al., "Presbytery of New York: Explanatory Statement," January 14, 1924, Box 12, Folder 34, "Polemical Publications, Articles, Sermons, Clippings, 1922–1924," PHS.

68. "A Protest," February 4, 1924, Box 12, Folder 33, "Guide to the Presbyterian Church in the USA Office of Stated Clerk Records," PHS.

69. Walter D. Buchanan, Albert D. Gantz, and John McNeill, "Fosdick Case Complaint of Walter D. Buchanan and Others to the 136th General Assembly

of the Presbyterian Church in the U.S.A. against the Presbytery of New York," May 3, 1924, 46, Box 12, Folder 34, "Polemical Publications, Articles, Sermons, Clippings, 1922–1924," PHS.

70. Mendenhall to John Foster Dulles, April 15, 1924, JFDP, Box 6, Reel 2.

71. John Foster Dulles to Finney, April 17, 1924, JFDP, Box 6, Reel 2.

72. John Foster Dulles to Charles Wood, May 13, 1924, PACC, Box 2.

73. Foster explained the role and workings of the Judicial Commission upon the request of the librarian of Harvard University Law School. John Foster Dulles to Eldon R. James, November 24, 1924, PACC, Box 2.

74. "Text of Report of the Judicial Commission regarding the Complaint against the New York Presbytery," *New York Times*, May 29, 1924, Box 12, Folder 34, "Polemical Publications, Articles, Sermons, Clippings, 1922–1924," PHS.

75. Fosdick, *Living of These Days*, 171.

76. Miller, *Harry Emerson Fosdick*, 132–33.

77. John Foster Dulles to Allen Macy Dulles, June 2, 1924, PACC, Box 2.

78. Timothy N. Pfeiffer, oral interview, October 14, 1965, New York City, conducted by Richard D. Challener, JFDOHC.

79. Pfeiffer, oral interview.

80. Coffin to John Foster Dulles, March 20, 1925, PACC, Box 2.

81. The Presbyterian Church in the U.S.A. in the General Assembly, 1925, in the Matter of the Complaint of Albert D. Gantz and others against the Synod of New York: Memorandum for Respondent, 7, PACC, Box 2.

82. Mendenhall to Coffin, Brown, and John Foster Dulles, June 24, 1925, JFDP, Box 7, Reel 2.

83. John Foster Dulles to Coffin, December 9, 1925. See also Coffin to John Foster Dulles, December 7, 1925, JFDP, Box 7, Reel 2.

84. Memorandum on Behalf of the Presbytery of New York, Respondent, 3.

85. Memorandum on Behalf of the Presbytery of New York, Respondent, 6–7.

86. Van Dyke to John Foster Dulles, January 25, 1926, PACC, Box 3.

87. Brown to John Foster Dulles, January 8, 1926, JFDP, Box 7, Reel 2.

88. Coffin to John Foster Dulles, January 8 and January 12, 1926, JFDP, Box 7, Reel 2.

89. Coffin to John Foster Dulles, October 15, 1926, JFDP, Box 7, Reel 2.

90. John Foster Dulles to Bennett, May 13, 1926, JFDP, Box 7, Reel 2.

Chapter 4

1. John Foster Dulles, "The Church's Contribution to a Warless World," speech given at Bushnell Memorial Hall, Hartford, CT, October 11, 1939, JFDP, Box 289.

2. Eleanor Lansing Dulles, *John Foster Dulles: The Last Year* (New York: Harcourt, Brace & World, 1963), 152.

3. Travel Notes, "St. Lawrence Trip," circa 1935, July 21–August 17, JFDP, Box 278. The gaff rig is a horizontal pole that supports a four-cornered sail at the top. The backstay and shroud are cables that support the spar, or the mast.

4. Travel Notes, "St. Lawrence Trip."

5. Eleanor Lansing Dulles, *John Foster Dulles*, 154.

6. Avery Dulles, oral interview, July 30, 1966, Woodstock College, MD, 14, conducted by Philip A. Crowl, JFDOHC.

7. Roswell Barnes, oral interview, July 24, 1964, New York City, 35–36, conducted by Philip A. Crowl, JFDOHC.

8. Avery Dulles, oral interview, 15.

9. Ronald W. Pruessen, *John Foster Dulles: The Road to Power* (New York: Macmillan, 1982), 94.

10. Pruessen, *John Foster Dulles*, 87.

11. John Foster Dulles and Morris Hillquit, "The Power of International Finance," speech and discussion at Foreign Policy Association, March 28, 1928, 8, JFDP, Box 289.

12. Martin Erdmann, *Ecumenical Quest for a World Federation: The Churches' Contribution to Marshal Public Support for World Order and Peace, 1919–1945* (Greenville, SC: Verax Vox Media, 2016), 166.

13. John Foster Dulles to Osler, November 22, 1927, JFDP, Box 8, Reel 2.

14. John Foster Dulles to Claude W. Cole, September 3, 1929, and Claude W. Cole to John Foster Dulles, September 15, 1929, JFDP, Box 9, Reel 2.

15. Claude W. Cole to John Foster Dulles, March 2, 1930, JFDP, Box 9, Reel 2.

16. John Foster Dulles to Claude W. Cole, February 23, 1933, JFDP, Box 11, Reel 2.

17. Pruessen, *John Foster Dulles*, 138–39.

18. John Foster Dulles, "The Road to Peace," *Atlantic Monthly*, October 1935, 492, JFDP, Box 281.

19. John Foster Dulles to Sedgwick, May 1, 1935, JFDP, Box 14, Reel 3.

20. John Foster Dulles, "The Road to Peace," 492.

21. John Foster Dulles, "The Road to Peace," 492.

22. John Foster Dulles to Sedgwick, May 1, 1935.

23. John Foster Dulles, "The Road to Peace," 493. Hereafter, page references to this work will be given in parentheses in the text.

24. Thomas Hobbes, *Leviathan*, ed. C. B. Macpherson (New York: Penguin Books, 1986), 190.

25. Albert N. Keim, "John Foster Dulles and the Federal Council of Churches, 1937–1945" (PhD diss., Ohio State University, 1971), 18–19.

26. Sedgwick to John Foster Dulles, May 17, 1935; contract from the *Atlantic Monthly* agreeing to pay $175 to John Foster Dulles, June 5, 1935; John Foster Dulles to Edward Weeks, August 2, 1935; Aswell to John Foster Dulles, September 10, 1935, JFDP, Box 14, Reel 3.

27. John Foster Dulles to the Japanese ambassador, October 1, 1935; Luther to John Foster Dulles, September 25, 1935; Rosso to John Foster Dulles, September 28, 1935, JFDP Box 14, Reel 3.

28. Cromwell to John Foster Dulles, October 1, 1935; Dodds to John Foster Dulles, September 25, 1935; Clothier to John Foster Dulles, September 25, 1935; Stone to John Foster Dulles, October 4, 1935; Scharf to John Foster Dulles, November 5, 1935; Poole to John Foster Dulles, November 26, 1935; Edith F. Dulles to John Foster Dulles, September 23, 1935, JFDP, Box 14, Reel 3.

29. John Foster Dulles, "Peaceful Change within the Society of Nations," Stafford Little Foundation Series, March 19, 1936, 5, JFDP, Box 289. Hereafter, page references from this work will be given in parentheses in the text.

30. Albert N. Keim, "John Foster Dulles and the Protestant World Order Movement on the Eve of World War II," *Journal of Church and State* 21, no. 1 (Winter 1979): 74.

31. John Mackay, oral interview, January 9, 1965, Chevy Chase, MD, 6, conducted by Philip A. Crowl, JFDOHC.

32. Samuel McCrea Cavert, oral interview, July 29, 1965, New York City, 1–2, conducted by Richard D. Challener, JFDOHC.

33. Cavert, oral interview, 2.

34. John Foster Dulles, "The Problem of Peace in a Dynamic World," *Religion in Life: A Christian Quarterly* 6, no. 2 (Spring 1937): 207, JFDP, Box 281 (emphasis added).

35. John Foster Dulles, "As Seen by a Layman," *Religion in Life: A Christian Quarterly* 7, no. 1 (Winter 1938): 40, JFDP, Box 281.

36. John Foster Dulles, "As Seen by a Layman," 36.

37. John Foster Dulles, "As Seen by a Layman," 37.

38. Keim, "John Foster Dulles," 76.

39. John Foster Dulles, "As Seen by a Layman," 40.

40. John Foster Dulles, "As Seen by a Layman," 41.

41. John Foster Dulles, "As Seen by a Layman," 44.

42. Brandt to John Foster Dulles, October 18, 1938, JFDP, Box 17, Reel 3.

43. Curtis to John Foster Dulles, July 15, 1939, JFDP, Box 18, Reel 4.

44. John Foster Dulles to Curtis, July 19, 1939, JFDP, Box 18, Reel 4.

45. John Foster Dulles, *War, Peace, and Change* (New York: Harper & Brothers, 1939), 115.

46. Coffin to John Foster Dulles, December 20, 1938, JFDP, Box 17, Reel 3.

47. John Foster Dulles, *War, Peace, and Change*, 119.

48. Barnes to John Foster Dulles, January 5, 1939, JFDP, Box 18, Reel 4.

49. John Coleman Bennett, oral interview, May 13, 1965, New York City, 22–23, conducted by Richard D. Challener, JFDOHC.

Chapter 5

1. John Foster Dulles to Henry Sloane Coffin, May 20, 1940, Box 7, Folder 30, "General Secretary John Foster Dulles, June 1922–January 1951," PHS.

2. Lillias Dulles Hinshaw, oral interview, May 29, 1966, Washington, DC, 56–57, conducted by Philip A. Crowl, JFDOHC.

3. Robert F. Hart, oral interview, July 6, 1965, Chaumont, NY, 15, conducted by Philip A. Crowl, JFDOHC.

4. Arthur Dean, oral interview, May 20 and July 13, 1964, New York City, 41, conducted by Philip A. Crowl, JFDOHC.

5. Avery Dulles, oral interview, July 30, 1966, Woodstock College, MD, 36–37, conducted by Philip A. Crowl, JFDOHC.

6. Avery Dulles, oral interview, 22.

7. See Dean and Hart, oral histories, for example.

8. Lillias Dulles Hinshaw, oral interview, 47–51.

9. Lillias Dulles Hinshaw, oral interview, 48.

10. Jonathan C. Brown, "In Memoriam: John W. F. Dulles (1913–2008), Pro-

fessor of Latin American Studies; Son of Former Secretary of State," *Perspectives on History: The Newsmagazine of the American Historical Association*, December 1, 2008, https://www.historians.org/publications-and-directories/perspectives-on-history/december-2008/in-memoriam-john-w-f-dulles.

11. Marquis Childs, oral interview, January 12, 1966, Washington, DC, 38–39, conducted by Richard D. Challener, JFDOHC.

12. John W. F. Dulles to John Foster Dulles, December 3, 1958, JFDP, Box 128, Reel 50. See correspondence between John and Foster in Dulles, John W. F., JFDP, Box 6, 8–16, 31, 59, 69, 91, 102, 115, 128, 139.

13. Avery Dulles, SJ, *A Testimonial to Grace and Reflections on a Theological Journey* (1946; reprint, Kansas City, MO: Sheed & Ward, 1996), 3–9. Hereafter, page references to this work will be given in parentheses in the text.

14. Avery Dulles, oral interview, 27–28.

15. Childs, oral interview, 37–38.

16. Dean, oral interview, 39.

17. See Avery's correspondence with Foster in Dulles, Avery, JFDP, Box 8–18, 26, 41, 69, 80, 91, 102, 115, and 128.

18. Glassford to John Foster Dulles, October 14, 1945, and telegrams from Florence Snell (Foster's secretary) to John Foster Dulles, October 18, 20, 26, 1945, JFDP, Box 26, Reel 6.

19. See, for example, Leonard Mosley, *Dulles: A Biography of Eleanor, Allen, and John Foster Dulles and Their Family Network* (New York: Dial Press / James Wade, 1978), 54, 80–83, and Townsend Hoopes, *The Devil and John Foster Dulles* (New York: Little, Brown, 1973), 43.

20. Hart, oral interview, 7.

21. Travel log, "Menemsha," August 12–31, 1933, PACC, Box 5.

22. Hart, oral interview, 34.

23. Firm of Osler, Hoskin, and Harcourt to John Foster Dulles, July 15, 1941, JFDP, Box 20, Reel 4.

24. Hart, oral interview, 33.

25. Richard K. Benson, oral interview, July 8, 1965, Chaumont, NY, 15, conducted by Philip A. Crowl, JFDOHC.

26. John Foster Dulles to Hart, September 30, 1941, JFDP, Box 20, Reel 4.

27. Hart, oral interview, 35.

28. Hart to John Foster Dulles, May 1, 1943, JFDP, Box 22, Reel 5.

29. Hart, oral interview, 38–39.

30. Hart to John Foster Dulles, July 5, 1943, JFDP, Box 22, Reel 5.

31. "Life at Duck Island Retreat Described by Foster Dulles," *Picton (ON) Gazette*, June 11, 1958.

32. "Life at Duck Island Retreat Described by Foster Dulles."

33. Diary of trip to Duck Island, April 8–April 23, 1944, PACC, Box 8.

34. "Life at Duck Island Retreat Described by Foster Dulles."

35. Hart, oral interview, 29.

36. See Reinhold Niebuhr, "Leaves from the Notebook of a War-bound American," *Christian Century*, October 25, 1939, 1298–99; November 15, 1939, 1405–6; December 6, 1939, 1502–3; December 27, 1939, 1607–8.

37. Draft of "The American Churches and the International Situation," JFDP, Box 19, Reel 4. Henry P. Van Dusen enclosed the draft in a letter to John Foster Dulles, January 19, 1940.

38. John Foster Dulles to Van Dusen, January 16 and March 18, 1940, JFDP, Box 19, Reel 4.

39. John Foster Dulles to Debevoise, April 30, 1940, JFDP, Box 19, Reel 4.

40. The speech was "America's Role in World Affairs," given to the YMCA in Detroit on October 28, 1939, JFDP, Box 289.

41. Rogers Lamont to John Foster Dulles, April 31 [*sic*], 1940, JFDP, Box 19, Reel 4.

42. John Foster Dulles to William R. Castle, November 8, 1940, JFDP, Box 19, Reel 4.

43. Memorandum from John Foster Dulles, October 4, 1940, Box 7, Folder 30, "General Secretary, Dulles, John Foster, June 1922–January 1951," PHS.

44. John Foster Dulles, "The American Churches and the International Situation," December 12, 1940, 1, 5–9, JFDP, Box 19, Reel 4.

45. John Foster Dulles, "The American Churches," 7.

46. Henry P. Van Dusen, oral interview, May 27, 1965, Princeton, NJ, 8, conducted by Richard D. Challener, JFDOHC.

47. Roswell Barnes, oral interview, July 24, 1964, New York City, 8–9, conducted by Philip A. Crowl, JFDOHC.

48. See Mark G. Toulouse, *The Transformation of John Foster Dulles: From Prophet of Realism to Priest of Nationalism* (Macon, GA: Mercer University Press, 1985); Martin Erdmann, *Ecumenical Quest for a World Federation: The Churches' Contribution to Marshal Public Support for World Order and Peace, 1919–1945* (Greenville, SC: Verax Vox Media, 2016); and Andrew Preston, *Sword*

of the Spirit, Shield of Faith: Religion in American War and Diplomacy (New York: Anchor, 2012).

49. "Statement of Guiding Principles," in *A Message from the National Study Conference on the Churches and a Just and Durable Peace*, March 1942, JFDP, Box 290.

50. John Foster Dulles, "Peace without Platitudes," *Fortune*, January 1942, 14, PACC, Box 7.

51. John Foster Dulles, "The American People Need Now to Be Imbued with a Righteous Faith," in *A Righteous Faith for a Just and Durable Peace*, October 1942, 5, JFDP, Box 282.

52. John Foster Dulles, "The American People," 11.

53. "A Christian Message on World Order," July 1943, 19, JFDP, Box 293.

54. John Foster Dulles, "Toward World Order," March 5, 1942, 11, PACC, Box 7.

55. "The Churches and the Dumbarton Oaks Proposals," November 28, 1944, 2, JFDP, Box 283.

56. John Foster Dulles, "Pillars of Peace," *Social Progress*, May 1943, 10, JFDP, Box 283.

57. John Foster Dulles, Memorandum of Conference with the President at the White House on Friday March 26, 1943 at 12:45 p.m., 4, JFDP, Box 283.

58. Department of State, *Postwar Foreign Policy Preparation, 1939–1945*, Department of State Publication 3580, General Foreign Policy Series 15 (Washington, DC: GPO, 1949), 20. Quoted in Frederick S. Dunn, *Peace-making and the Settlement with Japan* (Princeton: Princeton University Press, 1963), 3–4.

59. John Foster Dulles, "The Churches and a Just and Durable Peace," Cleveland, Ohio, January 16, 1945, 1–2, JFDP, Box 26, Reel 2.

60. John Foster Dulles to G. Bromley Oxnam, April 5, 1945, Box 31, Folder 15, "JFD Resignation, April 1945–December 1949," PHS.

61. See correspondence between John Foster Dulles and Arthur Vandenberg, February 17, 22, 28; March 5, 6, 7, 12, 20; April 6; and June 30, 1945, JFDP, Box 27, Reel 6.

62. Vandenberg to John Foster Dulles, June 30, 1945, JFDP, Box 27, Reel 6.

63. See John Foster Dulles, "The Charter—a Great Document of Human Rights," *Post War World* 2, no. 4 (July 10, 1945): 1–3.

64. John Foster Dulles, "The General Assembly," *Foreign Affairs*, October 1945, 11, JFDP, Box 295.

65. See Bernard M. Baruch, statement to the United Nations Atomic Energy Commission, June 13, 1946; John Foster Dulles to Baruch, July 3, 1946, JFDP, Box 28, Reel 7.

66. John Foster Dulles, "The Atomic Bomb and Moral Law," *Christian News-Letter* 251 (January 9, 1946): 12, JFDP, Box 28, Reel 7.

67. John Foster Dulles, "Thoughts on Soviet Foreign Policy and What to Do about It," *Life*, June 3 and 10, 1946, 22, JFDP, Box 284.

Chapter 6

1. *Hearings before the Committee on Foreign Relations, United States Senate,* Eighty-Second Congress, Second Session on Japanese Peace Treaty and Other Treaties Relating to Security in the Pacific, January 22, 1952, 56 (statement of Alexander Wiley), JFDP, Box 61, Reel 22.

2. John Foster Dulles, statement to New York City police commissioner, June 14, 1942, PACC, Box 7.

3. John Foster Dulles, statement to New York City police commissioner.

4. Pistol License Application, Police Department, City of New York, completed by John Foster Dulles, n.d., PACC, Box 7.

5. John Foster Dulles, interview, "US and Russia Could Agree but for Communist Party's Crusade," *US News and World Report*, January 21, 1949, 34, JFDP, Box 297.

6. John Lewis Gaddis, *The Cold War: A New History* (New York: Penguin Books, 2005), 9.

7. Winston S. Churchill, "Iron Curtain Speech, March 5, 1946," Fordham University Modern History Sourcebook, https://sourcebooks.fordham.edu /mod/churchill-iron.asp.

8. "George Kennan's 'Long Telegram,'" February 22, 1946, Wilson Center: Digital Archive; International History Declassified, reprinted in US Department of State, ed., *Foreign Relations of the United States, 1946*, vol. 6, *Eastern Europe; The Soviet Union* (Washington, DC: United States Government Printing Office, 1969), 696–709, http://digitalarchive.wilsoncenter.org/document/116178.

9. "President Harry S. Truman's Address before a Joint Session of Congress, March 12, 1947," Avalon Project: Documents in Law, History and Diplomacy, Yale Law School, Lillian Goldman Law Library, https://avalon.law.yale .edu/20th_century/trudoc.asp.

10. Gaddis, *The Cold War*, 30–36.

11. Gaddis, *The Cold War*, 42.

12. Statement by Acting Secretary Dean Acheson, Department of State Press Release No. 892, December 10, 1946, JFDP, Box 28, Reel 7.

13. See Mark G. Toulouse, *The Transformation of John Foster Dulles: From Prophet of Realism to Priest of Nationalism* (Macon, GA: Mercer University Press, 1985), and Mark Toulouse, "Working toward a Meaningful Peace: John Foster Dulles and the FCC, 1937–1945," *Journal of Presbyterian History* 61, no. 4 (Winter 1983): 393–410.

14. "A Christian Message on World Order," July 1943, JFDP, Box 293.

15. Statement on Control of the Atomic Bomb, Executive Committee of the Federal Council of Churches of Christ in America, September 18, 1945, JFDP, Box 283.

16. John Foster Dulles, "The Atomic Bomb and Moral Law," *Christian News-Letter*, January 9, 1946, 12, JFDP, Box 284.

17. John Foster Dulles, Memorandum of Conference with President Truman in the White House, March 16, 1946, JFDP, Box 29, Reel 7.

18. John Foster Dulles, "Thoughts on Soviet Foreign Policy and What to Do about It," *Life*, June 10, 1946, 38, JFDP, Box 284.

19. "Soviet-American Relations," Commission for a Just and Durable Peace, October 11, 1946, Box 29, Reel 7.

20. John Foster Dulles, "Thoughts on Soviet Foreign Policy," 39.

21. Address by John Foster Dulles at the First Presbyterian Church, Watertown, NY, August 28, 1949, PACC, Box 11.

22. Senator Dulles of New York spoke for ratification of the North Atlantic Treaty (*Congressional Record* 1949, 95, pt. 7:9491), PACC, Box 11.

23. Senator Dulles of New York spoke for aid to the members of the European Pact (*Congressional Record* 1949, 95, pt. 10:13337), PACC, Box 11.

24. John Foster Dulles, *War or Peace* (New York: Macmillan, 1950), 6.

25. Frederick S. Dunn, *Peace-Making and the Settlement with Japan* (Princeton: Princeton University Press, 1963), 54–62.

26. Dunn, *Peace-Making*, 77.

27. Douglas MacArthur, Memorandum on the Peace Treaty Problem, June 14, 1950, 1, JFDP, Box 49, Reel 16.

28. Douglas MacArthur, Memorandum on Formosa, June 14, 1950, 1, JFDP, Box 49, Reel 16.

29. Dunn, *Peace-Making*, 86.

30. Vandenberg to Acheson, March 31, 1950, JFDP, Box 47, Reel 15.

31. John Foster Dulles, *War or Peace*, 122.

32. John Foster Dulles to Acheson, March 29, 1950, JFDP, Box 47, Reel 15.

33. Acheson to John Foster Dulles, March 30, 1950, JFDP, Box 47, Reel 15.

34. Bernard C. Cohen, *Political Process and Foreign Policy: The Making of the Japanese Peace* (Princeton: Princeton University Press, 1957), 126.

35. Cohen, *Political Process*, 134.

36. Cohen, *Political Process*, 136.

37. John M. Allison, oral interview, April 20, 1969, New York City, 7, conducted by Richard D. Challener, JFDOHC.

38. John Foster Dulles, Top Secret Memorandum on Japan Situation, July 6, 1950, JFDP, Box 49, Reel 16.

39. John Foster Dulles, prepared portion of radio interview, CBS, Washington, DC, July 1, 1950, JFDP, Box 54, Reel 19.

40. Digest of Discussion, Study Group Report on Japanese Peace Treaty Problems, Council on Foreign Relations, October 23, 1950, 3, JFDP, Box 54, Reel 19.

41. Digest of Discussion, 5.

42. Allison, oral interview, 17.

43. Press Conference with Mr. Sakai, representing the Japanese press, September 15, 1950, 5, JFDP, Box 54, Reel 19.

44. Shigeru Yoshida, Prime Minister's Report to the Diet regarding Dulles Conferences, February 13, 1951, JFDP, Box 53, Reel 18.

45. Katsuo Okazaki, oral interview, October 2, 1964, Tokyo, 4, conducted by Spencer Davis, JFDOHC.

46. John Foster Dulles, Address to the Australian Institute of International Affairs, Sydney, Australia, February 19, 1951, JFDP, Box 303.

47. John Foster Dulles, Remarks at a Luncheon Tendered by the Institute of Pacific Relations, Manila, Philippines, February 12, 1951, JFDP, Box 303.

48. John Foster Dulles, "Answer to Soviet Charges against Japanese Treaty," *New York Times*, September 3, 1951, JFDP, Box 304.

49. Annex 1: Statement Made at the San Francisco Conference on September 5, 1951, by John Foster Dulles on Behalf of the United States Delegation, Japanese Peace Treaty and Security Pacts, JFDP, Box 61, Reel 22.

50. *Hearings before the Committee on Foreign Relations, United States Senate,*

January 22, 1952, 5–14 (statement of John Foster Dulles, personal representative of the president on the Japanese peace treaty).

51. John Foster Dulles, interview, "Impressions of Japanese Peace Treaty Conference," September 11, 1951, JFDP, Box 53, Reel 18.

52. Colina to John Foster Dulles, October 26, 1951; Sacasa to John Foster Dulles, October 29, 1951; Valenzuela to John Foster Dulles, November 6, 1951; del Rio to John Foster Dulles, October 25, 1951, JFDP, Box 53, Reel 18.

53. John Foster Dulles, "A Diplomat and His Faith," *Christian Century,* March 19, 1952, JFDP, Box 285.

54. *Hearings before the Committee on Foreign Relations, United States Senate,* January 23, 1952, 77–86 (statement of A. J. Muste).

Chapter 7

1. Avery Dulles, SJ, *John Foster Dulles: His Religious and Political Heritage; The Flora Levy Lecture in the Humanities,* ed. Maurice W. duQuesnay and Albert W. Fields (Lafayette: University of Southwest Louisiana, 1994), 22.

2. Presidential Proclamation 2914 of December 16, 1950, by President Harry Truman Proclaiming the Existence of a National Emergency, December 16, 1950, Docs Teach, https://www.docsteach.org/documents/document/presiden tial-proclamation-2914-of-december-16-1950-by-president-harry-truman-pro claiming-the-existence-of-a-national-emergency.

3. Proclamation 3004—Control of Persons Leaving or Entering the United States, January 17, 1953, National Archives, https://www.archives.gov/fed eral-register/codification/proclamations/03004.html#1.

4. Du Bois to John Foster Dulles, February 22, 1957, James Aronson–W. E. B. Du Bois Collection (MS 292), Special Collections and University Archives, University of Massachusetts Amherst Libraries, http://credo.library.umass.edu /view/full/mums292-b001-i021.

5. Kent v. Dulles 357 U.S. 116 (1958), in Legal Information Institute, Cornell Law School, https://www.law.cornell.edu/supremecourt/text/357/116.

6. Richard H. Immerman, ed., *John Foster Dulles and the Diplomacy of the Cold War* (Princeton: Princeton University Press, 1990), 10.

7. See, for example, Richard H. Immerman, *John Foster Dulles: Piety, Pragmatism, and Power in US Foreign Policy* (Wilmington, DE: Scholarly Resources, 1999); Richard H. Immerman, *John Foster Dulles and the Diplomacy of the Cold*

War; William Inboden, *Religion and American Foreign Policy, 1945–1960: The Soul of Containment* (Cambridge: Cambridge University Press, 2008); Michael Doran, *Ike's Gamble: America's Rise to Dominance in the Middle East* (New York: Free Press, 2016), to name a few.

8. Dwight D. Eisenhower, oral interview, July 28, 1964, Gettysburg, PA, 6–7, conducted by Philip C. Crowl, JFDOHC.

9. Richard Nixon, oral interview, March 5, 1965, New York City, 6, conducted by Richard D. Challener, JFDOHC.

10. Eisenhower, oral interview, 5.

11. John Lewis Gaddis, *The Cold War: A New History* (New York: Penguin Books, 2005), 32.

12. John Foster Dulles, "A New Foreign Policy: A Policy of Boldness," *Life*, May 19, 1952, 11–14, JFDP, Box 286.

13. *Hearing on the Nomination of John Foster Dulles, Secretary of State-Designate, to the Committee on Foreign Relations, United States Senate*, Eighty-Third Congress, First Session, January 15, 1953 (statement of John Foster Dulles), 6, JFDP, Box 310.

14. John Foster Dulles, Speech to American-Japan Society, Tokyo, Japan, February 2, 1951, JFDP, Box 303.

15. John Foster Dulles, "A New Foreign Policy," 6.

16. John Foster Dulles, "A New Foreign Policy," 7.

17. John Foster Dulles, Speech before the Council on Foreign Relations, New York City, January 12, 1954, 3–4, 8, JFDP, Box 322.

18. Gaddis, *The Cold War*, 68.

19. James Shepley, "How Dulles Averted War," *Life* 40, no. 3 (January 16, 1956): 70.

20. Shepley, "How Dulles Averted War," 78.

21. Shepley, "How Dulles Averted War," 78.

22. Richard H. Parke, "Stevenson Gibes at the President as Inept 'Coach,'" *New York Times*, February 26, 1956, 1.

23. John Foster Dulles, Opening Statement, Secretary Dulles' News Conference of January 17, 1956, 1, JFDP, Box 105, Reel 41.

24. Samuel McCrea Cavert, oral interview, July 29, 1965, New York City, 39, conducted by Richard D. Challener, JFDOHC.

25. John Mackay, oral interview, January 9, 1965, Chevy Chase, MD, 14–16, conducted by Philip A. Crowl, JFDOHC.

26. O. Frederick Nolde, oral interview, June 2, 1965, New York City, 13–14, conducted by Richard D. Challener, JFDOHC.

27. "The Power of Moral Forces," in *The Spiritual Legacy of John Foster Dulles: Selections from His Articles and Addresses*, ed. Henry P. Van Dusen (Philadelphia: Westminster, 1960), 225.

28. Robert Purcell, oral interview, July 15, 1965, New York City, 34, conducted by Richard D. Challener, JFDOHC.

29. See Leonard Mosley, *Dulles: A Biography of Eleanor, Allen, and John Foster Dulles and Their Family Network* (New York: Doubleday, 1978), for a comprehensive look at the relationship among the three siblings.

30. Mosley, *Dulles*, 300–301.

31. See John Foster Dulles, Statement made at Trophy Races, July 15–17, 1955, JFDP, Box 91, Reel 45.

32. Manning to Hart, November 11, 1957, Crescent Yacht Club, Chaumont, NY, http://www.crescentyachtclub.org/NewWeb/wp-content/uploads/2020/02/DullesTrophy.pdf.

33. Dana Adams Schmidt, "John Foster Dulles Dies; Special Funeral Decreed; Geneva Talks to Suspend," *New York Times*, May 24, 1959, 1.

34. Eleanor Lansing Dulles, *John Foster Dulles: The Last Year* (New York: Harcourt, Brace & World, 1963), 229.

35. John Foster Dulles, Statement Accepting the Position as Special Consultant to the President, April 23, 1959, JFDP, Box 370.

36. Eleanor Lansing Dulles, *Chances of a Lifetime: A Memoir* (Englewood Cliffs, NJ: Prentice Hall, 1980), 275.

37. Eleanor Lansing Dulles, *John Foster Dulles*, 231.

38. Eleanor Lansing Dulles, *John Foster Dulles*, 232.

39. Townsend Hoopes, *The Devil and John Foster Dulles* (Boston: Little, Brown, 1973), 486.

40. Dwight D. Eisenhower, "John Foster Dulles: The President's Tribute," *New York Times*, May 25, 1959, 1.

41. "Dulles Formulated and Conducted US Foreign Policy for More Than Six Years," *New York Times*, May 25, 1959, https://archive.nytimes.com/www.nytimes.com/learning/general/onthisday/bday/0225.html?scp=1&sq=.

Epilogue

1. Louis Jefferson, *The John Foster Dulles Book of Humor* (New York: St. Martin's, 1986), 131.

2. "Carol Burnett Showcases Her 'Lost Episodes,'" Paley Center for Media, September 16, 2015, https://www.youtube.com/watch?v=6HHcX_M_eMs.

3. Jean Edward Smith, *Eisenhower in War and Peace* (New York: Random House, 2012), 552n.

4. Mark Russell, "Dull, Duller, Dulles," *New York Times*, July 13, 1986, https://www.nytimes.com/1986/07/13/books/dull-duller-dulles.html.

5. Richard H. Immerman, ed., *John Foster Dulles and the Diplomacy of the Cold War* (Princeton: Princeton University Press, 1990), 10.

6. See Charles Murray, *Coming Apart: The State of White America, 1960–2010* (New York: Crown Forum, 2013).

7. Secretary Dulles Press Conference, London, April 13, 1954, Geneva Conference, April–July 1954, JFDP, Box 81, Reel 31.

8. Allen H. Kitchens and Neal H. Peterson, eds., *The Geneva Conference*, vol. 16, *Foreign Relations of the United States, 1952–1954*, ed. John P. Glennon (Washington, DC: United States Government Printing Office, 1981), 1715.

9. Harry S. Truman, "Inaugural Address, January 20, 1949," in *The Annals of America*, vol. 16, *The Second World War and After, 1940–1949*, ed. Mortimer J. Adler and Charles Van Doren (Chicago: Encyclopaedia Britannica, 1968), 562.

10. See Will Herberg, *Protestant—Catholic—Jew: An Essay in American Religious Sociology* (New York: Doubleday, 1955).

11. Raymond Haberski Jr., *God and War: American Civil Religion Since 1945* (New Brunswick, NJ: Rutgers University Press, 2012), 23.

12. Fulton J. Sheen, *Communism and the Conscience of the West* (New York: Bobbs-Merrill, 1948), 55. Quoted in Haberski, *God and War*, 27 (emphasis Haberski's).

13. See Jon Butler, *Awash in a Sea of Faith: Christianizing the American People* (Cambridge, MA: Harvard University Press, 1990).

14. Two years later, in 1956, Congress directed that the national motto be changed to In God We Trust. That same year, Eisenhower ordered that the motto be inscribed on American currency.

15. Andrew Preston, *Sword of the Spirit, Shield of Faith: Religion in American War and Diplomacy* (New York: Anchor, 2012), 7–8.

16. See Justin B. Litke, *Twilight of the Republic: Empire and Exceptionalism in the American Political Tradition* (Lexington: University Press of Kentucky, 2013), and John D. Wilsey, *American Exceptionalism and Civil Religion: Reassessing the History of an Idea* (Downers Grove, IL: IVP Academic, 2015), for intellectual histories of American exceptionalism that consider the idea's complexity and various manifestations.

17. John Foster Dulles, "A Policy of Boldness," *Life* 32, no. 20 (May 19, 1952): 146.

18. John Foster Dulles, "A Policy of Boldness," 146.

19. John Foster Dulles, "A Policy of Boldness," 127.

20. Richard M. Gamble, *The War for Righteousness: Progressive Christianity, the Great War, and the Rise of the Messianic Nation* (Wilmington, DE: ISI, 2003), 5.

21. Gamble, *The War for Righteousness*, 30–38.

22. Gamble, *The War for Righteousness*, 30–38.

23. Allen Macy Dulles, *The True Church: A Study (Historical and Scriptural)* (New York: Revell, 1907), 270.

24. Allen Macy Dulles, *The True Church*, 283–84.

25. Allen Macy Dulles, *The True Church*, 289.

26. Lionel Curtis, *Civitas Dei* (London: Allen & Unwin, 1950), vii.

27. Curtis, *Civitas Dei*, 742–43.

28. John Foster Dulles to Curtis, November 4, 1937, JFDP, Box 16, Reel 3.

29. Samuel Goldman, *God's Country: Christian Zionism in America* (Philadelphia: University of Pennsylvania Press, 2018), 133.

30. See William Zukerman, "Dulles, Israel, and American Jews," *Jewish Newsletter* 9, no. 13 (June 22, 1953): 1–2, JFDP, Box 73, Reel 27. Zukerman, the editor of *Jewish Newsletter*, expressed grave concern that Foster was withdrawing American support for Israel and appeasing its Arab enemies.

31. JFD Statement before the Senate Foreign Relations Committee, February 24, 1956, JFDP, Box 104, Reel 40.

32. Bernard Katzen to Roderic O'Connor, October 21, 1954, JFDP, Box 82, Reel 32.

33. JFD Statement before the Senate Foreign Relations Committee, February 24, 1956.

34. "Cultural and Scientific Aid to Israel," July 17, 1956, JFDP, Box 104, Reel 40.

35. Elson to John Foster Dulles, September 30, 1953, JFDP, Box 69, Reel 25.

36. William Macomber to John Foster Dulles, August 22, 1957, JFDP, Box 116, Reel 45.

37. Elson to John Foster Dulles, January 3, 1958, JFDP, Box 128, Reel 50.

38. This section on Foster and Israel has been adapted from John D. Wilsey, "Wondrous Chasm between Jacksonianism and Progressivism? Response to Michael Doran's 'The Theology of Foreign Policy' in *First Things*," *Providence: A Journal of Christianity and American Foreign Policy*, April 19, 2018, https://prov idencemag.com/2018/04/wondrous-chasm-jacksonianism-progressivism-re sponse-michael-doran-theology-foreign-policy-first-things-zionism-andrew -jackson-john-foster-dulles/, with kind permission from Mark Tooley, editor in chief of *Providence*.

39. Martin Luther King Jr., "My Pilgrimage to Nonviolence," September 1, 1958, Martin Luther King, Jr. Research and Education Institute, Stanford University, King Papers, https://kinginstitute.stanford.edu/king-papers/doc uments/my-pilgrimage-nonviolence. Originally published in *Fellowship* 24 (September 1, 1958): 4–9.

40. Anthony Leviero, "Eisenhower Picks a 'Cold War' Chief," *New York Times*, February 17, 1953, 16.

41. John Foster Dulles, Remarks before the United Negro College Fund, March 20, 1955, JFDP, Box 99, Reel 37.

42. See Martin Luther King Jr., "I Have a Dream," Address Delivered at the March on Washington for Jobs and Freedom, August 28, 1963, Martin Luther King, Jr. Research and Education Institute, Stanford University, King Papers, https://kinginstitute.stanford.edu/king-papers/documents/i-have-dream-ad dress-delivered-march-washington-jobs-and-freedom.

43. William I. Hitchcock, *The Age of Eisenhower: America and the World in the 1950s* (New York: Simon & Schuster, 2018), 217.

44. Hitchcock, *The Age of Eisenhower*, 241.

45. Richard Weaver, *Ideas Have Consequences* (Chicago: University of Chicago Press, 1948), 176.

46. *CIL* 11.6243, 6–8.

47. William Inboden, *Religion and American Foreign Policy, 1945–1960: The Soul of Containment* (Cambridge: Cambridge University Press, 2008), 22.

Index

Note: *Bold page numbers refer to illustrations.*

Acheson, Dean, 7, 150, 158, 159
Adams, Sherman, 201
Adenauer, Konrad, 185, 186
Advisory Committee on Problems of
    Foreign Relations (1939), 142
AFME (American Friends of the
    Middle East), 199–200
Agnew, George P., 91
Alexander, George, 87, 91
Alexander II, 31–32
Allen, Florence, 85
Allen, Henry Tureman, 85
Allied Supreme Command, 80
Allies, 35, 74, 80, 135, 139
Allison, John, 161
"American Churches and the Inter-
    national Situation, The" (JFD),
    137
"American Churches and the
    International Situation, The"
    (Niebuhr), 134
American exceptionalism, 152, 194,
    195–96, 203
American Friends of the Middle East
    (AFME), 199–200

American indispensability, 17, 76, 82,
    84, 134, 181, 194, 196, 203
Anderson, Harriet, 61
ANZUS alliance, security treaties
    with, 165
atomic weapons
    deployment of, 146, 149, 154, 177
    as deterrence, 177
    international control of, 143, 154
    JFD's view of, 143–44, 153, 154, 156
Auburn Affirmation (1923), 89, 90
Augustine, 197
Australia, 161, 162, 163, 165, 175
Austria, 107
Avery, Janet Pomeroy. *See* Dulles,
    Janet Pomeroy Avery
Axis powers, 113, 135, 139, 140, 152

Baker, Conrad, 30
Barnes, Roswell, 99, 120, 136, 138, 141,
    179, 185
Baruch, Bernard, 42, 74, 75, 143
Baruch Plan (1946), 143
Belgium, 102, 105
Bennett, James E., 95

Bennett, John Coleman, 121
Benson, Dick, 131
Bergson, Henri, 7, 112
Berman, Pemberton ("Pem"), 122, 186
Bernadotte Plan, 199–200
Blaine, James, 32
"Blizzard of '88," 44
Borton, Hugh, 157
Borton Group, 157
Brandt, Joseph A., 119
Briand, Aristide, 105
brinkmanship. *See also* massive retaliation policy
  art of, 178
  criticism of, 9, 17, 178–79, 180
  informed by JFD's morals, 173, 181–82
  JFD's marriage proposal as, 64
  JFD's shift to, 179–80
  of John F. Kennedy, 180
Britain, 105, 106, 107
Brown, William Adams, 94, 95, 136, 193
Brownell, Herbert, 202
Bryan, William Jennings, 88–89, 92
Bunyan, John, 185–86
Burnett, Carol, 188
Burnham, Caleb, 39
Butler, Jon, 193
Byrnes, James F., 130, 142–43, 150

Carnegie, Andrew, 80
Carnegie Endowment for International Peace, 80, 150
Case, Everett, 160–61

Catt, Carrie Chapman, 77, 85
Cavert, Samuel M., 117, 179, 180, 181
CFM (Council of Foreign Ministers), 150, 152, 164
Challenge of the Present Crisis, The (Fosdick), 87, 88
Chamberlain, Neville, 107
Chamorro, Emiliano, 72
change, JFD's views on
  analogy for, 101–2
  human resistance to, 109, 144
  as inevitable, 86, 101, 108, 109, 110, 112, 114, 152, 196–97
  as necessary, orderly, and peaceful, 101, 108, 109–10, 112
  peril of relaxation and, 144
  vs. progress, 114
  religious commitments and, 17, 18, 68, 69, 84–85, 86, 196–97
  vs. status quo, 79, 111, 144
Cheves, Langdon, 26
Childs, Marquis, 125–26
China, 146, 149, 164–65, 169, 174, 191, 192
Chou Enlai, 191
Christian Amendment, 193
Christianity and the Social Crisis (Rauschenbusch), 201
"Christian Messages to the Peoples of the World" (Commission for a Just and Durable Peace), 138
Christmas traditions, 52
church, JFD's views on
  criticism of, 133
  peril of relaxation for, 142

recovery of dynamic faith in, 97,
118, 139, 142, 189, 195
role in peace efforts, 10, 108, 115,
118, 120, 134, 137, 138, 139–40
role in public education, 141–42
usefulness of, 11
"Churches and Dumbarton Oaks,
The" (Commission for a Just and
Durable Peace), 138
Churchill, Winston, 147–48, 185
civil religion, American, 192–93, 194,
196
Civil Rights Act (1957), 202
Civitas Dei (Curtis), 198
Clarke, William Newton, 193
Clothier, Robert, 113
Clover, Dora, 61
Clover, Richardson, 61
Coffin, Henry Sloane, 89, 93, 94, 95,
120
Cohen, Bernard C., 158, 159–60
Cold War
as ideological confrontation,
147–48, 153
JFD's view on armaments during,
147, 156
religious framing of, 192, 193
WWII as setup for, 147–48, 153
Cole, Cecil, 103–4
Cole, Claude W., 53, 103–4, 131
Cole, Sarah Ann, 131
Colfax, Schuyler, 31
Colina, Rafael de la, 166
collective security
as indispensable to peace, 181

in JFD's discussions with Eisenhower, 172
as League of Nations goal, 115
through Japanese treaty, 160, 162,
175
through massive retaliation policy,
176, 177
through North Atlantic Treaty, 156
through Pacific treaties, 165, 175
Commission for a Just and Durable
Peace (Dulles Commission)
chaired by JFD, 8–9, 15, 133, 134,
137–38
Christian leaders mobilized by,
139, 141–42
conferences held by, 139
creation of, 134, 137
JFD's resignation from, 142
"Statement of Guiding Principles"
(Six Pillars), 138, 141–42
themes of, 134, 138, 139–41, 142, 143,
144, 167
Commission on International Justice
and Goodwill (FCC), 77
Committee on War (New York Presbytery), 83–84
Committee to Study War (New York
Presbytery), 77
Communism
Christian overlap with, 155
vs. fascism, 153, 155, 156
vs. free world, 151
JFD's opposition to, 17, 41, 151, 153,
155–56, 168, 170–71, 182, 189
as priority in JFD's Japan treaty
work, 159–64, 166

Communism and the Conscience of the West (Sheen), 193
Conference on the Cause and Cure of War (1925), 77, 85
containment policy, 9, 173, 174, 175, 177
Coolidge, Calvin, 85
Cooper, George, 13
Cooper, Herb, 13
Corwin, Edward, 119
Council of Foreign Ministers (CFM), 150, 152, 164
Council on Foreign Relations, 161
Covenant of League of Nations (1919), 109, 111–12, 116
Crescent Yacht Club, Chaumont, NY, 184
Cromwell, William Nelson, 62–63, 113
Culbertson, William Smith, 86
Curtis, Lionel, 119, 198, 203
Czechoslovakia, 107, 149

Daladier, Edouard, 107
Davis, Norman, 74, 75, 76
Dawes, Rufus C., 102
Dawes Plan, 102, 103
Dean, Arthur, 125, 129, 161, 186
Debevoise, Thomas, 135
De Civitate Dei (Augustine), 197
deterrence
  by American forces in Japan, 162
  atomic weapons as, 177
  effectiveness of, 178
  JFD's changing view of, 115, 152
  in JFD's massive retaliation strategy, 175–77, 178
developmentalism, 196–97

Dewey, Thomas, 11, 150–51, 202
"Diplomat and His Faith, A" (JFD), 167
disarmament, forced, 163
Docherty, George M., 192
Dodds, Harold, 113
domino theory, 163
Doolin, Paul, 126–27
Douglas, William O., 170
Douglass, Frederick, 31
Drezner, Daniel, 6
Du Bois, Shirley, 170
Du Bois, W. E. B., 170
Duck Island. *See* Main Duck Island
Dulles, Allen Macy (JFD's father)
  American Theological Society co-founded by, 21
  anti-Catholic views of, 129, 172
  birth of, 39
  concern about JFD's engagement, 64
  courtship of Edith Foster, 37, 38
  death of, 12, 39
  education of, 27
  European trip with children, 51
  family heritage valued by, 45
  farewell sermon of, 19, 21
  fishing outings, 42
  JFD influenced by, 23, 40–41, 43, 171, 197–98
  JFD's birth, 45
  marriage of, 38
  memories of JFD, 44, 46–47
  ministry career of, 10, 39–40, 45
  personality of, 52
  philosophy of, 40

religion in family life of, 11–12, 23, 48, 129

Sunday routines of, 42, 48–49

theology of, 39, 40, 198

view on fundamentalist-modernist conflict, 69

Dulles, Allen Welsh (JFD's brother)

birth of, 47

as CIA director, 5, 183

meeting with Hitler, 2

personality of, 183

relationship with JFD, 42, 49, 53, 60, 183

on Sullivan and Cromwell's Berlin office closing, 14

Sunday routines, 48–49

Dulles, Avery (JFD's son)

birth of, 20, 70

career as Catholic theologian, 5, 20, 21, 125, 130

education of, 124, 125, 126

at First Presbyterian Church anniversary celebration, 20

memories of JFD, 10, 99, 100, 101–2, 128, 169

polio contracted by, 130

relationship with JFD, 125, 126, 128–30

religious commitments of, 20, 126–27, 128–30

sailing and travels with JFD, 12, 123, 124, 130–31

Dulles, Clover Todd (JFD's sister-in-law), 183

Dulles, Edith Foster (JFD's mother)

broad experiences of, 22, 34–36

concern about JFD's engagement, 64

courtship of Allen Macy Dulles, 37, 38

education of, 34, 35, 37

JFD encouraged by, 67–68, 113

JFD influenced by, 22, 38–39, 43

JFD's birth, 45

loss experienced by, 35–37, 68

love of outdoors, 35

marriage of, 38

memories of JFD, 46–47

personality of, 52

religious experience of, 36–37, 68

Sunday routines of, 42

travels with children, 22, 50–51

values of, 22, 36, 38

Dulles, Eleanor Lansing (JFD's sister)

on Auburn house parties, 53

birth of, 47

career of, 5, 183–84

childhood memories of, 12

Dulles history recorded by, 183

education of, 183

on Grandfather Foster's entertaining, 60–61

living with JFD and Janet, 64

marriage of, 71

memories of JFD, 50, 52, 53, 59, 97, 98

memories of Mary Parke McFerson Foster, 29–30

relationship with JFD, 183–84, 185

on Sunday routines, 42

Dulles, Harriet Lathrop Winslow (JFD's grandmother), 26

Dulles, Janet Pomeroy Avery (JFD's wife)
death of, 186
engagement to JFD, 64
at JFD's death, 185
at Main Duck Island, 13, 131, 132–33
marriage of, 64–65
sailing with JFD, 97, 123, 130
travels with family, 124
Dulles, John Foster ("Foster")
American moral leadership emphasized by (see United States, moral leadership of)
American unity urged by, 196
analogies from sailing and nature, 99, 100, 101–2, 133–34, 182, 184
anti-Catholic views of, 129
authoritarian regimes tolerated by, 182
binary frame of, 6, 41, 149, 151
birth of, 32, 44–45
brinkmanship of (see brinkmanship)
cancer treatments received by, 184–85
career overview, 7–8
Carnegie Endowment for International Peace chaired by, 150
change, views on (see change, JFD's views on)
as chief foreign policy adviser, 150–51, 158, 202
childhood activities of, 12, 22, 34, 42, 47, 49–50, 52, 53
childhood pets of, 41–42, 49
childhood travel experiences of, 46, 47, 50–51

"Christian lawyer" goal of, 8, 22, 57
church, views on (see church, JFD's views on)
church and denominational leadership roles of, 69, 70, 77, 83–84, 90–96
civil religion/progressive Christianity of, 10, 190, 193–94, 203
collective security promoted by, 156, 160, 162, 172, 175, 176, 177, 181
commitment to freedom, 171–72, 189
Communism opposed by, 17, 41, 151, 153, 155–56, 168, 170–71, 182, 189
complexity of, 17, 171, 189–90, 203–4
containment policy criticized by, 9, 173, 174, 175, 177
as Council of Foreign Ministers adviser, 150, 164
courtship of Janet Pomeroy Avery, 60, 63–64
criticism of, 6, 14–16, 17, 133, 136, 173, 188–89 (see also under brinkmanship; massive retaliation policy)
death of, 5, 13–14, 171, 172, 185–86
diplomatic missions of, 7
Dulles Commission leadership (see Commission for a Just and Durable Peace)
early career of, 60–63, 69, 71–72
economic interdependence valued by, 82–83, 141

education of, 7, 48, 54–55, 56,
57–61, 63, 68
extended family gatherings, 12, 23,
42, 52
family traditions valued by, 21,
42–43, 52, 125, 130, 190
FCC leadership roles of, 154, 159,
179–81 (*see also* Commission
for a Just and Durable Peace)
federalism promoted by, 116
foreign policy adjustments,
179–80, 189, 194
foreign policy consistency, 171, 172,
179, 181, 189, 195
in fundamentalist-modernist controversy, 68, 69, 90–96, 171
Geneva Conference delegation led
by, 191
German business ties of, 14–16
Hitler and, 1–2, 14, 153
human dignity central for, 137, 171,
189
humanity of, 14, 189, 190, 204
influenced by Allen Macy Dulles,
23, 40–41, 43, 171, 197–98
influenced by Edith Foster Dulles,
22, 38–39, 43
influenced by John Watson Foster,
8, 21–22, 23, 34, 43, 80, 171
influenced by Will Stevens, 49–50
intellectual development of, 55, 57,
100–108
intellectualism critiqued by, 115, 117
internationalism, views on, 140,
144, 194, 195
isolationism opposed by, 182, 195
Israel, views on, 199–200

Japanese peace treaty drafted by
(*see* Treaty of San Francisco)
Kellogg-Briand Pact critiqued by,
106, 115
Latin American diplomatic efforts,
72–73
law practice at Sullivan & Cromwell, 7, 14–15, 62–63, 69, 76, 102,
104, 151
leadership style of, 138
legacy of, 5–6, 18, 185, 186–87
liberation policy of, 9, 173–75
love for outdoors, 98–100, 130, 182
love of sailing, 12, 22, 49, 50, 53,
97–98, 123, 130, 182–83, 184
Main Duck Island enjoyed by, 13,
53, 103–4, 131–32
marriage of, 17, 64–65
massive retaliation policy of (*see*
massive retaliation policy)
military career of, 69, 73
moral law central for (*see* moral
law, JFD's application of)
nationalism of (*see* nationalism)
on national self-interest *vs.* righteousness, 122, 135
nature and moral order, views on,
17, 133–34, 144
nicknamed "Foster," 45
nuclear weapons, views on, 143–44,
153, 154, 156
Oxford Conference on Church
attended by, 116–18, 120, 180
parenting style of, 12, 21, 64, 70,
123–26, 128–30, 126
peace, views on (*see* peace, JFD's
views on)

personal defense valued by, 146

personality as a child, 44, 46–47, 50, 53

personality as an adult, 13, 16–17, 46, 50, 65, 70, 122–23, 188

philosophical development of, 59, 108–14

post-Versailles remedial efforts of, 138, 159

pragmatic worldview of, 65–66, 86, 101, 112, 152, 199

preaching of, 77

private life of, 6–7, 16–17, 188

public persona of, 17, 46, 188

race, views on, 200–202

realism, views on, 82, 115, 151, 168

relationships with children, 21, 123–26, 128–30

relationships with siblings, 183–84

relationship with Dwight Eisenhower, 172

relationship with Woodrow Wilson, 76, 108, 114

religious calling of, 100

religious consistency of, 17–18, 23, 66, 189, 195

religious development of, 100–108

religious ebb and flow of, 10, 11, 23, 59, 65, 67, 68, 118, 120–21

religious lineage of, 27–28

religious pragmatism of, 10, 17, 65, 68, 120–21, 152, 189, 199

religious-professional life intersection for, 11, 66, 78, 182

religious upbringing of, 10, 11–12, 23, 41–42, 45, 48, 65, 68, 129

robbery of, 145–46

at San Francisco Conference, 133, 142–43, 166

at Second Hague Conference, 7, 8, 46, 55, 56–57

as senator, 151, 155, 156, 159

sense of Christian duty, 99

sense of humor of, 122–23

social life of, 46, 52–53, 54, 55, 60–61

sovereignty system critiqued by, 110–12, 114

as special consultant to Eisenhower, 185

as special counsel for Central American affairs, 72

on spiritual conversations, 67

universality, views on, 118, 154, 167, 168

as US secretary of state (*see* US secretary of state, JFD as)

at Versailles Peace Conference (*see* Treaty of Versailles)

war, views on (*see* war, JFD's views on)

on War Industries Board, 74

on War Trade Board, 73

work ethic of, 99–100

work relationships of, 13–14

Dulles, John Watson Foster (JFD's son), 5, 97, 123, 125–26, 130, 131

Dulles, John Welsh, 26–27, 38

Dulles, John Welsh II, 27, 39

Dulles, Joseph, 26

Dulles, Joseph Heatly ("Uncle Joe") (JFD's uncle), 27–28, 45, 51

Dulles, Joseph Heatly (JFD's great-grandfather), 26, 27

Dulles, Lillias. *See* Hinshaw, Lillias Dulles

Dulles, Margaret (Mrs. Margaret Dulles Edwards) (JFD's sister), 47, 48, 51, 52–53

Dulles, Margaret Welsh (JFD's great-grandmother), 26

Dulles, Mary Elizabeth, 26

Dulles, Nataline (Mrs. Nataline Dulles Seymour) (JFD's sister), 41, 47–48, 60

Dulles, Sophie Heatly (JFD's great-great-grandmother), 26

Dulles, William Winslow, 27

Dulles Commission. *See* Commission for a Just and Durable Peace

Dulles family
   Eleanor's historical records of, 183
   family tree, 24
   mission tradition of, 26–27
   origins of, 26–28
   pets, 41–42, 49
   Princeton tradition of, 27, 54

Dulles International Airport, 6

Dumbarton Oaks Conference (1944), 140–41

Dunn, Frederick, 157, 158

Dyke, Tertius van, 70, 71, 77, 89, 95

Earle, Edward M., 86

East Germany, 146, 149

economic interdependence, 82–83, 141

Edwards, Margaret Dulles (JFD's sister), 47, 48, 51, 52–53

Eisenhower, Dwight
   baptism of, 193
   civil religion revival led by, 192, 193
   grand strategy of, 173
   at JFD's funeral, 186
   on JFD's legacy, 5, 186–87
   JFD's roles with, 151, 172–73, 185
      (*see also* US secretary of state, JFD as)
   massive retaliation policy of, 177
   relationship with JFD, 172–73

Eldredge, Art, 182

Elliston, Herbert B., 161

Elson, Edward L. R., 185, 192, 193, 200

Engert, Cornelius, 200

Erickson, John A., 83

Evans, Anthony H., 83

exemplarism, 194

family trees, 24–25

Far Eastern Commission (FEC), 162

fascism, 147, 155

Faubus, Orval, 202

Federal Council of Churches (FCC), 77, 134–37, 154, 159, 179–81. *See also* Commission for a Just and Durable Peace

federalism, 116

Fellowship of Reconciliation, 167

Finney, Bill, 90–91

First Presbyterian Church, Manhattan ("Old First"), 87, 88–89

First Presbyterian Church, Watertown, 19–20, 39, 41, 52
fishing, 34, 42, 47, 49–50
Flanders, Ralph E., 193
Flick, Friedrich, 15
Foch, Ferdinand, 80
Forster (Foster), George, 28
Forster (Foster), Jane, 28
Fosdick, Harry Emerson, 87–88, 90–92, 193
Foster, Alexander "Sasha," 37
Foster, Alice, 38
Foster, Eleanor (Mrs. Eleanor Foster Lansing) (JFD's aunt), 52
Foster, Eleanor Johnson (JFD's great-grandmother), 29
Foster, John Watson ("Grandfather Foster") (JFD's grandfather)
  birth of, 29, 70
  career of, 21–22, 29, 30–34
  Christmas letter to JFD, 52
  education of, 30
  entertaining power players, 60–61
  family cottage built by, 42
  family traditions valued by, 21
  fishing outings, 34, 42, 47
  with JFD at Second Hague Convention, 7, 8, 46, 55, 56
  JFD influenced by, 8, 21–22, 23, 34, 43, 80, 171
  loss experienced by, 37–38
  marriage of, 29
  personality of, 29
  as Republican, 71
  Sullivan & Cromwell connection, 63, 71

travels with family, 50–51
Foster, Mary Parke ("Parkie") (JFD's aunt), 38
Foster, Mary Parke McFerson (JFD's grandmother), 29–30
Foster, Matthew Watson (JFD's great-grandfather), 19, 21, 28, 29
Foster, Sarah McLoud Kazar, 29
Foster (Forster), George, 28–29
Foster (Forster), Jane, 28–29
Foster family, origins of, 25, 28–29
France, 79, 101, 102, 105, 106, 107, 111, 115
freedom
  Communist threat to, 168, 171, 172, 192
  intellectual, 40, 141, 171
  JFD's commitment to, 171–72, 189
  moral and religious foundations of, 10, 40, 121, 140, 171, 176
  vs. political stasis, 174
  religious, 40, 89, 141
Frémont, John C., 30
Fuller, Carlos, 90, 94–96
fundamentalism, 197
fundamentalist-modernist controversy
  developments in, 87–89, 91–92, 93
  JFD's involvement in, 68, 69, 90–96, 171
  progressive Christianity and, 193–94

Gaddis, John Lewis, 147, 149, 174, 177
Gamble, Richard M., 196
Garfield, James A., 35

Garry, Fred, 20

Geddes, Eric, 75

Geneva Conference (1954), 191

Germany, 102, 105, 106, 107, 111, 135, 152

Gladden, Washington, 193

Glassford, William, 130

God's Country (Goldman), 199

Goldman, Samuel, 199

Goodnow, Frank J., 85

Graham, Billy, 192–93

Grant, Ulysses S., 31

Great Depression, 104–5, 106

Grew, Joseph, 161

Gromyko, Andrei, 186

Haberski, Raymond, 193

Hague Conferences (1899, 1907), 81

Hall, Cameron Parker, 90, 94–96

Hammarskjöld, Dag, 186

Harrison, Benjamin, 8, 31, 47

Hart, Robert, 131, 132, 134, 182–83, 184, 186

Hatch, Harold A., 83, 84

Hawaii, 22, 32

Hayes, Rutherford B., 31

Heatly, Sophie (Mrs. Sophie Heatly Dulles) (JFD's great-great-grandmother), 26

Henderson, New York, 12, 23, 42, 47, 48–49, 50, 52, 65

Herberg, Will, 192

Herblock, cartoons of, 9, 189

Herter, Christian, 185, 186

Hibben, John Grier, 55, 61, 89

Hill, Bob, 126

Hinkle, Beatrice, 85

Hinshaw, Lillias Dulles (JFD's daughter)

birth of, 70

career of, 130

education of, 122, 125

marriage to Robert Hinshaw, 13, 131

memories of JFD, 11, 122–23

relationship with JFD, 97, 122–23, 124–25, 130–31

Hinshaw, Robert, 13, 131

Hiroshima, 154

Hiss, Alger, 150

Hitchcock, William I., 202

Hitler, Adolf, 1–2, 14, 106, 107, 111, 153

Hobbes, Thomas, 110

Ho Chi Minh, 190–91, 192

Hocking, William, 179

Holmes, Oliver Wendell, 61

Hoopes, Townsend, 12, 64, 186

Hoover, Herbert, 78–79

"How Dulles Averted War" (Shepley), 178

Hughes, Charles Evan, 79

Hull, Cordell, 142

Huston, Bruce, 184

"I Made a Fool of Myself over John Foster Dulles" (Burnett), 188

Immerman, Richard H., 171, 188

Immigration and Nationality Act (1952), 170

imperialism, 194

"Importance to the United States of

the Economic Provisions of the
Treaty of Versailles" (JFD), 78–79
Inboden, William, 204
Indochina, 178, 190–91
intellectual freedom, 141, 171
intellectualism, 115, 117
internationalism, 140–41, 144, 194,
195
International Roundtable of Chris-
tian Leaders (1943), 139, 152, 179
International Studies Conference
(1937), 117
isolationism, 182, 195
Israel, 199–200
Italy, 105, 106, 107, 135
"I Was a Nominal Christian" (JFD), 8

Jackson, C. D., 186, 201
Japan. *See also* Treaty of San
Francisco
American occupation of, 157, 161,
162, 167
Hiroshima and Nagasaki bombing,
149
JFD's view of, 97, 107
security treaties with, 165, 175
steps toward WWII, 106
Versailles Treaty mandates, 106
Washington Conference naval
limitations, 105
Japan's Policies and Purposes (Saito),
113
Jefferson, Louis, 18
Jensen, Erik M., 62
Johnson, Eleanor (Mrs. Elea-

nor Johnson Foster) (JFD's
great-grandmother), 29
"Just and Durable Peace, A" (Commission for a Just and Durable
Peace), 138

Kazar, Sarah McLoud (Mrs. Sarah
McLoud Kazar Foster), 29
Keim, Albert, 112, 116, 118
Kellogg, Frank B., 105
Kellogg-Briand Pact (1928), 80, 105,
106, 109, 111, 115
Kennan, George, 148, 157, 174, 181
Kennedy, John F., 6, 180
Kent, Rockwell, 170
Kent v. Dulles (1958), 170
Kim Il-sung, 149
King, Martin Luther, Jr., 201
Kinzer, Stephen, 6
Korean peninsula, 149, 160, 174, 191
Korean War, 160, 169, 174, 191

Lamont, Rogers, 135–36
Lamont, Thomas, 74, 75
Lansing, Eleanor Foster (JFD's aunt),
52
Lansing, Robert ("Uncle Bert"), 12,
52, 71–72, 73–74
Lazelle, Ebenezer, 39
League of Nations
Covenant of, 109, 111–12, 116
failure of, 105, 138
Germany's withdrawal from, 106
JFD's support for, 85
pre–WWII events and, 106–7

US opposition to, 79, 81, 105, 106, 139

Versaille Treaty and, 106

in Wilson's peace program, 115

"Leaves from the Notebook of a War-bound American" (Niebuhr), 134

Lee, Ivy, 88

Leech, Henry, 14

Lehman, Herbert, 151

Leviathan (Hobbes), 110

liberation policy, 9, 173–75

Life in India (John Welsh Dulles), 26

Li Hung Chang, 32–34

Lincoln, Abraham, 30

Locarno Treaty (1925), 105–6, 109, 111

"Long Range Peace Objectives" (Commission for a Just and Durable Peace), 138

"Long Telegram" (Kennan), 148, 174, 181

Luther, Hans, 113

MacArthur, Douglas, 157–58

Macartney, Clarence, 88

Machen, J. Gresham, 95

Mackay, John, 116, 117, 179–80, 181

Macmillan, Harold, 185, 188

Macomber, Phyllis Bernau, 13, 188

Main Duck Island, 13, 53, 103–4, 131–33

Malik, Yokov, 164

Manning, A. P., 184

Mao Tse-tung, 146, 149

Maritain, Jacques, 127

Marsden, George, 89

Marshall, George C., 150, 185

Marshall, Thurgood, 202

Marshall Plan, 174

massive retaliation policy

brinkmanship and, 178, 179–80

criticism of, 9, 179–80

as deterrence strategy, 175–77, 178

drawbacks of, 177

informed by JFD's morals, 173, 181–82

JFD's shift to, 17, 179–80

success of, 178

Mathews, Shailer, 193

Max of Baden, 74

McCarthy, Joseph, 150, 170

McCormick, Vance, 73

McFerson, Mary Parke (Mrs. Mary Parke McFerson Foster) (JFD's grandmother), 29–30

McIntire, Carl, 17, 192

McIntyre, James Francis, 192

McKee, Benjamin Harrison, 47

Mendenhall, H. G., 90, 94, 95

Menemsha, 97–98, 130, 131

Merrill, William Pierson, 77, 89, 91

Metcalf, Willis, 53

Miller, Everard "Pat," 54, 57, 59

Miller, John Franklin, 61

modernism, 69, 89, 95. *See also* fundamentalist-modernist controversy; progressive Christianity

Molotov-Ribbentrop Pact (1939), 107

Monnet, Jean, 185, 186

moral law, JFD's application of American leadership responsibility (*see* United States, moral leadership of)

changing foreign policy views and, 144, 151–52, 155

consistent commitment to, 68, 168, 181, 189

as Dulles Commission theme, 139, 140, 141, 167

freedom and, 171, 176

in Japanese peace treaty, 167–68

in liberation policy, 174

in rejection of Communism, 17, 41, 151, 153, 155–56, 168, 171, 189

universality and, 118, 151, 154, 167

Morton, Oliver P., 30, 31

Moscow Declaration (1943), 140

Mosley, Leonard, 183

Murray, Charles, 190

Murray, John Courtney, 192

Mussolini, Benito, 107

Muste, A. J., 167–68, 181

"My Pilgrimage to Nonviolence" (King), 201

Nagasaki, 154

National Conference on the Christian Way of Life, 77

National Day of Prayer, 193

nationalism. *See also* American exceptionalism; United States, moral leadership of

JFD's shift to, 144, 151–52, 172, 180, 190, 194–95

JFD's warnings about, 119–20, 122, 135, 181

National Presbyterian Church, Washington, DC, 200

National Security Council (NSC), 157, 177

National Study Conference (1945), 139, 140, 142

nation-deity/nation-devil concept, 119–20, 181

"New Foreign Policy, A" (JFD), 174, 175–76

"New Knowledge and the Christian Faith, The" (Fosdick), 88

"New Look" grand strategy, 173

New York Presbytery, 77, 83–84, 88–89, 92

New Zealand, 161, 162, 163, 165, 175

Nichols, Robert Hastings, 89, 91, 93

Niebuhr, Reinhold, 134–35

Nixon, Richard, 172–73

Nkrumah, Kwame, 170

Nolde, Fred, 179, 180

North Atlantic Treaty (1949), 156

North Korea, 149, 160, 169, 174

Noyes, Frances, 61

Noyes, Frank Brett, 61

NSC (National Security Council), 157, 177

Okazaki, Katsuo, 162

Oldham, John H., 116–17

Oliver Brown v. Board of Education of Topeka (1954), 202, 203

O'Ryan, John F., 85

Osler, Britton, 103

Oxford Conference on Church (1937), 116–18, 120, 180

Pact of Paris (Kellogg-Briand Pact), 80, 105, 106, 109, 111, 115
Pashkoff, W. A., 37
Passport Act (1926), 170
peace, Hobbes's view of, 110
peace, JFD's views on
   active effort required for, 17, 79, 80, 181
   causes and definition of, 41, 108–9
   change and, 108–9
   collective security necessary for, 181
   critique of realist efforts, 115
   critique of treaty/sovereignty system, 110–12, 114
   influenced by Oxford Conference, 116–18
   nationalism *vs.* internationalism and, 140, 144, 151–52
   peril of relaxation and, 134, 142, 143, 144, 153–54
   retributive *vs.* restorative, 159, 167
   role of church in, 10, 108, 118, 120, 137, 138, 139–40
   universality of, 168
"Peaceful Change within the Society of Nations" (JFD), 114, 116
"Peace without Platitudes" (JFD), 138, 139
Peale, Norman Vincent, 192
Pearson, Drew, 14
Pepper, Claude, 15, 17
personification of the nation, 119
Pfeiffer, Timothy, 92
Philadelphia Overture, 88–89, 92
Philippines, 163–64, 165, 175

Pilgrim's Progress (Bunyan), 185–86
Pledge of Allegiance, 193
Poland, 107
"Policy of Boldness, A" (JFD), 195
Policy Planning Staff, 157
Poole, D. C., 113
Potsdam Conference (1945), 149
pragmatism
   in JFD's religious views, 10, 17, 65, 68, 120–21, 152, 189, 199
   in JFD's worldview, 65–66, 86, 101, 112, 152, 199
Pre-Armistice Agreement, 74, 75
Presbyterian Church, 88–89, 93, 95. *See also* fundamentalist-modernist controversy
Preston, Andrew, 194
Princeton
   as Dulles family tradition, 27, 54
   JFD's alumni involvement with, 55
   JFD's education at, 7, 48, 51, 54–55, 56, 57–60
"Problem of Peace in a Dynamic World, The" (JFD), 117, 180
progress, 114, 196, 197, 201
progressive Christianity, 190, 193–94, 196–98, 203
Pruessen, Ronald, 15–16, 71, 73, 79, 102, 104
Purcell, Bob, 182–83, 184

Rabb, Maxwell, 202
race, 200–202
Ramsay, Mebane, 83
Rauschenbusch, Walter, 87, 193, 201
realism, 82, 115, 151, 168

Red Scare, 150, 170

relaxation, peril of, 134, 142, 143, 144, 153–54

religious exceptionalism, 194, 195, 203

religious freedom, 141

reparations, 163, 165, 171. See also Versailles Reparations Commission

Republican National Committee, 193

Republic of Korea, 149, 160, 165, 169, 174

Reston, James, 164

Rhee, Syngman, 160

Ride through Palestine, The (John Welsh Dulles), 26

"Righteous Faith for a Just and Durable Peace, A" (Commission for a Just and Durable Peace), 138

Rio, Felix Nieto del, 166

"Road to Peace, The" (JFD), 108–9, 112–13, 114, 116, 119

Rockefeller, John D., Jr., 88

Rockefeller, John D., III, 186

Rome-Berlin Axis agreement (1936), 107

Roosevelt, Franklin Delano, 141, 142

Roosevelt, Kim, 200

Rosso, Augusto, 113

Rusk, Dean, 186

Russell, Mark, 188

Russia. See Soviet Union

Sacasa, Guillermo Sevilla, 166

sailing
  JFD's analogies from, 99, 100, 101–2, 184

JFD's love for, 12, 22, 49, 50, 53, 97–98, 123, 130, 182–83, 184

Saito, Hiroshi, 113

salvation, ethical, 198

San Francisco, Treaty of. See Treaty of San Francisco

San Francisco Conference, 133, 142–43, 166

Scharf, Madeleine, 113

Schweiger, Beth Barton, 1, 4

Scopes trial (1925), 88–89

Second Hague Peace Conference (1907), 7, 8, 46, 55, 56–57

Sedgwick, Ellery, 108

Senate Committee on Foreign Relations, 165–66, 199

sentimentalism, 115–16

Sewall, Bevan, 86

Seymour, Nataline Dulles (JFD's sister), 41, 47–48, 60

"Shall the Fundamentalists Win?" (Fosdick), 87

"Shall Unbelief Win?" (Macartney), 88

Shedd, Edward, 54

Sheen, Fulton, 127, 192, 193

Shepley, James, 178

"Six Pillars of Peace" (Commission for a Just and Durable Peace), 138, 141–42

Smuts, Jan, 75

Sousa, John Philip, 47

South Korea, 149, 160, 165, 169, 174

sovereignty system, 110–12, 114, 138

Soviet espionage, 149–50

Soviet Union
atomic bombs deployed by, 146,
149
Churchill's view of, 147–48
expansionist acts of, 149
in Japan peace treaty process, 160,
164–65, 166, 181
JFD's Cold War view of, 143–44,
146–47, 151, 153–54, 155–56, 160,
176–77, 194
JFD's early view of, 135, 155
postwar posture of, 148
Spaak, Paul-Henri, 186
Spanish Civil War (1936), 107
Speer, Robert, 77
Spellman, Francis Cardinal, 192
Spencer, Anna Garlin, 85
Stalin, Joseph, 149, 153, 174
Stassen, Harold, 183
"Statement of Guiding Principles"
(Commission for a Just and Du-
rable Peace), 138, 139, 140–41, 167
"Statement on Control of the Atomic
Bomb" (Commission for a Just
and Durable Peace), 138–39
Stevens, Will, 49–50
Stevenson, Adlai, 178–79
Stone, Harlan, 113
Sudetenland, 107
Sullivan, Algernon Sydney, 62
Sullivan & Cromwell, 7, 14–15, 62–63,
69, 76, 102, 104, 151

Taft, Helen, 61
Taft, Robert, 182
telos, 196

Testimonial to Grace (Avery Dulles),
128
Theology for the Social Gospel, A
(Rauschenbusch), 193
38th Parallel, 149
Toulouse, Mark, 23, 151–52, 172, 180,
190
*Transformation of John Foster Dulles,
The* (Toulouse), 151–52
treaties, success and limitations of,
110–12, 141
Treaty of San Francisco (1951)
goals and vision for, 157–58,
159–60, 161–62
JFD's faith and morals as influence
on, 153, 159, 167, 168
JFD's role in, 7–8, 9, 151, 158–60,
162, 165–66, 167, 181
opposition to, 167–68, 181
Soviet criticism of process, 164–65,
166
success of, 147, 166, 167, 181
unity among delegates of, 166
urgency of, 156–57, 160
Treaty of Shimonoseki (1895), 21–22,
32–34
Treaty of Versailles (1919)
European fulfillment of, 105–6
flouted by Germany, 106, 107, 111
JFD's efforts to remediate, 138
JFD's role in, 67, 78–79
limitations and failure of, 106, 111,
138, 147, 159, 163, 167
US rejection of, 105
WWII and, 76
True Church, The (Allen Macy
Dulles), 21, 40, 129, 197–98

"True Church, The" (Avery Dulles), 21

Truman, Harry
atomic energy control discussed with JFD, 154
on Cold War struggle, 192
foreign policy of, 9, 173, 176
Japan peace treaty supported by, 7–8, 158, 159, 166
McCarthy's crusade countered by, 150
Pacific security treaties submitted for Senate ratification, 165
travel restrictions enacted by, 169–70
Zionist policies of, 199–200
Truman Doctrine (1947), 148–49, 174
Tucker, Henry St. George, 141

Underbluff, 42, 49
United Nations, 139, 141, 174
United Nations Charter (1945), 139
United Negro College Fund (UNCF), 201
United States
American exceptionalism, 152, 194, 195–96, 203
faith in human liberty lacking in, 176
religious trends in, 190, 192–93
viewed by JFD as Christian nation, 69, 78, 155, 193, 195
United States, moral leadership of
in defeating Communism, 9, 10, 151, 154, 155, 171, 193, 195

as God-given responsibility, 9, 10, 153
in modeling tolerance, 155, 167
moral and physical qualifications for, 151, 153, 172, 181, 194–95, 203
as unselfish, 181–82, 195
Universal Christian Conference on Life and Work, 77
"Universal Church and a World of Nations, The" (JFD), 117
universality, JFD's view of, 118, 151, 154, 167, 168
Upper Silesian Coal and Steel Company, 15
US secretary of state, JFD as
approach to role, 189–90
as career goal, 8, 34, 151
massive retaliation strategy, 176
tenure of, 7, 9, 172, 173, 185
travel restrictions during, 169–70
world events during, 152, 158, 169–70

Valenzuela, J. E., 166
Vandenberg, Arthur, 143, 158
Van Dusen, Henry P., 90, 93, 122, 136, 137, 161, 186
Van Kirk, Walter, 136, 179
Versailles Peace Conference (1918), 67, 69, 85
Versailles Reparations Commission, 69, 74, 75–76, 152, 159, 163
Versailles Treaty. See Treaty of Versailles
Victor, Royal, 72

Vietnam, 190–92

Vinson, Fred, 173, 202

Wagner, Robert, 151

Waldegrave, Granville, 37

war, JFD's views on

banning of, 80–81, 84

causes of, 109

change-stasis metaphysic applied
to, 68, 69, 86, 112, 144, 174

definition of, 114

economic motives and, 85, 86

human and spiritual forces in, 137

individual and national responsibility in, 110, 134–35

internationalism and, 79–83, 105–6

interventionism and, 135–36, 152

as not inherently evil, 84

as standard for settling disputes,
108

as unavoidable risk, 178

War, Peace, and Change (JFD), 113,
119, 181

war fever, 115–16

War or Peace (JFD), 151, 156, 158

Warren, Earl, 186, 202–3

Washington Conference (1921, 1922),
79, 82, 105–6

Washington Naval Treaty (1922),
109, 111

Weaver, Richard, 204

Welles, Sumner, 142

Welsh, Margaret (Mrs. Margaret Welsh Dulles) (JFD's
great-grandmother), 26

"When Morning Gilds the Skies"
(hymn), 11, 19

Wiley, Alexander, 145

Willard, Frances, 193

Wilson, Woodrow

diplomatic efforts of, 73–76, 114–15,
116

as JFD's professor, 56, 71

relationship with JFD, 76, 108, 114

Robert Lansing's ties to, 71

war declared on Germany by, 35

Winslow, Harriet Lathrop (Mrs.
Harriet Lathrop Winslow Dulles)
(JFD's grandmother), 26

Winslow, Miron, 26–27

Wolfe, Paul, 185

Wood, Leonard, 186

Woolley, Mary E., 85

"Work, for the Night Is Coming"
(hymn), 185

World Court, 84, 85, 115

World War I, 74–76, 80, 83, 102–3.
See also Treaty of Versailles

World War II

as clash of ideologies, 140, 152, 153

end of, 143

factors leading to, 106–7, 138

as moral crisis, 134–35, 139, 140

as setup to Cold War, 147–48, 153

Yoshida, Shigeru, 9, 162

Titles published in the

LIBRARY OF RELIGIOUS BIOGRAPHY SERIES

Orestes A. Brownson: American Religious Weathervane
by Patrick W. Carey

The Puritan as Yankee: A Life of Horace Bushnell
by Robert Bruce Mullin

A Life of Alexander Campbell
by Douglas A. Foster

Duty and Destiny: The Life and Faith of Winston Churchill
by Gary Scott Smith

Emblem of Faith Untouched: A Short Life of Thomas Cranmer
by Leslie Williams

Her Heart Can See: The Life and Hymns of Fanny J. Crosby
by Edith L. Blumhofer

Emily Dickinson and the Art of Belief
by Roger Lundin

God's Cold Warrior: The Life and Faith of John Foster Dulles
by John D. Wilsey

A Short Life of Jonathan Edwards
by George M. Marsden

Charles G. Finney and the Spirit of American Evangelicalism
by Charles E. Hambrick-Stowe

William Ewart Gladstone: Faith and Politics in Victorian Britain
by David Bebbington

One Soul at a Time: The Story of Billy Graham
by Grant Wacker

A Heart Lost in Wonder: The Life and Faith of Gerard Manley Hopkins
by Catharine Randall

Sworn on the Altar of God: A Religious Biography of Thomas Jefferson
by Edwin S. Gaustad

The Miracle Lady: Katherine Kuhlman and the Transformation of Charismatic Christianity by Amy Collier Artman

Abraham Kuyper: Modern Calvinist, Christian Democrat
by James D. Bratt

The Religious Life of Robert E. Lee
by R. David Cox

Abraham Lincoln: Redeemer President
by Allen C. Guelzo

*The First American Evangelical: A Short Life of **Cotton Mather***
by Rick Kennedy

***Aimee Semple McPherson**: Everybody's Sister*
by Edith L. Blumhofer

*Mother of Modern Evangelicalism: The Life and Legacy of **Henrietta Mears***
by Arlin Migliazzo

*Damning Words: The Life and Religious Times of **H. L. Mencken***
by D. G. Hart

***Thomas Merton** and the Monastic Vision*
by Lawrence S. Cunningham

*God's Strange Work: **William Miller** and the End of the World*
by David L. Rowe

***Blaise Pascal**: Reasons of the Heart*
by Marvin R. O'Connell

*Occupy Until I Come: **A. T. Pierson** and the Evangelization of the World*
by Dana L. Robert

*The Kingdom Is Always but Coming: A Life of **Walter Rauschenbusch***
by Christopher H. Evans

*A Christian and a Democrat: A Religious Life of **Franklin D. Roosevelt***
by John F. Woolverton with James D. Bratt

***Francis Schaeffer** and the Shaping of Evangelical America*
by Barry Hankins

***Harriet Beecher Stowe**: A Spiritual Life*
by Nancy Koester

***Billy Sunday** and the Redemption of Urban America*
by Lyle W. Dorsett

***Howard Thurman** and the Disinherited: A Religious Biography*
by Paul Harvey

*Assist Me to Proclaim: The Life and Hymns of **Charles Wesley***
by John R. Tyson

*Prophetess of Health: A Study of **Ellen G. White***
by Ronald L. Numbers

***George Whitefield**: Evangelist for God and Empire*
by Peter Y. Choi

*The Divine Dramatist: **George Whitefield** and the Rise of Modern Evangelicalism*
by Harry S. Stout

*Liberty of Conscience: **Roger Williams** in America*
by Edwin S. Gaustad